A LIFE WITH

CLAW

THE PETER CLOHESSY STORY

A LIFE WITH

CLAW

THE PETER CLOHESSY STORY

ANNA GIBSON-STEEL

HEROBOOKS

HEROBOOKS

PUBLISHED BY HERO BOOKS
1 WOODVILLE GREEN
LUCAN
CO. DUBLIN
IRELAND
www.umbrellapublishing.ie
Hero Books is an imprint of Umbrella Publishing

First Published 2014

A CIP record for this book is available from the British Library

ISBN 978-0-9526260-3-9

Printed in Ireland with Print Procedure Ltd
Cover design and typesetting: Jessica Maile
Cover photographs: Inpho
Munster and Ireland photographs: Inpho
Personal photographs: The Clohessy family collection

Daddy Noel, Love Always

INTRODUCTION

'Do you want a drag?'

Once upon a time... not quite, the fairytale began at Crescent College Comprehensive in Limerick. I was 14 years old when I first met Peter Clohessy at what we used to call "the hole" which was a not so-secret place to smoke.

These were Peter's first words to me.

The rest as they say is history – 33 years later, 25 of them in marriage, and it hasn't been boring! The journey has been more roller-coaster than motorway for sure, but I would not change one day of it.

This book is the story of that journey and while I may well be viewing a different movie than some of the friends and characters in our lives, this is how the story was for me. I'm pretty sure that Peter will not have the same perspective as I have. In fact I'm certain he won't, as our different views on life have led to many a row over the years!

Peter was asked many times to write the story of his rugby life and his answer was always that if he did, he could only tell the naked truth and that would definitely upset too many of his friends. It got me thinking that a female perspective would be an interesting alternative, so this is a personal account that won't include an avalanche of match stats or results, except where they are an integral part of the story.

But the motivation was inspired by our 8 year old Harry. He rushed into the house one day, bursting with excitement. His friend, Jack Nicholas had shown him a YouTube clip of Peter scoring a try for Ireland. I was shocked by his excitement.

'But Harry... you've seen Daddy play on video before?'

His reply was the defining moment that conceived this book.

'I have never seen Daddy play!'

I then realised that recording these stories was important for all three of our children.

While I rarely missed a match that Munster and Ireland played from 1993 to 2002, the memories for me were as much about the aftermath and the characters who filled our lives as the games themselves.

I had briefly thought about calling this book "The Life and Times of a HAG". A Has-Been WAG (wives and girlfriends), but in truth I never considered myself such a person in any sense of the word. The term WAG didn't exist in the days when Peter played professional rugby, however the ethos around it did, although not to the same extent as today perhaps.

At any rate this book is to be taken and read in a light-hearted manner. We shouldn't take ourselves too seriously, in life or on the rugby field, and my intention is to inform and entertain and, perhaps, dispel a few myths along the way.

To Peter, this book is a thank you from my heart, for everything that you have done for me. I also have to say that this book was an easy project because, over the years, you created enough fantastic memories to write 10 books!

I could not have asked for a better partner, teacher, and soul mate. I love you eternally.

To everyone reading this book, all I can wish is that you enjoy the story of our journey in life so far.

Anna Gibson-Steel, October 2014

CONTENTS

PROLOGUE

I was upstairs on the phone engrossed in conversation with my detective friend, Jane Murphy when there was a huge bang and the house shook.

I assumed that Peter had dropped the big trailer loaded with rubble outside the back door. So I continued chatting. Fifteen minutes later, Cian Clohessy was calling me loudly.

'Peter just drove up...' he shouted.

'Come down and give out to him Anna... he forgot to collect Luke and me... and bring us down to the fire.'

I came downstairs and opened the back door.

Peter was standing there.

There was no skin on half of his face, or on his right arm. My immediate thought was *Thank you God for not letting him die.* It was only then that I realized that the bang was actually an explosion.

Thank God he hadn't taken the kids with him.

That was my very next thought. Earlier, Peter had told our eldest son, Luke that he would be burning rubbish in the back field, and when Luke excitedly asked if he could go with him Peter, as always, said yes. It was either divine intervention or the fags that saved the kids that day.

Peter was supposed to be off the cigarettes, but he was smoking on the quiet. So when he was going to the garage down the road to buy petrol for the fire, he didn't bring Luke because he wanted to have a sneaky fag. In the meantime, Luke's cousin Cian had called over and the boys were engrossed in a PlayStation game, so they didn't hear Peter calling them. That is how he came to drive to the field in the jeep on his own.

Peter definitely used one of his nine lives that Monday evening in early April. He was standing beside the jeep, and had poured all the petrol onto the rubbish. But as it was a humid evening the fumes were still in the air, so Peter stood back to light a bit of paper to throw on it. As soon as he clicked the lighter however the whole thing exploded. The flames just shot up at me, Peter later explained to me. He remembered keeping his eyes closed. Fortunately, because he was fit, he reacted instantly by rolling around in the grass to put out the fire on his arm and face. He could smell his skin burning as he did so. He then got up straight away and drove back to the house in the jeep.

His face looked like a pizza.

We rang our good friend and former team doc, Mickey Griffin who lived nearby, and he told us to come up immediately to his house. Mickey later admitted that his first instinct was to put Peter into a cold shower, but the burns looked so severe he second-guessed himself. So we got back into our car, and took off to the Regional, our local hospital in Limerick.

Peter was sitting in the front seat.

He was very quiet.

A dozen times, I must have asked him if he was, 'Okay?'

'Yeah…' is all he replied.

On the way Mickey called a skin surgeon in Galway Hospital, Dr Mick McGann who confirmed that Mickey's first instinct had been correct. Cold water was what was needed instantly. When we got to the Regional the three of us quickly found ourselves in one of those small cubicles, dosing Peter with cold water for an hour and a half as we'd been advised by Dr McGann. Having our own doc with us that evening was crucial to Peter's recovery, as they wouldn't have okayed the water treatment without Mickey's insistence.

Peter was still quiet. The shock was setting in. At the time I was trained as a Reiki Master, and I knew that this was one of those defining moments, where I either stepped up or stepped out. So I decided that even though I was in the hospital with a medical doctor, I was going to follow my instincts.

I stood behind Peter and put my hands on his shoulders and closed my eyes.

'Anna… are you going asleep?' Mickey asked.

'No' I replied.

Nothing else was said.

He slept that night. Actually he was in a *coma*, with all of the sleeping pills he had been given. His arm was covered in gauze, but the staff in the hospital decided not to cover his face.

The next day I drove Peter to the burns specialist in Galway, and once he checked the skin he informed us that Peter would need grafting in a week's time. The burns were so deep, he explained.

On the drive home a compilation CD that Paul O'Connell had made for us was playing *Something Inside So Strong* by Labi Siffre, and it seemed as though it had been written just for Peter. Len Dineen, one of Limerick's best known journalists and radio personalities, had asked for an interview live on air, something I had encouraged Peter to do on the drive to Galway as our phones had been hopping once the news of the incident had got out. Peter had chatted casually with Len for 10 minutes.

'I always knew you'd go out with a bang… but this is taking the p***,' I happily informed my husband.

Peter had returned from Paris the day before the fire, where he played the last of 54 games for Ireland and taken his final bow at the end of the 2002 Six Nations Championship in a city which had done more than any other to present the full character, A to Z of Peter Clohessy, to the world.

Three weeks later, back in France, there was also the *little* matter of a Heineken Cup semi-final against Castres in Peter's last playing diary.

In the Stade de France, in Eddie O'Sullivan's first year as national coach, Ireland had suffered their second record defeat of that particular Championship. It was a massive disappointment for the Irish supporters, particularly as the previous four meetings between the countries had been titanic toe-to-toe battles. This time the French had trotted out a 44-5 victory, but for Peter the 80 minutes he spent in the front row with Keith Wood and John Hayes for company, and with the formidable trio of Pieter de Villiers, Raphael Ibanez and Jean Jacques Crenca facing them, had been as intense as ever to the bitter end.

As an opponent, de Villiers had it all. He was a great scrummager, but he could also move around the field like a wing forward. Peter was *going out* against the very best opponent anyone could have handpicked for him!

'Let's win this one for Claw...!' Fester had demanded of the team before leaving the dressingroom.

It was easier said than done, however. The front row had held solid for most of the afternoon, but there were problems elsewhere... everywhere, really. It was like being transported back to the mid-90s when bashings by the French were annual events. And when their supporters, on this occasion, got into full voice Peter could feel their front row strengthen further.

At the final whistle, there was only deflation.

It was not the finale Peter would have chosen. The home supporters in the stadium had resorted to Mexican waves long before the final whistle. Six years earlier they had also hit Ireland for over 40 points, but the mood was wholly different, as that was the day Peter found himself in the mother of all battles – not that every game in Paris ever managed to avoid some degree of such a motherhood – and was cited for stamping on Olivier Roumat's head. He was quickly banned for 26 weeks.

As I had known Peter from such a young age, I had always known that he lived his life on the edge. I would witness many occasions in his playing career when he would admit to me afterwards that... 'the *red mist* descended'.

I also knew Peter well enough to know that his nature is incredibly kind and compassionate, and that he is not naturally a violent person.

He is loyal beyond reason.

He is also true to himself.

Therefore, when anyone tests this loyalty, or encroaches in that direction, he will not back down. It is his natural instinct to protect those he cares for – this includes family, friends, teammates, his club, his province and his country, and indeed his own boundaries.

I have always known that any time Peter has reacted on the field, it was never a random act, or something that was without provocation.

That is not to say that I agreed with all of his reactions. But what I came to understand, is this... the motivation behind any action he has ever taken are values of loyalty, and a heartfelt need to protect those he cares for!

It took him a few years to get the red mist under control. I also knew that Peter felt remorse after any such incident, so there was never any need for me to make him feel worse by going on about it. There were plenty of other people more than willing to do that. My role was to support my husband.

And, because I knew who he was, and what he stood for in his life and on the rugby field, that was not a difficult role for me at any time in *my* life.

Marcus Horan, who had been waiting patiently in the wings for Peter to retire for the previous number of years, got an awful slagging from the lads in the days that followed the explosion.

'F*** it, Marcus... there was no need to set him on fire!'

Marcus heard that from more than one friend in the dressingroom, though being the gentleman that he is I knew that he felt sorry for Peter. But, of course, he was equally entitled to be excited about finally taking over the red No.1 shirt for good, and actually getting his hands on that shirt in a Heineken Cup semi-final would have been a dream come true. There was no way anyone expected Peter to make the huge game against Castres.

That game against one of Munster's greatest rivals over the previous two years was due to be Peter's second last game of rugby. If they could win!

It was also huge for Munster supporters who paid out so much money for so many years and followed the lads all over Europe, and who now had the European final in the Millennium Stadium in Cardiff within their sight. They were backing the team with every fiber in their bodies to grasp the Holy Grail at last. A defeat in Beziers would perhaps bring a cruel ending to an amazing era for everyone.

For Peter, who would play no more! For Gaillimh perhaps, as Mick Galwey had fought harder than any man to get Munster to the very top in Europe, and for the team's coaches, Declan Kidney and Niall O'Donovan who were definitely also standing down once Munster had given their all that season.

The desperate fight to become European champions had begun when the Heineken Cup started in 1995. After all sorts of difficulties on the road, and some torturous adventures in France against a variety of teams, Munster had been on the brink for three years of bringing it all home.

There had been a gut-wrenching one-point defeat by Northampton in the final in Twickenham in 2000, when all our hopes exploded, and then a semi-final loss in Lille against Stade Francais the following spring. Another game lost by one precious, cruel point.

Beziers and Cardiff, we had firmly believed in our hearts, were our final two glorious destinations.

Back at that time, when I had begun my journey into the world of Alternative and Complimentary Medicine, Peter had paid a scant passing interest. While he clearly saw how I had recovered from my injuries suffered in a car accident some years earlier thanks to CAMs, he always kept his distance. Great for you love, but not for me thanks, was his general attitude.

But now I had a captive audience of one.

His body had gone into shock so he was in bed for a couple of days sleeping. He slept and I worked continually on him using Reiki. Peter has always had great healing power, so I'm sure it was a combination of both, but the following week when we went back to Galway the specialist couldn't believe how well the burns were healing. He told us there was no grafting needed. He also said that there was a small chance Peter would be fit for the semi-final. The new skin was growing, and Munster's medical team was also more hopeful and had ordered a special lycra-based protector to cover his arm, on the long shot that he might be able to play some part in the match in Beziers.

To keep up his fitness Peter went playing indoor soccer with the lads, and on one such occasion he banged his arm against David Wallace. A small circle of the new skin fell off there and then and, to this day, that remains the only small scar to remind him of the incident that could have taken his life.

A small white circle on his right elbow.

Marcus Horan couldn't believe his eyes!

'A f****** phoenix rising from the ashes!' he proclaimed.

And indeed he did.

Peter has defied many laws in his lifetime as a prop forward for his proud club Young Munster, and for Munster and Ireland. On this occasion in 2002 he had also defied the law of nature.

'Mam & Dad.

'Little did I know when we were kids and ye were bringing us to all the Internationals home and away, and I use to queue to get the Irish players' autographs in The Shelbourne Hotel after matches, that years later I would be the one at the other end of the queue.

'We had so many great times together as you brought us all over the world to matches. It is a credit to you, that now your children are doing the same with their kids. Thanks for all the happy memories and support.

'Love always.'

– Peter

CHAPTER 1

Unlike most Limerick children, I wasn't raised at the side of a rugby pitch. Instead, I was found at the side of a soccer pitch, as my very British Dad, Harry Gibson-Steel was a complete soccer alickadoo, as they would say in rugby circles.

Dad had moved to Ireland in the late 1950s and married Helena Gannon, who was at least 20 years younger than him – we never knew how much younger! His second love was soccer, though Mam would argue that soccer was Dad's first love!

In addition to devoting himself to Limerick, he also served as chairman of the League of Ireland in the mid-sixties. So my Sundays were spent at the Markets Field in Limerick, or at some windswept football ground in places with strange names. To this day I'm not exactly sure where Ballybofey is!

This changed dramatically once I went to Crescent Comprehensive for my secondary education, and I immediately took to the definitely more exciting game of rugby, not to mention a better social scene! The pure excitement of borrowing a Crescent jersey, and painting our faces for a schools cup match was an eagerly anticipated and integral part of school life. Chants would be practiced in the central area for days prior to matches. Mind you, as supporters we came in for more flack than any other school, as the female contingent were definitely screamers – sometimes I actually found it hard to listen to our lot myself!

What an education though, and I'm not talking about the academic side at Crescent, although that was great also. I'm talking about real life skills, and listening to and observing boys and their points of view was invaluable. Having gone to a convent all-girls primary school, with just one older brother (who at that time wasn't too bothered in hanging out with his nuisance of a younger sister), I had no idea that boys thought so differently to us girls! My life education began in earnest as I found myself more comfortable in the company of boys more often than not. Somehow their conversations were more interesting to me. I never had any time for silly gossip (though I do enjoy a good juicy story!) or for make-up, dancing or singing. Shopping was my one female vice and one that I have perfected to an art form over the years, and I owe a huge debt, figuratively and literally, to the Munster and Ireland fixtures lists for bringing me to so many shopping paradises over the years.

In hindsight, my "emotional education" at Crescent was an intrinsic foundation that stood me in good stead during my "WAG" years. I took with me from those school years many nuggets of wisdom, which are as relevant today as they were back then, despite the fact that many things have changed dramatically in all of our lives. The most dramatic and relevant change naturally is social media – and it is important to point out to anyone born since the early nineties that for a great many of the rugby years contained in this book mobile phones did not exist. Email did not exist. There was no Skype, no texting, no Twitter, and nobody carried a camera around with them, except reporters occasionally.

So, that meant no communication with a partner unless each of us were at a landline! This, naturally, had very obvious advantages to maintaining an "old boy" society where there were many unwritten rules, most of which isolated women from knowing what really went on in camp, or in cities and countries far from home!

No, that's not true… it just isolated partners and wives!

My emotional survival and, indeed, the maintenance of our relationship owed a great debt to the knowledge I gained at Crescent Comp about boys and their thinking. For starters, I learned my place, how to be accepted, how to keep my reactions to myself but, actually, as I've written already, I genuinely enjoyed the company of boys. They tended to be refreshingly honest in their opinions, and less judgmental than us girls. Their ability not to need to divulge every detail of an event is a double-edged sword however, and also facilitates the storage of many under-cover events!

In many ways, I realize that had Peter and myself not met at such a young age we probably would never have made it together in later life. We often joke that we are so different it is quite incredible that we ever *worked* as a couple, but perhaps these differences are the magic glue.

It was Sammy Flemming who first told me, 'Peter Clohessy is spotting you'. I had no idea who Peter was, but at break that school day I found out when he offered me that 'drag' of his cigarette.

He seemed nice, but for some reason I didn't take much notice of him. We did however become good friends and hung around together with others. Then, one afternoon, he finally plucked up the courage to ask me to the pictures.

I told him I would think about it.

I also told him to call in to me the next day in Tony Ward's sports shop where I worked on Saturdays in the centre of the city. There I had become friends with Eliz McCrory who worked part-time in the shop also, and first thing that Saturday morning I had told her about Peter asking me out.

'How will I say no… in a nice way to him?'

I asked Eliz that question half a dozen times that morning, though I have absolutely no memory of what she told me back. I desperately did not wish to hurt his feelings. So, to ease myself free of any guilt, I nicely stepped around his invitation to the pictures and encouraged Peter to ask my friend Sarah out instead!

Tony Ward's sports shop was an interesting place to work, as many young people used it as an impromptu clubhouse where all sorts of plans were hatched. My Dad who was retired also became part of the furniture there, and I'm sure it was through his encouragement that Tony played and won an FAI cup medal with Limerick United in 1982.

Eoin Hand, whom Mickey Webb and Dad had signed as Limerick's player-manager, was also a regular in the shop. Eddie O'Sullivan often called in as well. Limerick has always had a great respect and love of sport and that shop seemed to cross all divides. Dave Maheady, who was Tony's partner in the shop, was always great fun to work with, and he was way ahead of his time with his passion for fitness. Dave would come into work after training the Limerick football team the night before and boast about how many "hughies" he had caused – that's how many players he had left on the side of the pitch throwing up from the physical exertion of his training programme!

There were three floors to the shop that had been converted into a fitness centre with weight machines, once again way ahead of their time. This was one of only two gyms in Limerick city in the eighties.

I liked Peter, but as a friend only. I continued to encourage him to ask Sarah out instead, but for many months we did socialise together. Our friendship grew as he dated my friend and, one night, I suddenly had to admit to myself that I fancied him!

I also admitted this to Peter.

So he broke it off with Sarah and we started going out. My guilt was assuaged as I later was instrumental in matching Sarah with her husband, Len Dineen! Peter and I did the usual thing of *off* and *on*, for a couple of years. I went to Cape Cod for the summer of my Fifth Year in Crescent, and went back to the States again after my Leaving Cert in 1985, which broke the heart of Peter's mother… not Peter.

Meg Clohessy still recounts how she cried while I was gone each of those summers. Not because she missed me, but because Meg maintained that

I was the only person who could keep Peter out of trouble! Although we both enjoyed our freedom in the summer of 1985, the moment we met that September when I returned to go to secretarial college our relationship was *back on*, and despite many ups and downs over the following years, here we are with our three children... 21 year old Luke, 15 year old Jane and Harry, our eight year old.

Limerick.

'Thanks for all your support and banter over the years, it is what makes Limerick such a great city, and makes me proud to be a Limerickman.'

– Peter

CHAPTER 2

Peter was born on March 22, 1966, in St Anthony's Nursing Home in Limerick city. By then his Mam, Meg O'Halloran already had three children... Gerard, Margaret and Deirdre, and Deirdre was just 11 months old when Peter was born which meant that they became great playmates. In fact, it seems that Dee was even better at rugby than Peter when they played on the Under-10s. Len Dineen senior still recounts how Dee had her hair short and they pretended she was a boy so she could compete in the Community Games! After Dee, Meg and Noel Clohessy welcomed "young Noel" into the world, and then Desmond some years later.

Meg was born in Thomondgate to Peter Fox-O'Halloran and Monsie O'Halloran, so they were "soda cakes" as all the people from Thomondgate were nicknamed – a name that carried down from the tradition of women baking soda cakes and leaving them on their garden walls to cool down.

Peter always remembers his Grandad with great fondness, and he often talks about his Grandad playing with his hair for hours on evenings when he lived with them in Monaleen. He was a great rugby player and he had captained Garryowen in his time. On any occasion I have heard people speak of him they have voiced a great respect for this gentle man. If there was ever gossiping or arguments going on Meg would always quote her Dad's favourite saying… 'Say nothing and saw wood'. My understanding is that he was a wise and compassionate man, who did indeed have an influence on Peter's formative years.

Peter's Dad, Noel whom everyone called "Daddy Noel" was born to Nelly Quinn and Martin Clohessy who lived in Janesboro. He was one of a family of five boys and one sister, Olive. Daddy Noel was an incredibly hard worker, and he became a very successful builder. Therefore all of his brothers – Cyril, Tony, Johnny and Michael – and indeed most of their children all worked in Noel's business at some stage, as did their extended families. Noel instilled this hard work ethic in his own boys, and Ger, Peter, Noel and Des all learned invaluable skills on building sites around Limerick. Daddy Noel was a tough taskmaster, but incredibly fair, and everyone learned to respect him. He was especially generous, and never held back on providing his family with every type of luxury.

Yet there were never ever any airs and graces about him. Because I met Peter at school I had no idea that his family was financially secure and, as I lived in the city and Peter lived on the other side of Limerick, we would always hang out at my house. One day, however, when we were off school Peter called to my house with his seven years-old brother, Des whom he had collected from the dentist.

'Do you want to come over to our house?' Peter asked me out of the blue. On the bus to Monaleen I was extremely nervous about meeting Peter's family for the first time, and as we got closer to the back gate to their house, I buckled.

'I'll wait for you out here,' I announced.

From this back gate, I could just see one window of the house in the distance. But, next thing I could hear a voice calling me in. I had been spotted, and Peter was sent out to fetch me. I nervously went in the non-descriptive back door, and then found myself in a kitchen that simply took my breath away. It was enormous. The only place I'd seen a kitchen like it was on the *Brady Bunch* television show.

Then this woman appeared.

'Hi love… cuppa tea?'

She spoke with a strong Limerick accent, and I immediately assumed she must be some woman who worked for the family. This fantastically posh house couldn't belong to someone who spoke like that!

We have laughed about my first impressions many times over the years, but Meg welcomed me with open arms into her family. Peter and Des then showed me around the whole house. I was still speechless… split level, six bedrooms, en-suites here and there… and this was in the eighties!

Clearly I didn't manage to hide my disbelief very well, so Peter and Des proceeded to tell me that there was a swimming pool in the *wing* where their parents' bedroom was, and of course I totally fell for it.

When I got back to my house my Mam, who was a brilliant mid-wife was on her day off and was doing housekeeping in the dining room. She looked at me, and quickly asked, 'What's wrong love?'

'Oh Mam… I can't bring Peter here anymore,' I told her, foolishly. Our house was an ancient Georgian number, four-storeyed over a basement and was always needing repair.

'Why not?' she asked.

'I've just been to his house… and they even have a swimming pool there!' I'm not sure if Mam was surprised or not, but I was in shock, as I had known Peter for a while at that stage, and I had no inkling that they were wealthy.

Money certainly hadn't changed the Clohessys though, and they stayed true to their belief of *family first*. Daddy Noel was always helping people out but he would never say very much about it to anyone.

He also gave his children their every wish, and in 1981 he took the whole family to New York and Disney World for the Christmas holidays. Meg had brought her magnificent full-length fur coat for the stopover in New York. In Florida, her coat was stolen from the hotel room, but the hotel refused to take responsibility as they couldn't believe that anyone would bring a fur coat to Florida. In true Daddy Noel style, when they arrived back home in Limerick he just went out and bought Meg a new fur coat!

Peter and Daddy Noel always had a special bond that Peter's siblings would tease him about regularly, and their relationship was copper-fastened when Peter was in third class in primary school. He was playing Community Games rugby for Regional against Our Lady of Lourdes, and got injured. When they brought him home Meg refused to take him to the hospital as he was covered in mud, and insisted on putting him into the bath and scrubbing him clean first of all.

When he was finally brought to the hospital and X-rayed it transpired his leg was broken in four places!

This led to Peter being off school for many months during which time he went to work daily with Daddy Noel. Peter loved having his Dad all to himself during this time (and, curiously, I see history repeating itself with our youngest, Harry who insists on having his Dad all to himself!). At any rate, Peter learned that working was far more exciting than school, and after that experience he completely lost interest in being in school at all. Back at Crescent Comp I would see Peter throw his school bag into his locker before we went for the bus home and I could never understand how he got away with that. I was at the same school… and my teachers wouldn't have tolerated no homework from me!

When they had moved to the beautiful house in Monaleen, Daddy Noel built stables at the back of their home because over the years he bought ponies for the kids when they spent their summers in Kilkee. Meg was very uncomfortable with the ponies, and Peter still takes off how she used to roar 'Get him OUT… get him OUT' whenever he brought "Magoo", his pony into the kitchen of their house in Kilkee!

During Aga Khan season they would set up jumps in their front garden and the kids would pretend to be the horses as they jumped the course against the clock. Peter had a competitive edge even then, and he used to enjoy tormenting the locals in Kilkee each year by winning the musical chairs and the beach racing on "Princess". The locals would be all decked out in their fine silky jockey gear, and their saddles would be gleaming, and they'd watch Peter turn up in his jeans. They'd then have to watch him ride "Princess" bare back, as the girth used to give her blisters!

He also mastered the Donkey Derby two years in a row – helped a little by the pepper that he would put up the donkey's rear end!

Peter's sister, Mags had a special interest in the horses too, hence the stables at the house in Monaleen, though I'm not sure how impressed the neighbours were when Peter would ride "Princess" bareback through the housing estate in the evenings!

This experience on ponies led to Peter's later love of fox hunting during his adult life. He never wishes to see a fox caught, but he adores the dangerous aspect of jumping a high wall and not knowing what may be on the other side! Hunting became especially important to him when he retired from rugby. His character is such that he needs to have that rush of adrenalin on a frequent basis. A lot of professional sportsmen suffer physiologically and emotionally when they suddenly go from one or two games and contact training sessions every single week, to nothing much at all. Peter would have been no different, but he purposely sought to fill any possible void once his professional rugby days were at an end.

He is a natural huntsman. This is partly due to the fact that he has an instinctive and finely tuned reflex system, and is very quick to react wisely in emergency situations. It's part of who he is, and always has been and even though I have worked for years as a Healthcare Therapist, complete with first aid training and experience, he is the one person I want around when our kids get injured.

Over the years, he has rescued children from drowning on summer holidays. But I think there was something divine at work one New Year's Day when Peter went hunting that morning in early January, 2008. He was in two minds that morning whether to go or not?

At the same time, he had promised his hunt pals that he would be their designated driver that day and he didn't want to let down his hunting buddy, John Hourigan.

Off he went on the Scarteen Hunt in Tipperary.

At one point during the hunt something made Peter look back into the last field they had come through, and he saw a rider down. He quickly turned around and rode back, and found a young girl unconscious on the ground. We would later find out her name was Aoife, and she was 13 years old. She had fallen off her pony "Robbie" and suffered a compound fracture of the skull. She was unconscious.

Aoife's mouth was firmly shut. Another lady rider arrived and was looking over the girl and warned Peter, who was bending over her, not to move her neck!

'F*** her neck… she's not breathing!' Peter replied.

He could see she was turning a poor colour and there was blood flowing from the back of her head. Peter knew how fatal it could be for someone swallowing their own tongue. He had heard about it, though he'd never helped someone in an emergency situation like this before. Immediately, he sought to open Aoife's mouth but struggled to do so. He couldn't believe how hard it was to force her jaws open, but he finally managed it, and probed into her mouth with his fingers and released her tongue. She began a very shallow breathing. It was a major effort to get the rescue services to her as she was in the middle of many fields. Over hedges and ditches the petite young girl was lifted, before she was rushed to Clonmel Hospital and then brought to the neurological unit at Cork University Hospital. Aoife survived, and is now back to full health and with her parents she kindly called into Peter a few weeks after the accident to thank him for his actions that morning.

The Fanning family had a gift for Peter, and Aoife's mother said that the doctors told them when they got to the hospital that they didn't think that she would make it such was the severity of the fracture to her skull. But for Peter's reactions on the day she certainly would not have lived, they told us.

Naturally, in keeping with his general character, Peter didn't even mention the incident to me on the telephone after the hunt. He waited until he got home to tell me what had happened. Later that evening he did admit to being a little shaken by it all, particularly as he was thinking that could easily have been our Luke or Jane on the ground.

During every school holiday Peter happily went to work with his Dad and he learned so many skills at an early age.

One morning, during our early years together, I remember coming upon Peter as he worked on the roof of Saint Alphonsus Redemptorist Church in the city, and he slid down scaffolding from a great height to come and chat with me. When we were finished, he jumped into a big orange and blue truck twice his height and drove away. He was 15 years old!

He told me that the previous day he had gone to Dublin in that same truck with his Dad, and Daddy Noel had let him drive the truck home from Dublin!

History has repeated itself with our children, and living on a farm has allowed them to drive at a very young age also. On one occasion I was showing Keith Wood's wife, Nicola around our new house in Murroe when we had just moved in. We were upstairs when I saw Nicola turn a little pale.

She looked at me with a horrified expression.

'Is that Luke driving that jeep?' she asked in a quiet voice.

'Oh yeah…' I answered nonchalantly.

'But… but… is that Alexander in the front?'

Alexander was Nicola and Keith's toddler.

'Oh, gosh… I'm sorry Nic… is that ok with you?'

'Luke has been driving for years,' I assured her. 'He's very safe!'

Luke was 10 years old at that time!

By the time Peter got to his Junior Certificate he was out of school more often than he was in. And on the days that Meg thought she had got him into school, he would take off with his pal, Billy Meehan on Billy's Honda 50. He'd arrive home at the appropriate time so Meg didn't know any different.

Fr Todd Morrissey, Principal of Crescent Comprehensive at that time, actually took a handle on the situation and advised Meg and Noel that their son would be better off working on the building sites. So, there and then, Peter happily said goodbye to his formal education and embraced his life skills' education.

To this day Peter is a magnificent Mr. Fix It, and at heart he is an engineer.

There were great advantages to having a boyfriend who was working, and driving around the place, while I was still at school. Daddy Noel had given all the boys access to cars and jeeps, even before they were old enough to legally drive them! So on my 16th birthday Peter taught me how to drive in the Clohessy's green Land Cruiser in the car park of the Crescent Shopping Centre.

This ability to get from A to B any time he wished also allowed all of Peter's friends to share in a great sense of freedom. None of us would ever get bored, we had so many options and choices to make for ourselves. For instance, as we got older, we would drive to the Worlds End in Castelconnell, and after being in the pub all night we'd go swimming, with the lights of the jeep surveying the river! I never worried on these adventures. Peter was always very protective of me and I would be mildly amused, and becoming mildly irritated, whenever he insisted that I was not to swim even though the other girls were in the water!

One night, Sarah McDonogh (later Dineen) dived off the top board. I watched half horrified. It was just as well Peter didn't let me swim that same night.

Though I would never have been that brave or daft!

This freedom also created some friction as I suspect always happens between the friends and the *girlfriend*, as we both competed for Peter's time.

So during our teenage years there was a mutual love-hate relationship between myself, and Pod (Pat O'Donnell), Mikey Clohessy, Snap (Brendan Ryan), Billy Meehan, Ger Enright and a few others, as I occasionally *took* Peter from them and visa versa! When they subsequently found their own girlfriends they began to get an understanding of how this system works!

Peter was lucky that his Dad had created a business for them to work in, because all the rest of Peter's friends ended up emigrating in the late eighties. Only two of that original group now live back in Ireland. But it is fantastic to have great friends who live in exotic places such as Long Island (Pod), and we have enjoyed many visits in recent times, when the 25 year gap melts into insignificance as the foundations of an old lasting friendship are re-kindled, and we watch our children interact and muse at the fact that we were that same age when we hung out together.

One of the highlights of the 2013 Lions tour to Australia was having lunch with Snap and his beautiful family in Melbourne. And the invitation to visit Mickey in San Francisco is a tempting one that I'm sure we will exploit in the near future.

Although the rugby genes clearly were inherited from the O'Halloran side of the family – Meg's dear brother, Pete was a great soccer and rugby player – Peter credits his uncle, Tony Clohessy as the one who encouraged him to get serious about playing rugby with Young Munster. Each day on the building site, Tony would try to steer Peter in the direction of Greenfields.

It is because of this that Peter once again began playing rugby in his late teenage years, just because he loved the thrill of it. That love of playing was part of growing up in that Monaleen house, where one of the corridors, four feet wide and thirty feet long, was the boys' pitch late at night. Ger, being the biggest, was always made to play on his knees, and he would partner Dee, against Noel and Peter. These great battles always ended up in tears, usually with Noel crying because he wasn't on the winning team.

The high priority of *family first*, was embedded in the children by Daddy Noel and Meg from the start, and if you crossed one Clohessy you crossed them all! This mafia-type family protection was an intimidating force to be reckoned with. Their bonds were super glue, and even though there are six bedrooms in the house all four boys slept together in the smallest room. Peter in a single bed and Ger, Noel and Des in the "pissy" double bed! Sorry Noel!

Noelie used to love his grub. When Ger was old enough to go out to the pub at weekends, he would bring home burgers, fish and chips from Donkey Fords chipper in the city. He would put a burger on Noel's chest as he slept, and they would all watch in laughter as Noel's nose would begin to twitch. He would half-open his eyes, eat the burger and go straight back to sleep!

Noelie was his Auntie Majella's favourite, and many is the time that he bawled as they would slag him that he was in love with Auntie Majella. She was Meg's sister, who lived with them after Grandad O'Halloran died, and how she had the patience to put up with those lunatic children I will never know. She is a lady who has the patience of a saint. When she started dating John Mullane he was quickly named "John will kill me", as Majella would be panicking getting ready for her dates and she would repeatedly be heard saying 'John will kill me... John will kill me' out loud. All the Clohessys agreed that house was never the same after Majella and John got married, and she moved out.

Without exception every member of my family adored Peter Clohessy. He could do no wrong. Once my father got over the fact the 'he plays with a pill-shaped bloody ball', he welcomed Peter with open arms, and was unashamedly proud when Peter got his first Ireland caps at Under-25 and B level in the early nineties.

When Peter would call to our house, Nana, Mam and my uncles would flap over him with cups of tea, sandwiches, cigarettes, even the remote control – his wish was their command. Nana was always saying 'Poor Peter'. To which I would reply 'Yeah... and isn't it such a shame he married... ME!'

My Mam would also go to great lengths each year to find a unique birthday present for Peter, which wasn't easy as he literally did have everything! I remember her delight when she located, of all things, a solid silver retractable toothpick! In later years when Mam lived with us, even when she was incredibly ill, her love and admiration for Peter never waned. In fairness to Peter, this love and respect was well earned as he was always very good to my family. He never once complained about any of them staying with us or visiting, and was always first to lend a hand in a crisis. Only those that truly know him enjoy his natural loyalty and thoughtfulness, and find the gentleman that lies beneath his seemingly gruff exterior.

Young Munster.
  All my Young Munster friends.
  'The best rugby days of my life were spent
with you lot... without what you taught me,
the rest of the story wouldn't have happened.
  'Thank you.'

                                    – Peter

CHAPTER 3

At the height of Peter's rugby career, I was often asked what it was like to be married to someone *famous*, but I'm sure those people didn't realize that when I met Peter he wasn't even on the Crescent school team. He had left school in 1982 after his Inter Cert and didn't play club rugby again until Young Munster asked him to play on their Under-18s. So Peter has always been the same to me as the day I first met him.

The fact that he played professional rugby for Munster and Ireland was just an interesting twist on the roller-coaster ride! Some of the best days out, however, were with Young Munster. The fun after those matches in the clubhouse was second to none. It was a hot bed of die-hard characters, from the older generations of the Harry Butterfields, to my parents' generation of the Geraldine Quinlivans. These people would make fun in a bucket.

While most visiting teams were intimidated on the pitch at Tom Clifford Park in Greenfields, they would all agree that the craic and welcome in the clubhouse after the game was fantastic. Young Munster's reputation preceded the club everywhere. The late, famous actor Richard Harris once told the story that his Mother insisted that he played with Young Munster because she wanted him playing with them and not against them! Mind you, if she only knew that was no guarantee of safety!

After one match against Cork Constitution, the players were talking about how Peter Meehan tore into a ruck and raked the back of his own men. Finally, one of his teammates piped up.

'What the f*** were you playing at Peter?'

'Sorry about that,' he replied, '... but Bradley (Michael Bradley, the Cork Con and Ireland scrum-half) was underneath you!'

The club's reputation was big – good in a big way, or bad in a big way – depending on someone's perspective!

When St Mary's came down from Dublin to play Munsters in one of many important All-Ireland League games, at the time when John "Paco" Fitzgerald was the captain of Young Munster, everyone was really excited at getting stuck into them.

It had emerged earlier in the week that Mary's had been telling people that they were going to *Jurassic Park*, in reference to the movie out at the time in which dinosaurs and all sorts of large, dangerous creatures were on the loose on a sub-Tropical island.

In the pre-match warm up, Paco was sharing this with his teammates in a rather excited way. But he got over excited... and then he got confused, and then he let out a roar before he led Munsters out the door of their dressingroom.

'We'll show them...

'We'll give them f****** ostriches!'

Peter, to begin with, enjoyed playing wing forward with underage teams in Young Munster. No matter how late he may have been out on the Saturday night he would always be on time for the match on Sunday... and, if he was late, it was because he had to call to Billy Meehan's house to drag him out of bed!

It was Roy Grant who told Peter to switch to prop.

The team was short a prop at the time.

Peter refused.

'If you don't go in there,' continued Roy, '... you're not playing for me!'

The following weekend, for the first time ever, Peter slept it out and he was late getting to Derryknockane. He was annoyed with himself as he knew that

Roy would think that he wasn't going to turn up. When Peter got there the match had already started and Roy, rightly so, gave out stink. However he did eventually put Peter on… in the front row rightly enough!

And to his surprise Peter enjoyed it and realised the front row wasn't as bad as he thought. If it was good enough for Dermot "Tessie" O'Brien, Fintan Costelloe and Pat Kilbridge, it was good enough for him. In latter years, Roy would proudly always remind Peter that he was the one who had *made* him into a prop.

Peter did get a reprieve for a while, however. 'I got a break for about three years,' he likes to remember when asked about turning into a prop forward. 'Unfortunately, Roy had a stroke… and he lost his memory… but then three years later Roy got his memory back again!'

Peter didn't expect to make the Munsters senior team anytime soon as they had a superb tight head prop in Johnny Murphy. But coming up to a semi-final of the Munster League against Shannon, Johnny went down with the flu – it was a big surprise when Peter was picked to play for the seniors.

He was propping that day against Tomas Healy, and when the first scrum collapsed, Tomas duly stood on Peter's hand.

'Welcome to the big time,' he added.

I believe he was duly reminded of that afterwards… and on many occasions! Peter's immediate success as a prop was down to the fact that he had Ray Ryan in the second row. Ray was consistently strong and also played from the heart.

While passion fuelled Young Munster, and made the crucial difference for them on many a close call, their coach Tony Grant was also a formidable character. He was very dedicated and in many ways far ahead of his time. He would even try to educate the lads about the effects of drinking – not that they listened!

He also was one of the first coaches in Limerick to do pre-season training, and he would bring the team up to Cratloe Woods, where he would run with them himself. Peter recently thought of Tony when he heard Johnny Giles reminisce that, in his day at training, you were told, 'If your grandmother is in your way… kick her'. Tony's approach was similar.

Munsters had a Munster Cup replay against Bohs one Monday evening, and Tony had warned the team they were not to go out drinking on the Sunday night. So, to distract themselves, Peter and Ray decided they would go and play a game of pitch and putt in Clonlara. However, they decided to play for a pint per hole! They assumed that they would be evenly matched so that the bet was safe enough.

Ray beat Peter by six holes, and they duly went to the local pub to clear the bet. There they played darts. Peter lost again, but decided to make a stand at the rubber rings board, by which stage they were p*****!

The two boys consoled themselves by reasoning that because they were far away in the country – Clonlara, for heavens sake! – nobody would ever know what they had been up to? The next evening in the dressingroom before the game, Tony Grant was going ballistic, roaring about how he had asked the team not to drink and how he had heard that two of them had gone on the lash.

Ray and Peter cast each other a very guilty look. Then Tony shouted, 'Mul… Miko… outside… NOW!'

Johnny Maloney and Miko Benson trooped out the door behind Tony. Peter and Ray heaved a sigh of relief. But, even Tony Grant knew there was nothing he could do to interfere with Thursdays!

Thursday night training for Munsters was pitch, pub, and Ted's Nightclub, and always in that order, though occasionally some bright spark would decide to add a house party to the scheme of things.

It was mandatory, and hard to escape. Some tried. One evening Paco decided – more likely it was his wife, Caroline's idea! – to arrive at Greenfields in his tracksuit so he couldn't possibly even think of going out afterwards with the rest of the boys. In the showers, after training, the others were busy sprucing themselves up and the temptation was simply too much for Paco – he hightailed it to the Crescent Shopping Centre and bought himself some clothes!

Match days in those early years were very special, simply because the local rivalry between clubs, and the stakes, were always very high. The club was a birthright that nobody dared swap. It was in the blood and any club transfer was seen as high treason.

In those days too, almost every man, woman and child in Limerick understood the game, and had an allegiance and loyalty to one club or another. This was why rugby blossomed in Limerick. The other unique aspect to rugby in Limerick was that it crossed all social classes.

In the bigger cities rugby was a *posh* game, but not so in Limerick where the "docker" played against the "doctor". And, of course, Thomond Park was and hopefully will always remain a very special place, principally because the home crowd is so knowledgeable about the game. The arrival of the Heineken Cup and, along with it professionalism in the game, has diluted this rivalry dramatically. We have a whole generation of children and young adults who are dedicated to Munster, and will never know of the passion that existed in the clubs in the eighties.

The craic on the "popular side" of Thomond Park at a club match had to be witnessed to be believed. And there were always a few *wits* who, as well as being the creators of much sideline laughter, instigated many a row also. The like of Harry Butterfield, who would walk up and down the sideline, would always rise to the challenge of taunts from rival supporters.

It was all par for the course, and would be resolved in the clubhouse over a pint afterwards. The community spirit that club rugby created was warming and all-embracing. This was especially evident at funerals. Then, all of a sudden, club loyalties would be set aside and rugby supporters would unashamedly demonstrate their deep respect for one another's families.

While the new *club* Munster is incredibly special in many ways, it owes a great debt that can never be fully repaid to the foundations that were put in place by so many dedicated club members down through the generations. And this same community spirit propelled Munster to great heights and massive success as the club members who had fought in the trenches of club rugby quite naturally transferred their allegiance to *club* Munster.

In a way the clubs were sacrificed for Munster.

The difficulty now, that the last generation of club supporter is depleting, is that the next generation of supporters do not have this local spirit as their foundation. The challenge for Munster going forward is to re-create that all-encompassing community spirit – but thankfully those in charge of the province seem to realise this, as they have recently employed some home grown coaches, like Anthony Foley and Niall O'Donovan, who understand where everything comes from!

Each club in the city had its own particular style, characteristics, and traditions! For Young Munster, the club's unique personality dated back beyond the winning of the Bateman Cup in 1928, when the winners of the four provincial Cups came together to make certain who was the best team in Ireland – and Munsters were crowned No.1.

My dear Nana, who would have been 26 years old at the time, often spoke of how she had never seen anything like the celebrations that went on in the streets of Limerick after that victory. The Yellow Road, which stretched from the railway station to Young Munster's playing fields, was synonymous with the club. As was Dodo Reddan, who lived on Reeves' Path, a road we walked as children on the way to school.

Dodo was a real Limerick character who rescued stray dogs, and she would wheel them around the city in a huge old fashioned pram. It became traditional for Dodo – and her pram and dogs – to be decked out in black and amber ribbons. They travelled to all the matches.

The diet of the "Cookies", as Young Munster supporters were commonly known, was also very traditional and, in Peter's house as in many others, "Packet and Tripe" would be served on the morning of a match – a skill that I have never chosen to learn! The whitish lining of a cow's stomach and the blue-black colour of pig's blood are delicacies I am willing to pass up on, though I'm just as happy to forget the "Crubeens" or pigs feet that would be unwrapped from tin foil on the train journeys to games away from home. I always politely declined any offers of a taste from my older travelling companions.

The many Cup finals that Munsters lost to Shannon at Thomond Park are by now carved in history, as are the pub crawls back into town, with stops at all the Thomondgate pubs – North Star, Bowles and Meaney's, before heading to Charlie St George's and Austin's. The sing-songs were amazing, from Meg's traditional rendition of *Barefoot Days*, to Johnny Brennan and *My Boy*. Ray Ryan would keep it current and play the guitar, and of course there were regular and random interventions of *Beautiful, Beautiful Munsters*! The night would be rounded off with a steak breakfast in Dirty Dicks at three and four o'clock in the morning!

Peter made so many lifelong friends from his memorable days with Young Munster, hence Ray Ryan was our Best Man, and 17 years later he became Harry's Godfather. We are still guaranteed a great night out with Ray and Trish, as he has a very quick turn of phrase, and is a wonderful entertainer with his guitar. That turn of phrase did have its disadvantages on occasions, however.

After one Munsters match in Dublin, Trish and I went to collect the boys from the train station in Limerick. Peter, to be fair to him on this one occasion, was sober but as Ray had been injured and hadn't played in the game he was a couple of hours and probably 10 pints ahead of Peter in the drinking stakes. The four of us went to the Texas Steak House for dinner, which was definitely not a smart idea as, at that time, the waiters used to wear holsters, with guns in them that looked very like the real thing.

I could tell from Ray that he was in divilment mood, and I purposely warned Peter to keep an eye on him. The dinner passed without incident, mainly because the two lads were so hungry. After we paid the bill we decided to head back to Munsters' clubhouse but, as we were crossing a very busy one-way Shannon St, there was suddenly screeching of brakes on all sides.

I turned around to see the traffic stopped. Worse, there was an unmarked detectives' car mounted on the footpath!

In the middle of the road, there was Ray.

He had a gun belonging to one of the waiters in his hand and he was pointing this gun at the traffic. For 'the craic', was his only explanation the next day! One poor driver stopped in front of him had turned pale in the face and was not having any craic at all. Meanwhile the detectives were high on adrenalin.

They were shouting at Ray.

They demanded to know what was in his hand?

'It's a Colt 45,' Ray shouted back at them, adding…

'What do you think it is?'

They then asked him what he was doing with it? But rather than give them an answer, Ray then thought it was a good idea to swivel the gun around with his finger like one of those cowboys in the movies, saying 'I was doing this!'

Then he swivelled it the opposite way and said, '… and I was doing this!' Myself and Trish watched dumbfounded. Peter then felt obliged to chime in. He explained to the detectives that the gun was belonging to one of waiters in the restaurant, and quickly the detectives escorted Ray back in that direction. Meanwhile I argued with Peter to get into my car.

Trish was crying.

Peter was getting angry.

He couldn't understand what all the fuss was about? He then decided that it was a very good time to air a grievance that he had been holding onto for a few days, with the detectives. He made it known to them in a loud voice that he was sorely disappointed with the degree of law and order the detectives in Limerick were bringing to the place. Because, it so happened, that same week Peter had caught two lads breaking into his warehouse. Detectives had arrived quickly enough to the scene alright once Peter made a phone call, and they took the lads away, but Peter had followed them. He watched as the detectives drove for a mile or two and then let the two lads out of their car and away home as if nothing had happened, and didn't even bring them into the Garda station for some questioning.

So, naturally, Peter Clohessy thought it was an appropriate moment to tell these other two detectives that instead of arresting his good friend Ray it would be more in their line of duty to arrest the real criminals of Limerick.

This piece of advice was not a big help.

For starters, it did not help Ray one little bit. He was duly taken away in the squad car. And he was informed that he might be charged for attempted hold-up with an imitation firearm!

This was really bad news, because Ray worked for De Beers, the diamond company at the time, and a zero criminal record was a term of contract. I wasn't long pointing out to Peter how his tactics didn't help his best friend.

We went in search of a friend we knew who, to be fair, really stuck his neck out and went to the Garda station and managed to have Ray released without charge.

Unfortunately when he got into the station, all he could hear coming from the cells in the back was someone happily singing away to himself.

'FREE... HE... NELSON MANDELA... AH... AH...'

Peter had his *moments* too.

Early in 1993, he was asked to *do* an official dinner in Longford Rugby Club, which meant turning up as a Guest of Honour and impressing people with his chat and general charming personality. Peter, to this day, rarely *does* events, and at that time he didn't have much interest either, but he negotiated that Ray and Trish could also come with us. At that stage both Trish and I were heavily pregnant. Trish had been told it was twins, but it transpired later on in her pregnancy that she was having triplets! Their baby Dawn was only nine months old at this point!

Neil Enright from Longford RFC invited us to stay at his house the night of the function, but Peter insisted that we stay at a local hotel instead. At the dinner dance, the four of us were treated like royalty.

If only Peter had behaved like royalty!

The boys of course were tucking into their pints and at some point Trish and I decided we had listened to enough nonsense out of them and we went off to our bedrooms. I awoke early as usual. No sign of Peter.

I rang through to Trish's room to discover there was no sign of her husband in her bed either. We had no choice but to wait, and wait, as there was no way of contacting the boys or finding out if they were indeed dead or alive.

Much later, my bedroom phone rang. Lo and behold it was one Peter Clohessy, full of the joys, telling me that they had gone out in Neil's boat, on a lake, to do some skiing after the dinner dance. And if skiing while p****d wasn't bad enough, when they finished skiing my husband proudly told me they then took to some shooting in Neil's back garden. Neil had a shotgun and they decided to take advantage of the beer bottles that they had been emptying all evening long.

I held my own fire. I had to because I was further informed that we were now invited to lunch at Neil's beautiful home, and I was to drive myself and Trish over there.

There was no point in having the row there and then. Best to bite my lip really hard, I thought, and be polite during lunch. Neil and his lovely wife were very welcoming, and to her credit if she was as annoyed as she should have been, she managed beautifully to keep it to herself.

Lunch was beautiful, and if our party of four had retreated home to Limerick at that point the weekend would at least have come to a dignified ending. Mind you, the only coherent people at the table were the females. Peter, at some point, had disappeared to the toilet. And he had not returned to the table.

After a reasonable length of time, it was up to me to excuse myself, and go and check on him. Indeed, the toilet door was still locked, but whoever was inside was completely unresponsive.

Peter, I knew, was on the other side of the firmly locked door! I tried my best to wake him up by knocking on the door, but no luck. There was no choice but to go back to the table and deliver the unfortunate news to our hosts. So now, here we were, having wrecked their garden, and about to do more damage.

The Enrights had to take their bathroom door off its hinges.

It wasn't a pretty sight on the other side of the door.

Peter on the toilet!

Snoring his head off!

The row, when it did commence with my husband, lasted much longer than the long smelly journey back to Limerick!

The lack of accountability and traceability, for a generation who were not equipped with mobile phones, created the perfect environment for men to go missing in action.

Before we married, and before Peter was even playing senior rugby, Young Munster had won the Munster Senior Cup. There were big celebrations, and I had left the clubhouse late that night.

The following day Peter was nowhere to be found. Myself and another girlfriend were distraught as we tried all the usual suspect places, but there was not a trace of Peter or his friends. In those days, my biggest concern was drink-driving. Inexplicably, it was *socially acceptable* to drive while drunk back then – like a lot of illegal activity in the Ireland of the seventies and eighties it was considered unfortunate if someone was caught!

It was the Monday night before Peter was back on the radar, when I discovered that they had driven to Kilkee at four o'clock in the morning! In a way I had no right to complain on the many, many subsequent times that the same thing happened. It's not like I didn't see it coming!

This was standard issue behaviour for rugby players, who lived in an old fashioned man's world, and one where a woman's place was believed to be in the home. I can now look back and admire my stamina, as I incessantly challenged the system – and Peter – for many years about the injustice of this mentality!

When we became engaged in 1987 I mentioned to Peter that I would like to keep my own name after we got married. He asked me was I seriously going to make an already ridiculously long name even longer by adding Clohessy?

'Of course not,' I replied.

'… I'm not taking Clohessy at all… I'm staying just Anna Gibson-Steel.'

He didn't agree. So I suggested that he should change his name to Gibson-Steel after we married.

'You must be f***** joking,' was his reply.

'You keep your own names… !' he added.

And that was the end of that argument. Except, of course I still had to have hard words with the Revenue Commissioners as they automatically changed my name to Clohessy without even asking me. I won that battle too.

Looking back on it now as a mother, I am amazed that my parents didn't show any resistance to my getting married at 21 years old. On the other hand Peter's mam, Meg still admits to being the only mother of the groom to be wildly ecstatic as she watched her son going up the aisle and he just one year older than me.

Such was her relief.

The only woman who appeared to be able to manage her son was getting full and legal responsibility for him.

Buddha Healy.

'The Duracell Bunny — the longest lasting rugby player ever. He got his first cap for Munster at an age when most players retire. Best remembered for the time in the scrum against Toulouse when he was heard shouting, "Mr Califrano... stop... you're hurting me!"'

— Peter

CHAPTER 4

People assume that Peter was dedicated and ambitious about his rugby career. He was as the years progressed, but this certainly was not the case before the game went professional. Peter played because he enjoyed the game. He hated training. And he wasn't one to watch matches incessantly on television either. Physical fitness was alien to him, although he did have a natural fitness from the manual work he did as a builder. On the minus side, however, he had begun smoking at the age of 10, a habit he continues to this day.

He doesn't do politics, although he is naturally a great people person. He is also blunt and incredibly funny, so he is not your typical role model rugby player. However, he was a rare talent on the field, in that he had the ability – despite fitness levels – to play from his heart with a passion that made him exceptional, and occasionally this passion was his downfall.

He has the energy of a *Braveheart* warrior, and is unstoppable when he locks in his target! And it was this quality more than anything else that meant many a rugby selector had to choose him for their team, despite themselves!

Peter's love of a good time was nearly his downfall at the beginning of his rugby career. The choice between having the craic with his best friends and playing a game of rugby was a tough one for him at that time.

One weekend he was due to head to Dingle with the lads, which included his childhood partner in crime, Pat O'Donnell, but things got complicated a few days before they were due to set off when Peter got a late call up to an Irish Under-21 trial in Dublin. His Dad was so proud, and when Peter returned home to Limerick on the Sunday night, he asked his son how he got on?

'Nawh... it didn't go so well,' said Peter.

Well, it couldn't have, considering Peter had set off for Dublin alright with his bag of rugby tricks but then decided to turn his car around at Roscrea and headed to Dingle with the lads instead! That was Peter, and furthermore he had no regrets either!

Peter remained at ease about his rugby career.

It was more difficult for me to be so easygoing. To get to Peter's second game for Munster in the late eighties, which was against Connacht in Galway, I had to travel with him the day before the game as we only had one car – I didn't know any of the partners of his teammates to try to work a car-pool.

The team was staying in the Corrib Great Southern Hotel, so I had booked my own room there also for both nights. However, I was very aware that I shouldn't have been there, so when I arrived I went to my room and I stayed there all evening, ordering room service for dinner and spending all my time on the telephone to my friends. Meanwhile, Peter was under orders to go for a few pints with the team!

For this pleasure I duly paid a hotel bill of £120 at a time when my month's wages from the bank were £300! If Munster beat Connacht that day they were going to share the Championship with Ulster, but to win the prize of the crystal Heineken bowl they would have to score five tries.

The late and great Colm Tucker was Munster captain.

'Our objective is to beat Connacht,' he announced in his warm-up speech, '... and f*** the fruit bowl.'

Munster did win, and they shared the Championship, and failed to earn the fruit bowl, but not that many people were around the place to take much notice! Supporting Munster in that day was neither stylish nor mandatory. That Sunday night in the Corrib there were about 50 Munster people in attendance, including the team itself! Nevertheless, even if the whole province was oblivious to what had been done, the following day was declared a National Holiday by all of us – by Mossie Finn, Kenny Murphy, Pat Cross, Colm Tucker, Niall O'Donovan, Terry Kingston, Paco, Donal Lenihan, Finbar Kearney, Pat Murray, Ralph Keyes, Michael Kiernan, and all their partners.

These were perhaps more innocent days, before the game became big, and winning and money became such a central part of everyone's lives.

We crawled home and got to Durty Nellies at around 9.0 p.m., and started again! And, naturally, everyone had work to get to the next day.

Innocent enough days indeed, though amongst the players from different provinces there was not much love lost at times. During this same period Munster played Ulster in Cork, and the team dinner was back at Cork Constitution's clubhouse, and that's where we were sitting at a table when one prominent Ulster, and later Irish rugby player, asked Peter for a light.

Peter handed over his lighter.

When he looked for it back, however, this *gentleman* threw it on the ground and told Peter to get down on his knees for it!

Like that was ever going to happen, Sir!

That same evening I was formally called upon by the Munster team management, asking me to calm Peter down – apparently I came in useful occasionally! I never understood that arrogance, or show of nastiness. Neither did Peter.

Worse, because after that same defeat by Ulster in Cork, three of the Munster squad were dropped – Michael Kiernan and Michael Bradley for their under-par performances, and Peter for an entirely different reason. The media was struggling to understand why Peter was dropped?

Soon enough a reason was unofficially floated that he had used sectarian remarks against Willie Anderson, which he had not, but I'm pretty sure that the row and the altercation in the clubhouse afterwards was the deciding factor.

It was another four years before Peter would play for Ireland. However, this was never something that he spoke about, or particularly aspired to. He was never one for dreaming or setting targets.

He would live in the moment and let tomorrow take care of itself. While I spent a lot of time trying to teach him otherwise, I eventually came to the conclusion that in fact he was absolutely right! That did not mean that he lacked dedication. He always gives his full attention to everything he does and as a result has been very successful at mastering whatever he decides to turn his hand to. Peter is emotionally intelligent, and has the ability to learn anything of his choosing, despite any high level of formal education. I am constantly amazed at how he can remember and handle his many business deals, he can recall any invoice amount almost on demand from memory, has employed hundreds of people locally for many years, runs a farm, is a fantastic horse rider... heck, he even won the *ICA Bootcamp* reality TV show! His cool head when others around him are losing theirs is fascinating to me. He can do a live interview at the drop of a hat, while a clatter of children are hanging out of him! In Kilkee he is like The Pied Piper.

He will pull into the pier in his boat, and children will ask for a spin and he'll rarely refuse. Much to my horror.

'PETER... do their parents KNOW that they are on that crowded boat...?

'Have they ALL got lifejackets...?'

But he loves children, and is totally cool with them, and has infinitely more patience than me and, as he doesn't do fear, health and safety would not be his strongest point either! But in a crisis he is the person I would most want beside me, and I know he would have made a fantastic paramedic amongst other things.

The key is that he truly does not care what anyone else thinks of him, he doesn't second-guess himself, and he never does *drama*. Never. Ever. And that's how it was from the very start before his Ireland career even came close to kicking off.

It was almost despite himself that he ever got capped for Munster and Ireland. Politically he came from the wrong club, and rugby was very political at that time. Local rugby fans in Limerick only had to point at a brilliant player like

Ger Earls, who was never capped by his country, to recognise the darkest politics involved in some rooms when selectors were meeting to choose a representative team. Add to that the fact that Peter took no prisoners on the pitch, not ever – nothing less would even occur to him – and it was obvious that he had to be extra special to make it to the top of the game in this country.

Peter's reputation on the pitch was earned, for sure. However, in all the altercations over the years, he was never one to hold a grudge, and after every game he would leave what happened on the pitch behind him. Sadly, this is not true of all rugby players, and I have witnessed a few occasions when opposition players took the lower road, running off to reporters to anonymously tell their side of what happened in a game. I always found it sad to witness this non-masculine behaviour from so-called macho men!

Interestingly, although Peter had many a famous, and infamous, scrap with lots of French opponents, they always had a fantastic respect for him. They loved his passion, as the French do as a race, and as a result they always wanted to meet like with like – with the result that they would try and take him *out* early on in every game! But, like Peter, they would shake hands afterwards and forget about the war.

And there were wars! In Paris during one of Peter's early Five Nations Championship games, events on the pitch were getting exceptionally heated. The entire French team was clearly on a mission to get Peter.

Noel "Noisy" Murphy, the former Irish and Lions forward and coach, who was manager of the Irish team, was hopping up and down on the sideline.

'Take him off… TAKE HIM OFF!' he roared.

'They are going to… KILL HIM!'

The French left many scars that day on his body but, as usual, Peter had no complaints, and in a way I viewed the treatment meted out by his opponents as an acknowledgment of how valuable a player he was!

Most people I've met over the years assume that being a WAG of a professional rugby player is a life filled with travel and glamour.

Oh really?

Firstly, it's important to put on record that things changed considerably when rugby went professional but before that day arrived rugby had a very busy social scene attached to it and this was purely stag orientated, first and last. This, of course, did not mean that there weren't any females at these social events. There were, so long as they were not a wife or girlfriend.

This can be a tad challenging for a marriage!

In the late eighties and early nineties zero information technology at hand facilitated many AWOL instances.

Hours after some of those Thursday evening training sessions with Young Munster I'd be pacing the floor at home – there was the added concern of the guys drinking as much as they wanted and then deciding to drive home.

Luckily I have always been blessed with many good friends, and in those days Majella Fitzgerald and myself soldiered together, and supported each other on many a late night and early morning, as we played that waiting game.

Years later, it is easy to laugh at some of the funny instances, but rest assured they were not even vaguely humorous at the time. But, wives do learn to adjust and after five years of marriage and the arrival of Luke, our first born, I was able to sleep and not waste my time pacing the floor anymore. Though that did not stop me from being woken up.

One Sunday Peter was playing against Garryowen, and being a clever girl I made sure that his car was left at home – at least I wouldn't have to worry about him driving home drunk. So I slept soundly until the phone rang at three o'clock in the morning.

Paco Fitzgerald was on the other end of the line, asking me if Peter was home yet with his car! I woke up fairly lively and asked Paco how long was it since Peter had left in the car?

'About half an hour... Anna,' Paco replied, as innocently as he could manage.

This was not good news.

Peter should have been well home in that time. So, what was I to do but call on my partner in war, Majella. In fairness it was one of the rare occasions when her husband, Mark was already at home, and to their great credit, both of them got up and came over to our house.

Mark said he would go looking for Peter, and suggested Majella would stay with me, but I was having none of it. Therefore we left Majella minding

Luke and I took off with Mark. Our first duty was to check the local roads for any sign of an accident. Thankfully, we could not find anything amiss. Then we checked outside Henry St Garda station in the city. No sign of Paco's car there either.

We tried the usual suspect haunts. No joy. Mark decided we should head out to Garryowen rugby club to have a look?

Lo and behold, parked outside the clubhouse was Paco's car. However, the windows were completely fogged up.

Mark told me to stay in his car.

He would go and check inside the car, he insisted.

Yeah, right…? Like I was going to let him do that!

The two of us took off in a sprint. Mark was anxious to get there first in the hope of doing some damage limitation, and he did prove himself fitter and faster than me. He opened the door of Paco's car… and closed it just as quickly.

He turned to me.

'Anna… don't open it…!' he ordered.

I had to give him credit for trying, but his advice was never going to be taken on board by me that night. I swung open the door of Paco's car and… there was Peter with a young girl, I thought for a second!

It took two or three seconds more for me to realize it was not my husband in the car. Dessie Clohessy was the luckiest guy on the planet that night that I didn't hit him! Peter's younger brother did look quite like him at that stage. In Paco's car, it was Dessie getting to know his latest conquest!

Back in Mark's car, I began to relax. At least Peter wasn't stuck in a ditch in Paco's car. Now I just had one of the usual cases of missing in action on my hands.

Mark and I headed home to Majella, who by now had gone through 20 Silk Cut in my kitchen! It was five o'clock in the morning when a taxi pulled up. Out of it staggered the elusive Peter, suitably locked!

Into the kitchen he marched, and thought it highly amusing to see all three of us sitting there at the table. He had no idea why Paco thought he had his car. Mind you, he could make no sense about anything really.

My rule No.1 on occasions like this was applied.

Rule No.1 when Peter disappeared and then suddenly reappeared hours, or half a day later, was not to go for him bald-headed. That was no way to get any information on where he had been, and what might have been going on. Instead I smiled lovingly.

I made him a cup of tea.

I sat him down and asked him all about the wonderful night he'd had. This rule, while painful to apply, always got results for me. I always got all of the information I wanted every time, and furthermore Peter never remembered telling me anything! Tactically this is a Churchill move, and it did indeed gain me much needed ammunition over the years. Plus, I was able to check out Peter's stories before he even woke up the following morning with his hangover.

Then it was time to pounce – when it hurts the most!

It's great that things have changed so much in terms of the acceptance of this type of carry on, and nowadays most guys wouldn't dream of behaving so selfishly.

Perhaps they may dream, but most of them wouldn't do it. But, like drink driving, that behaviour was accepted as the norm back then, and in fact you were considered a cranky WAG if you complained or kept your man on too tight a reign.

In so many ways the arrival of information technology has been useful in curbing the opportunities for the players to stray, but this has also got a massive down side and actually I feel a little sorry for players nowadays as nothing is sacred any more – and there have been plenty of cases where information is recorded and then used out of context, causing lots of unnecessary pain in relationships.

In the old days the lack of technology brought some level of protection, and the only danger was a tabloid reporter and photographer with a camera being in the right place at the wrong time!

Too often, however, that was also the case.

Munster had played Ulster in Belfast, and after the match the guys travelled as far south as Dublin. It was one of those times where Peter was clearly in the process of getting out of the dog house again, as he had promised me that he wouldn't be drinking.

He duly phoned from his hotel room in Dublin to say goodnight. And a good night it was, as I found out the following day in *The Star* newspaper!

The biggest headline was on page three. I heard later that the same headline was due for page one, except poor Princess Diana died that same night, so she relegated the rugby story to an inside page.

In fairness to the lads, someone got wind of the story and suggested that Peter tell me about it before I read the paper!

"Rugby aces in Night Club fracas at the Pod".

That was the headline. Alongside the article were two photographs, a half decent one of Peter, and one of Mick Galwey taken during a match that made him look like a complete thug! Gaillimh reckoned that it was Peter's First Communion photo, he looked so charmingly innocent.

Five of them had been refused entry into the nightclub, and they argued of course, but nothing more than that. However, someone saw a story in the making! And the story of a brawl was fabricated. This was one of the few times when I'm one hundred per cent certain the lads were telling the truth, because they threatened the newspaper with legal proceedings, and the newspaper printed an apology double quick in the end. The paper also said sorry in cash!

There was an added development though at this stage, because Peter and Gaillimh were now professional rugby players. The IRFU called them to a disciplinary meeting to decide if their actions had brought the game into disrepute, and this in turn had led to the lads having to take legal action to protect themselves.

We got a nice holiday thanks to *The Star*.

In a further interesting twist to the whole episode Noel "The Buddha" Healy also threatened to sue the newspaper for calling him an *International* rugby player.

Gaillimh.

'My partner-in-crime.

'What a laugh we had together. You made all the travelling so much easier. We always had each others backs covered.

'You were also the best captain I ever played under.'

– Peter

CHAPTER 5

I clearly remember how truly *glamorous* it was in the early professional days for rugby in Ireland, as I worked in the bank, Monday to Friday, and my Mam took care of Luke. And each weekend I would spend at home alone with my baby as Peter went to Dublin for training camp.

The lads would have to be in Dublin after their club games – they played with their clubs as well as their province back then – and report to The Berkeley Court Hotel on the Saturday night for a team meeting. Training was scheduled for Sunday. While some of the dedicated squad members would indeed get some much needed rest on Saturday night, so they would be fresh for work the next morning, I know for certain of two that NEVER did.

This pair knew the service lift, which took them down to the basement of the hotel car park, intimately. This was the pair's escape and return route. They would make their getaway while the management team were in the lobby at meetings, and return back well after the managers and coaches were in their beds.

Sunday morning training was the only obstacle they had to navigate, but there was always a plan – join the queue outside the team doctor's room, and present an un-diagnosable injury acquired during the previous day's match. Of course it had to be an injury not visible to the naked eye, but at the same time with enough symptoms to suspect something serious might have occurred.

This meant Peter and Gaillimh just had to watch the training on Sunday morning instead of taking part.

For some years this worked a treat for them, until a boy cried wolf.

Gaillimh, this particular Sunday morning, presented himself at the doctor's door with a massive hangover – oops... I mean, suspected pain in his neck!

Clearly he did a great job describing his symptoms as he was duly sent to the local hospital for an MRI. That was one more of the advantages of being a professional rugby player, no long waiting lists.

The scan confirmed Gaillimh's symptoms. He did indeed have a serious neck injury, and he ended up spending the week in hospital. In fact, the main Irish newspapers busily started writing his rugby obituary. He would never play for Ireland again, they imagined.

Turned out the hospital diagnosis was wrong. Gaillimh was still Gaillimh. There was absolutely nothing wrong with his neck, and he went on to play many more times for his province and country.

When camp ended the lads would then arrive back to our house. As we lived near the Dublin Road at the time it was where they would pool their cars, and then each of them would claim expenses for driving up to Dublin from Limerick. The others would spin off after arriving at our house, and Peter would slump into the armchair and sleep off his hangover! Oh, the glamour of being a WAG.

Once Peter made his way on to the Irish team, the pressure really ramped up – not for him, for me! As I worked in the TSB Bank, we remained open until 6.0 p.m. on Fridays, so I would work all week, then get into my car late on Friday evening to drive to Dublin, which could easily take three and a half hours in those pre-motorway days. The night before games I would stay with a friend as we were never allowed to be with the men the 24 hours before a match.

I'd head to The Berkeley Court in time for lunch before the match. While this concept sounds like fun, it rarely was, as these lunches were stuffy affairs with perhaps 20 WAGS, and up to 150 committee members with their wives.

Laughing was generally frowned upon at these lunches, and I was not blessed with a delicate laugh – Peter can find me in a room of 500 if I am having a good time. The hotel's long serving waiters Bobby and Fran provided me with entertainment during these lunches.

To be fair we would always be anxious for the lads pre-match, and I often didn't eat lunch, as the nerves would be getting the better of me. I know some of the other partners felt the same nerves, but the only partner who truly felt the same as I did before a game was Trevor Brennan's wife, Paula. Our fears were not founded on whether the team would win or lose, or whether Peter and Trevor might get injured. We were just sick with worry that the pair would lose their heads!

After a game, if we were playing at home, we would be allowed to meet with our partners under the old West Stand at Lansdowne Road, where I would then – nerves all gone – feast on the delicious sandwiches and mini desserts. The lads would appear all dapper in their No.1s (IRFU blazer and slacks), and bearing the obvious scars of battle in the form of bandages, stitches or crutches.

This quiet time under the stand was my favourite period as it gave the two of us 30 minutes of quality time to catch up for the first time in a long week. After that, the madness would begin again. We'd walk or bus it back to the hotel, squeeze through the throngs of supporters, find and say hello to whichever family members were around, check into our room – and I'd be due downstairs in a ball gown within 15 minutes!

I used to feel awkward in the early days, as I wasn't quite sure what I should do when Peter was approached by supporters? I did not mind them asking to chat, but if I spoke I might appear cocky, and if I didn't I may appear aloof. So I was always happiest if I could take a photo of them with Peter.

Peter always had the ultimate patience with supporters, and only twice have I seen him get angry. The first time was with an Irish rugby supporter after he had retired from the game, when one supporter simply didn't give a damn that Peter had his hands full.

We were on a family skiing holiday – the players were not allowed engage in dangerous sports while they were contracted to play, so this was a real treat for us all, despite making the big mistake of not learning to ski ourselves first before we took off. The holiday was challenging to say the least.

Eight year old Luke put on his skis and immediately took off down the slopes without any lessons. Jane was three, and she was having none of being left alone at ski class so I spent the first four days sitting under a tree watching her learn. Peter, of course, decided that he didn't need any lessons either!

He was well able to ski on his first morning, as he knew he would be because of his experience as a good water-skier. Though quite suddenly he discovered the difference between the two forms of skiing. On the water you let go of the rope, and you stop! On snow and ice Peter was flying down the slope with absolutely no clue as to how to put the brakes on, and early on day one he duly crashed into a carousel of fifty pairs of skis outside a restaurant.

Our very dear friend, Eimear Farrell was on the trip with us. Eimear started out as Luke's babysitter eight years earlier – and is still our children's second mother, as well as our trusted friend. Eimear got to her ski lesson each day, and on the last day she took the advice of the eight year old Luke when he told her that she would be well able to ski down the mountain directly to our hotel. Luke had been doing this each day for the full week.

Bad choice. Luke got down as usual without a bother, but Eimear tore her cruciate ligament in her knee and had to be rescued from the mountain. The medical centre was about 100 yards down the hill from our hotel. By the time we got down from the mountain to meet her Eimear was in a brace sitting in a wheelchair – and we were due to fly home the next morning.

Peter was still in his ski boots and he was trying to push Eimear in her wheelchair up a 45 degree, snowy and slippy, hill.

Enter an Irish autograph hunter.

He started off okay with Peter.

'I see you are a bit busy,' he chimed.

'But any chance of a photo with my young lad?'

Peter had three options.

One, let go of the wheelchair and risk killing Eimear altogether. Two, politely tell the autograph hunter 'no'. Three, lose it!

Peter chose the last option on this menu.

There were also occasions when people would be curious enough about

Peter that they would ask me questions about him, and I have always been polite in those circumstances, even when the question didn't warrant a polite answer.

'What's it like to be married to an animal?'

I've happily lost count of the number of times someone has chosen to ask me exactly that question in so many words. Thankfully my parents had taught me that sticks and stones could break my bones but names could never hurt me, so I would just smile and not respond.

I would never tell Peter about these sort of questions until the next day, because he has always been very protective of those he cares for, and he wouldn't hesitate to defend their honour. I often did wonder however what way minds work for some people? What a strange thought-process? And, more curiously, what reply did they expect from me?

In those days after Five Nations games, the players and partners would be spilt up, the boys having dinner at one hotel, and the WAGS at another – a very strange experience to be dressed in evening gowns at a huge gala dinner, which could have over 300 guests, all female.

I found these dinners hard work, having not seen our partners for at least a whole week, perhaps a couple of weeks depending on their schedule, and then to be sitting in a room filled with females who, with the exception of the WAGS, were almost all our parents' ages. They were the wives of the various committee members and back room staff, and some of them were very nice people but, equally, a good number of them suffered from big doses of feeling quite superior to ordinary mortals.

It was not how I would have chosen to spend my Saturday night after an International match. Also having been a rugby supporter for many years before Peter ever got capped, I was well aware of the craic I was missing in the local pubs!

Glamorous it may have looked, but fun it was not.

Also we had to try to be on the best of behaviour at our dinners. Occasionally there was a renegade in the group who would try to inject a bit of fun into the evening, and on one occasion one in our number started a table game which had us putting napkins on our heads. There was war afterwards. The members' wives were having none of it, and after that they insisted on tables being shared between the partners of the players and the members' partners.

The boys, on the other hand, were allowed do whatever they wanted at their dinner, with drinking games, food fights, and God only knows what else!

We would be returned to the team hotel, sedate and tired from a tedious evening, usually to discover that the boys were nowhere to be found – well, not all the boys, some were very dutiful and would return to the hotel to be with their partners.

Duty and Peter, however, were not words to be used in the same sentence after a big game! Even when his wife was heavily pregnant, and he had no mobile phone to keep in contact with her, *duty* and *Peter* remained poles apart. As was the case in Cardiff one night, when I arrived back to the hotel where the boys' dinner was on and there was no sign of my fella anywhere.

After interrogating some of his teammates, I was told he was gone to the bank.

The bank?

'Why would he go to a bank?' I asked.

Unless the bank was the name of a pub! I immediately pulled the pregnancy card (it had to have some advantages) to get him back to our hotel which was 20 minutes away in Newport, but Peter was not happy. As a way of placating him we stopped at the hotel bar so he could have a few more pints.

We went to bed around one o'clock in the morning, but soon enough there was a knock at our door. I opened it to find a player's wife, in her ball gown, frozen with the cold and very upset.

I ran a bath for her, and got a brandy from the mini-bar, and then got around to asking her what had happened? They had queued outside one of the nightclubs in Cardiff in a group. Her husband, who was ahead of her, got in. She didn't! Her husband didn't even notice.

She had to find her way 20 miles back to the team hotel.

Glamour my backside!

Dress code was always black tie, which is great when you are in a posh hotel. But a rugby season is mostly played out in the depths of winter and, while I do like fashion, being in a packed pub in a gown – whilst longing to fit in by wearing a pair of jeans – and then walking the cold streets of Cardiff,

Edinburgh, London, or Dublin in an off the shoulder number, is not pleasant at 4.0 a.m. It's especially unhelpful when you're with a man who is insisting on getting a kebab!

At this same time, people on the street would normally recognize Peter and the others, and want to pass on their congratulations for winning the match. Or, worse still, their opinion about why the match had been lost, and by whom?

It wasn't long before I made the decision that one drinker in the family was enough, and I could be of greater use being sober on these occasions. So, for home games at least, I would drive a gang to Lesson Street, and know that we would have a safe way back to our hotel, as taxis were impossible to find in Dublin in those days.

It also meant that I could *smell* trouble brewing and could take intermediary action if necessary.

Noel "Noisy" Murphy.
'The most likeable rugby rogue you could
ever meet.
'Always very good to me in good times and
bad... support like that I can never forget.
'Thanks Noisy.'

— Peter

CHAPTER 6

The first *media incident* in Peter's career, though it was more of a *media storm* for Peter and myself in the middle of it, happened in 1992 after Munster defeated the touring Australians in Musgrave Park. It was kicked off by the Australian coach, Bob Dwyer.

Dwyer's intention was to distract from his country's loss and he did so by damning Peter's scrummaging technique. He declared it illegal.

Dwyer actually lost his head completely once the game was over and branded the 'Munster No.3' – as he had never seen Peter before – a 'disgrace'.

The Aussies don't like losing. They have an interesting way of reacting when this happens, which is quite different to our British-inherited stiff upper lip, or take it on the chin attitude. Of course the newspapers didn't need to be asked a second time to take Dwyer's bait and they all ran headlines about Peter and the accusations levelled against him!

Suffice to say that all good teams will push the rules right to their boundaries to ensure a win. In Munster in particular we were on the receiving end many times of this 'win at all costs' belief, and even had to take it on the chin in a Heineken Cup final, thanks to Neil Back's mischief for Leicester in the dying minute of the 2002 decider.

It was our scrum in Cardiff that year. The biggest game in European club rugby and Back scooped the ball away just as Peter Stringer put the ball in, and broke our hearts, but in his head he did what he felt he had to do to save the day for Leicester. And that's what happened.

In Musgrave Park, that October afternoon ten years earlier, the Aussies were guilty of not reading the game's history books some time before the game. If they had, they would have known that no Munster team has ever laid on a red carpet for any group of tourists. Back in the sixties Munster had beaten another Australian touring team, 11-8, and was the first Irish provincial side to knock a national touring team off their pedestal.

The mighty All Blacks came a cropper in Thomond Park just over ten years later, when Munster's performance was later immortalized in John Breen's play *Alone It Stands* and twice in the eighties Australia had come back for more from Munster and got their fill of it. They had their strongest team out in 1984 and barely survived, so Dwyer made a big mistake in putting out his second string, as the papers labelled them, that day in 1992. Munster had every right to feel a little insulted. He underestimated the passion of the Munster team. Although it was a relatively *unknown* team, the grit and determination of Paul McCarthy, Terry Kingston, Ger Earls, Mick Galwey and Peter's brother Ger saw to it that the pack played fantastically.

It was 22-19 at the end of a long, bad-tempered afternoon, and how anyone could single Peter Clohessy out at the end of it all, as some sort of villain, was as crazy as it was foolish. A dropped goal in the 80th minute by Shannon's Jim Galvin won it. It was clearly more than Dwyer could stomach, because the final 10 minutes of the game became a pitched battle. Three times before that the French referee, a Monsieur Desclaux had called both captains together to give them a piece of his mind.

But in the 73rd minute the referee could only watch as half the players on the field forgot all about the game itself. It started when Paul McCarthy was elbowed by one of the Aussies, but when another Aussie was tripped a moment later, fists started to fly. Gaillimh and Garrick Morgan were caught wrestling on the ground in the middle of all this mayhem and the two of them were sent off.

The Aussies were the first to lose their heads early on in the game when they found out the extremely warm welcome that had been awaiting them. After that, fists and boots were at work in the rucks nearly all of the time.

Thankfully, when the last fight broke out Peter didn't notice until it was well under way. And what many people didn't notice during the fight was one funny moment when a Munster player in frustration kicked the tourists' stuffed Wallaby mascot into the stand.

Dwyer, however, had eyes only for Peter it seemed.

'We had been warned about him,' he stated angrily, '… and we now know why he was selected… he played a major role in the flare up.'

Not true. Peter had been nowhere near the flare up – for once, and much to his own annoyance in truth! Garrett Fitzgerald who was coach that afternoon, and now is the Munster CEO, rebutted Dwyer's claim. 'I just do not understand Bob Dwyer's comments. Peter Clohessy did the job we put him in to do… and why he has been singled out… I just cannot understand.'

Ciaran Fitzgerald was in his final days as Irish coach. He would resign the next month, as after the heroic performance from Ireland in the 1991 World Cup we lost seven games out of seven in 1992, including a torrid tour of New Zealand and a home defeat to the Australians, but he had watched Peter and the guys from the stand in Musgrave Park and admitted he was one of the proudest Irishmen in the ground. Fitzy, one of Ireland's greatest rugby warriors ever, another true *Braveheart*, said he had viewed the 'soul of Irish rugby' that Wednesday afternoon.

There were no official Press Officers at hand to advise players in those days, and the boys were pretty much left to their own devices in dealing with the media. So when we arrived at Jury's Hotel in Cork for the after-match dinner, it was Terry Kingston who pulled Peter aside and gave him his statement for the waiting press.

'I am very upset at what has been said,' the statement began. 'There is a referee and two touch judges on the field with a job to do. I will make no further comment on what has been said.'

Just as well Terry was on hand, because Peter was likely to have spilled out anything after the game!

The following morning all the papers were awash with headlines, with Bob Dwyer slating Peter. The following day we were still celebrating in a pub in Mallow on the way back to Limerick when Ger Clohessy got a phone call telling him that his dog, Sam had bitten the balls off the next door neighbour's dog.

'Did Sam read the papers too?' Gaillimh asked.

Intense media attention was a new experience for Peter and all of us at the tail end of that Australian tour in 1992. We all acted defensively and felt hurt at the time, though little did I know this experience was only preparing Peter for many *inquisitions* from members of the media that were to come.

What I have learned is that a lot of the time, when the dust settles, these worrying dramas have a way of sometimes turning into a positive. When Bob Dwyer singled out Peter after Munster's victory it left the national selectors unable to ignore his obvious talent any longer – in fact, he was capped for the first time for Ireland in the next Five Nations Championship. And he was never dropped from the front row after that – his unavailability for selection, however, was another issue!

After 1992, Peter had an interesting relationship with the media. Those members of the rugby media who actually knew him were very supportive of him, like Ned Van Esbeck and Gerry Thronley of *The Irish Times*, and of course the gentleman that was the late Karl Johnston, who wrote for the old *Irish Press*. But there were many others who took the view that he was a dangerous player who lived on the edge, and they refused to budge from that stubborn belief.

The one thing Peter has always done is speak the truth, whether his views are popular or not, and others who sit on the fence can find this quite distasteful. Unfortunately there has also been an acknowledged bias on the part of the national media generally towards Limerick. So from a "D4" perspective Peter Clohessy was a dangerous rugby player who was from the wrong club and the wrong city.

This became glaringly obvious when Peter was thrust into the spotlight a second time after an All-Ireland League game between Young Munster and St Mary's College in Greenfields exactly twelve months after the visit of Bob Dwyer's Aussies. It's fair to say that Munsters and Mary's built up a *special* relationship of their own in the early nineties, and in 1993 they got to know one another extremely well.

In February of that year Munsters had faced Mary's in the deciding game in the All-Ireland League, in the grand setting of Lansdowne Road. Both teams had won five games and drawn one that season, but Mary's held a big points advantage – so, as well as having *home* advantage, they only needed a draw to lift the trophy. However, Munsters brought a support to Dublin that day which made Lansdowne Road sound like Greenfields had been transported a couple of hundred miles to south Dublin.

It was a day to be remembered. Dodo Reddan was there to witness it, with her dogs, and the club's mascot Goat was present! I remember sitting in the old East Stand, with Trish Ryan, between us pregnant with four children, as we held our breath many times throughout the match. It had been 65 years since Munsters had been officially crowned the best team in Ireland. That's how far back it had been since the club's famous Bateman Cup win and there were not many people in the ground that afternoon who could remember that far back!

Ger Clohessy was captain of Munsters, and while he had to go off after four minutes with a hamstring injury, the tone of the game had already been set. In the first minute, in fact, there was a fight between the two packs. The mood did not lighten after that, but Munsters' coach Tony Grant knew his men would not back down. It was a game that Ned Van Esbeck stated in *The Irish Times* proved "the heartbeat of Irish rugby is still strong".

For RTE's rugby analyst, Brent Pope, who was the primary source of passion in the Mary's pack, the game was hardly memorable. He was sent off the field shortly before half-time for punching Munsters' centre, Francis Brosnahan, who suffered a hairline fracture of the cheekbone but was given the biggest roar of all when he appeared in front of thousands of our supporters at the railway station that evening. Peter was not there to savour his proudest moment as a Munsters man. He couldn't travel home and join the celebrations, as he had to report to The Berkeley Court for Ireland camp – that is not to say that he didn't celebrate well in Dublin, and I believe, though I'm happy I was not on the scene to witness it myself, that was the night the referee, Leo Mayne found Peter asleep on the footpath outside Jury's Hotel!

It was a very exciting time for Young Munster who didn't have a strong tradition of Irish players. I believe that this is not because they didn't have great players from time to time, but was definitely more to do with the politics that existed within the IRFU at the time. Which must have been the case considering that traditionally Young Munster had the biggest club membership in Ireland.

We had beaten Mary's 17-14, and Young Munster were champions of Ireland.

Mary's thought they should have won. They saw our out-half, Aidan O'Halloran kick a late penalty with inches to spare over the crossbar, and they watched a penalty of their own after that rebound off a post. Ger Earls had intercepted a pass and run 60 yards to get the try which really won the day. There were heroes everywhere. Peter and the entire front row had an outstanding game. Ray Ryan won some vital ball in the lineout. Everyone did what was asked of them.

'This could add 10 or 20 years to the lives of our supporters,' Munsters winning captain declared when he had the cup in his hands – a cup which was destined for a rosy reception in Greenfields, and in the Clohessy house.

The two teams met again the following October in an early round of the AIL, and this time Munsters felt right at home, winning 18-3. But the game was another bruising affair from the start and early on Steve Jameson, the Mary's captain, had flattened Ger Clohessy during a lineout. Particularly in those days, teams were warriors and rival packs fought in the trenches – and players stood up for each other no matter what. So it was only a matter of time before retribution would be delivered.

It duly was. When Jameson ended up on the wrong side of a ruck, Peter took the opportunity to deliver a serious raking. All Jameson said afterwards, when he was asked about the incident, was that the only thing he could identify was a 'black and amber sock'.

Physicality was not such a big thing in those days, and wounds were considered part and parcel of *the game*. The referees in those days were under intense pressure to have eyes in the backs of their heads, but only during the game would foul play on the pitch be noted, and justice duly delivered. That was it, pretty much. When the match was over the referee's job was done, which is so different to nowadays when any incident on the pitch can be investigated for days afterwards and the referee has all the time in the world to reconsider any decision he has made.

Occasionally, in the older days, there would be a complaint, or if a player had been sent off then the Munster Branch or the IRFU might ask for an investigation that might prompt a disciplinary hearing. Very occasionally a suspension would be handed out.

What happened after this particular All-Ireland League game, after St Mary's went home to Dublin, was unique. It made history in the game in this country.

A video tape recording of the match was acquired by an anonymous source, and it was submitted secretly to the IRFU to investigate the incident between Peter and Jameson – and, coincidentally, a long article appeared the day after in one newspaper condemning Peter. There were many aspects to this that should have been disturbing to the IRFU and the rugby loving public.

To begin with how was a video tape taken by some amateur or completely anonymous person allowed to be used as evidence when this had never been done before? Secondly, why was the identity of the submitter protected by the IRFU? Thirdly, after the IRFU used the video to take disciplinary action against Peter, why did they then change their disciplinary rules so that such dodgy evidence could never again be used against any player in the country?

The incident had become another one of those huge *media storms* – it featured on the evening news on RTE for many days.

Before the hearing in Lansdowne Road we met up with Gerry Casey, who captained Young Munster in 1986 and was Centenary President of the club in 1996, and John Quigley who was a barrister. I clearly remember waiting in the room while the committee finished their deliberations, and I started laughing at something or other – unusually Peter snapped at me.

'Keep it down… your laugh is like a foghorn…!'

Gerry Casey looked him straight in the face.

'Jesus, Claw… have you only noticed that now?'

When we drove out of the IRFU building after the hearing, Peter actually couldn't see the traffic to pull out, because there were so many flash photographers taking pictures in the car window. It was like they do when people are leaving court buildings! More than one newspaper the next morning speculated that Peter's rugby career was over. He had been banned from playing for 10 weeks.

On a brighter, and lighter side, on the drive to Dublin for that disciplinary hearing, we were pulled over for speeding. When the Garda arrived at the driver's window and looked inside, he shook his head.

'You've enough troubles at the moment,' he smiled, 'DRIVE ON…!'

Naturally there were plenty of opinions about this ban, some absolutely agreeing with it, and others forcefully against it. What has always inspired Peter, and humbled myself, were the efforts people would make to show their support – which always means a heck of a lot when you are going through a serious low.

Lots of people wrote to Peter.

Here's two examples, both of them from men in Leinster.

'Dear Peter,

'I feel awful over what has happened to you last night. However, it is only 10 weeks, so stay training, keep fit and in 10 weeks you will be back again. You owe it to your club Young Munster and all of its supporters.

'I remember seeing you play against Old Wesley last year. I was standing beside a woman and her two young boys wearing black and yellow scarves. They had come up by train and bought chips on the way out to Donnybrook. No flashy restaurants, and presumably not much money either, but they followed you and Young Munster, that was their escape from the doldrums of living, it was their enjoyment. You are a Munster man, you have spirit and drive, be patient and arrive back.

'Don't give up, that's the easy way out.

'I know you'll continue to play.

'God Bless you Peter.

'Best Regards,

'T O'G,

'Rathfarnham,

'Dublin.'

'Dear Peter,

'I have just watched the extract from the video which the gentleman from the paper claimed would show you kicking one of the St Mary's players recently and have come to the conclusion that it is just pure begrudgery and I hope you are not tempted to give up the game you play so well because of it.

'You have given Munster and Ireland something which is sadly lacking in Leinster (Dublin) rugby, namely a bit of bottle and pride in the jersey you wear. I and many thousands more are looking forward to seeing you wear the Young Munster, Munster and Irish, and BaaBaas and Lions jerseys, all the way from here to JoBurg in the next few years.

'I look forward to making your acquaintance some time.

I am a native of Tulla.

'Yours in Sport,

'DB,

'Dundalk RFC,

'Executive Committee Member, Leinster Branch IRFU.'

But there was an intrusive side of the media at work that brought great stress to Peter's parents, and our family. Not too many people in the media industry think often enough of the human impact of it all.

Yet again, however, little did Peter or I realize that this whole daunting experience was only preparing us, and my family, for something far more tragic and potentially overwhelming which was shortly to come.

Niallo.
'Always a players' man above all else... and still great company over a few pints.
And Kathy... who is always smiling.'

— Peter

CHAPTER 7

The year ended so differently to how it had begun, because in addition to the joy of winning the AIL with Munsters, Peter had finally been called up for his first Ireland cap, at 26 years of age, in the 1993 Five Nations Championship.

He actually got the *call* the week before the deciding AIL game against St. Mary's in Lansdowne Road but, typically, without even thinking for one second about the risk of injury, he immediately told the media he would be refusing to take the traditional "rest weekend" which new caps always availed of before they played their first game for their country.

The thought of Peter *resting* while Munsters fought for the title was, of course, absurd – but the media thought he was being incredibly unselfish. He wasn't, he was being Peter Clohessy. Next game, no worries, and so he played for Munsters and then had a week to prepare himself for the French!

Fitzy was gone. The new coach was Gerry Murphy, a Leinsterman, who had been a surprise choice and whom Peter always held in the highest regard. Noisy Murphy was still manager. But the Irish rugby public was still glum and expectations were at an all-time low after we lost the first game of the Championship to Scotland in Murrayfield. Most people thought Ireland looked dreadful, and the great Willie John McBride announced on behalf of everyone else in the country that the team had no spirit, no fire. A little bit of fury is needed, he explained.

Enter Peter!

The good wishes, cards, letters and phone calls that accompanied Peter's selection were incredibly heart-warming, and a huge surprise to all of us in the family. For instance, I remember Steve McDonogh of Garryowen ringing and offering his International match tickets to us, as he knew that Peter would only get six tickets, and the option to buy four more, and that it would be very difficult for us to get enough tickets for all of the family. The goodwill was spectacular.

It was only four months since Dwyer and his Aussies had left. In writing about Peter's selection for Ireland, all of the reporters dug back up the accusations, and the innuendo, surrounding his personal performance in that win in Musgrave Park. He was one of two new caps for the game in Lansdowne Road, the other being Ciaran Clarke from Terenure. Half of the pack was also changed for the French visit to Lansdowne Road. Peter was coming in at tight head for Paul McCarthy. Terry Kingston was back for Steve Smith. Neil Francis was in for Richard Costello, Mick Galwey was in for Noel Mannion. This, remember, was Gaillimh doing his Lazarus impression, because two weeks earlier he had made up his neck injury to have a handy Sunday morning, and found himself in hospital for most of the week with medical people thinking he was doomed never to play the game again.

Peter had been unable to nail down his place on the Munster team all through 1992, so now he had a chance to show to selectors, at provincial and national level, what he was made of and how he could change things for the better. Though this did not stop him deciding to take a rest on the Sunday morning of his big week and reporting to the Irish team doc with a knee injury. The newspaper reporters watching training were told that Peter was sitting things out as a *precaution*.

Indeed...

It's true to say that this was his chance to make a big and lasting impression. It had been three years since Ireland had won a Championship game in Lansdowne Road, only managing to beat Argentina, Japan and Zimbabwe in that long time in front of their own supporters. After one game at *home* Ireland were booed off the pitch by their own people! We had lost 10 games in a row, which was a record, and anyone having the time needed to skip back to 1881 in the history books to find the last time we were in such a bad state of affairs.

It was a changing of the guard, however. Peter had Nick Popplewell, an old hand in the front row with him, and Terry Kingston – who was actually a powerful scrummager, and served as a third prop in the front row. Peter and Poppy had already had some interesting front row *contests* under their belts, in club and inter-provincial games, but as the two of them got older and wiser they entered an unwritten agreement – they would not kill one another in scrums anymore and, instead, they would save their energy for getting on the ball and running around the pitch.

In those days games came infrequently compared to the hectic fixtures list the professional game lives with, and the most experienced man in the Irish pack was Neil Francis, who had the sum total of 19 caps for his country.

Peter's direct opponent was Louis Armary from Lourdes. He was playing his thirty-second game for France, and was a battered, crusty old prop who had seen it all and done it all on the International stage. Armary wasn't a huge man to look at, but Peter was about to discover that the technique employed by the Frenchman was brilliant. And he was incredibly strong.

Peter also found out very quickly that if he let his guard down, for one second… there would be a price to be paid!

In the first scrum, the hit was phenomenal. The Irish front row found itself going backwards even before the ball came in. It was a wake up call. At the second scrum, Peter was at least prepared for the incredible surge of power coming in his direction. It was, however, one of the few matches in Peter's career when he was happy to have the smallest number of scrums possible!

The French had no reason to fear Ireland, or hold any doubt in the world that they would not win handily enough. Three of their forwards had more caps than the whole of the Irish pack put together, and then behind the scrum they had Sella, Saint-Andre and Lafond, who were so dangerous, and were world stars. Phillipe Sella had played for France 86 times! Twelve months before, in Paris, the French had run in seven tries. They had hit a record total of 44 points.

When he had heard that he was chosen for Ireland, Peter had experienced an initial fear and wondered if he would be able to play at that level. *Will I be up to it?* he asked himself. At the same time he felt massively proud and honoured. Philip Danaher had warned him that after the first 10 or 15 minutes he would be gasping for air.

Philip was right. Peter was asking himself the question Philip told him would pop into his head.

What the f*** am I doing out here?

It was just as well he had been suitably warned. Peter felt his lungs were going to burst but, also as Philip had wisely told him, he quickly got his second wind. Then, the game flew by. At the final whistle Peter felt that he had only been on the pitch for half an hour.

We were never going to win. But we kept the French to half of the previous year's total, losing 21-6, and conceding two tries *only*!

That night, after the official dinner, Peter also discovered the other side of Louis, his first International opponent. Louis had not a word of English. Peter had zero French, but the pair had the best of nights together. In their first day and evening, the two of them had formed a formidable respect for one another.

It was defeat number 11 against the French, but the counting stopped there, thankfully. In March, our lads went to Cardiff and won 19-14, and for the first time in over two years there was no change made on an Irish team – and then a fortnight later the English turned up in Dublin and, level on points with France they had a Championship in their sights, but we won an epic confrontation 17-3, with Gaillimh getting a try which stirred everyone in the ground, and nearly everyone in the country who had been watching on RTE as well. Eric Elwood had come into the team and his kicking was perfect. Meanwhile, in the front row, Peter now looked a permanent fixture, and with Nick Popplewell and Terry Kingston they had totally out-scrummaged the English. He loved the fierceness of Internationals.

Especially, that game against England told Peter what he had been missing in his life up until then. It was a brilliant English team that had a total of over 450 caps between them – the two Underwoods, Jeremy Guscott, Stuart Barnes, Dewi Morris, Jason Leonard, Brian Moore, Jeff Probyn, Martin

Bayfield, Wade Dooley and Peter Winterbottom – they had household names in every position.

It was real do-or-die against the English, and it was clear that some guys on the English team did not come to Lansdowne Road to die. We poured through the English line and gave Dewi Morris a bit of a battering. We won the ball back again and again, and the team's rucking was first class with our guys always up in numbers. The blood was drained from our visitors long before the end, even though it was just 3-3 at half-time. We had the wind after that, and we were clearly winning the war. Gaillimh's try came when the game was won, but it put a cap on the whole day. It came from a bad pass from Will Carling, which Elwood picked up. He passed it out to Michael Bradley, who heard Gaillimh, he later recounted, charging up on his left. Gaillimh took the ball and made the whole day with a wonderful try.

The day after the win over England the Lions selectors were meeting in a hotel near Heathrow airport to make their final decisions on the squad to tour New Zealand that summer. Most people, including Irish rugby supporters, thought we would be lucky to have one player amongst the selection of 30 – that was "Poppy", but newspaper reporters were hinting that Peter had a decent chance of being a surprise choice, given that Jeff Probyn of England was 36 years old and the Welsh tight head, Hugh Williams Jones was not having a great season. Three of the Lions selectors were in Lansdowne Road to see the win over England, and to see their pack being shoved all over the place by our lads. There was England's Geoff Cooke who was manager of the Lions, another Englishman Derek Morgan, and IRFU president Ken Reid. Peter was not holding his breath that Reid would battle for him at the meeting in Heathrow!

And he was right, of course.

The Irish papers said there should be three Irishmen – Poppy, Peter and Gaillimh, and that Franno had an outside chance as well.

Poppy and Gaillimh got the votes alright, but Richard Wallace was the third Irishman selected and he was totally deserving of the honour. Vinny Cunningham was also called up to the tour squad later on as a replacement.

England's Jeff Probyn who was naturally disappointed at his own omission from the squad, commented, 'If you leave me at home… why not take Peter Clohessy?' And the Lions manager, Geoff Cooke also saw fit to add his tuppenceworth. 'I fully understand the disappointment in Ireland at their representation. However, I will say that the most unlucky player to be left out was Peter Clohessy… he came very, very near to making the squad.'

But Peter wasn't one little bit disappointed, because he does not *do* disappointments. He was not bothered watching any of the games on television either, as he was busy with his own work – and in the amateur game, time away from rugby squads and training camps was time to be treasured by hard work.

New Zealand won the Test series 2-1, and most commentators singled out the "tight five" and the front row as an area of weakness for the Lions, and the only man amongst that lot who got the thumbs up at the end of it was Poppy. He had a brilliant tour. The two Scots, Peter Wright and Paul Burnell were heavily criticised, and it was suddenly being said that Jeff Probyn and Peter should have been the two tight head selections all along.

Who cared?

Not Peter Clohessy, for one!

Peter would never waste one second of his life pondering what might have been? What if he *had* been chosen for the Lions? What if he *had not* been suspended for 10 weeks?

It simply is not his nature.

He picks himself up and gets on with it, and never looks back in anger, an attribute that I am still in the process of learning – and he is absolutely right, for I have found that when I do it is way easier to move on.

At that time in 1993 Peter worked with his brothers, Noel and Ger in the suspended ceiling business that Daddy Noel had created for them. They had a great deal of work on their hands, here and elsewhere.

Russia was opening up to Irish companies, headed by Aer Rianta opening a duty free store and bar in Moscow in a partnership with the Russian airline, Aeroflot. So, to pass the 10 weeks of his suspension, Peter had decided to join Ger in Russia where they were renovating The White House, the premier government building. The building served as the base for the government and the Russian Prime Minister, but had been left damaged for a long time after the country's constitutional crisis, and tank shelling had left black burns on the exterior leaving it not so *white* anymore. Though newlyweds liked to have their photos taken in front of it!

Peter was in charge of 70 Turkish labourers, whom he taught to hang suspended ceilings. They used to call him 'Chef' – which is chief, apparently, in Turkish. Again it is testimony to his superb emotional intelligence that he could teach that many men a new trade, even though their English was as non-existent as Peter's Turkish.

Conditions weren't great in Russia at that time, but the boys made the best of it in the Irish bars! On the streets at night they had to be careful, though. One evening in a taxi a man jumped from an overhead bridge and landed on the bonnet of the car. A very angry taxi driver got out, pushed the body off... and drove on!

Phone calls were weekly only, as the phone lines were very undependable and crackly. I had absolutely zero desire to go and visit while he was there, especially when he described to me how in their apartment cockroaches didn't think twice about scooting across the kitchen table.

In fairness to the Galweys and Danahers, they helped me pass many a quiet Sunday in those lonely days, as I stayed home with Luke who was five months old at the time. Mam took care of Luke in her house Monday to Friday while I worked in the bank, but weekends were just the two of us.

Gaillimh and Philip would stop on their way home from Ireland training on Sundays and the girls would come over to our place, and I would cook dinner for all of them. Joan Galwey, who has many talents, was also gifted with a camera, and I have many superb photos of that time thanks to her. It became a bit of joke between us that every time Peter rang from Russia, Gaillimh should answer the phone!

It was remarkable that Peter stuck Russia for those few months, as he was a great homebird, and never held any inclination whatsoever to travel.

On Christmas week there was an interesting development when the IRFU announced the "Ireland A" side to meet Scotland in Glasgow on December 28, with *A N Other* named in the tight head position. As Peter's suspension was due to end on Christmas Eve it wasn't okay for the union to officially pick him, but their intention was clear that they wanted him back. He had to quickly get his mind back on rugby, on that game, and also the Final Trial four days later – which was still part of the furniture before every Championship in the dying days of the amateur era – when the *Probables* lined out against the *Possibles*. Thirteen of the Irish team that had beaten Romania in November were named on the Probables (or Whites), with the addition of Pat O'Hara and the man who now had a few words of Russian under his belt. Again he was titled *A N Other*.

Ned Van Esbeck in the *Times* phoned me to ask how Peter was getting on in Moscow.

"He (Peter) has been training hard in Moscow," wrote Ned, adding "… under the supervision of his brother, Ger. He is especially pleased that the selectors have not lost faith in him."

Peter was fit and well when he came home, however, and he had also lost some weight. Must have been all that training every day! First thing he had to do when he finally got home was play 30 minutes for Young Munster against Old Wesley, with one of the Irish selectors, Pat Whelan looking at him. Pat duly gave the thumbs up to Noisy Murphy, the Irish team manager that evening and Peter was up and running again. In the "A" game against the Scots Peter had the pleasure of a young whippersnapper for company, a young lad by the name of Keith Wood.

The pair would grow into firm friends so fast! Keith was christened "Fester" because of his likeness to Uncle Fester in *The Addams Family*. But the "Festers" and the "Claws" got on like a house on fire – and once Keith and Nicola had their first child, Alexander we began a double family tradition of going to Bunratty Folk Park every Christmas with the kids, and also Nicola's parents, Jack and Gwen, to do our Santa photos. I even have a private photo of Keith and Peter together sitting on each of Santa's knees!

The "Ireland A" team, which was managed by Donal Lenihan, had Peter amongst mostly up and coming players. There were only two members of the *senior* squad told they were in need of putting in a good performance in Scotland, Peter and Simon Geoghegan, who the selectors deemed to be a little off his best at the tail end of the previous year. Geoghegan had blasted onto the Irish scene, first with Connacht where he had George Hook as his coach, and when he first flashed down the wing for Ireland he scored three of our 10 tries in the 1991 Championship. He was an Irishman with a London accent, and he loved playing in a green shirt. That's all he'd ever wanted to do, so Peter and himself gave the selectors all the answers they needed even though they lost by 15 points.

Simon took his rugby very seriously, to the point that he hated cigarettes anywhere near him. On one tour he walked the length of the bus to inform the bus driver that Peter and Rob Henderson were smoking down the back! Needless to say, they weren't all that happy with that sort of *professional* behaviour. That apart, Simon was one of the good guys in Irish rugby, even if himself and Jim Staples were *clean living* – and waited until their rugby careers had ended before they started drinking and smoking and carrying on like the rest of them!

In January, Ireland opened the Championship with a visit to Paris, and Peter and Simon were back on the team.

Also in January of 1994, the IRFU laid down new and very specific procedures for the citing of players and the manner in which video evidence of foul play could be presented. Any citing now could only come from either of the participating teams, or a Union or Branch official. Any complaint had to be submitted within seven days and video produced in evidence had to have been taken by an authenticated source – and verification of the source that was citing the player.

'Without prejudice to the justice and suspension imposed on Peter Clohessy,' stated the President of the IRFU, Michael Cuddy, 'no one could be happy with the circumstances surrounding the submission of the video and other elements of the affair. We want to make sure that some of the circumstances and events surrounding it cannot be repeated.'

Pity they didn't think like that at the time!

But yet again, Peter just welcomed the change so that no other player would have to endure similar stress.

That Christmas we celebrated the end of a long roller-coaster year with Luke's first Christmas, and we faced into 1994 with confidence that it would surely be a less tumultuous year?

Terry.

'Ter-Ter... a sensible head, most of the time!

'Many's the time I heard you say, "Claw don't"... which saved me often. Anna mentioned Clodagh in the book crying, but I only remember Clodagh crying with laughter. Thanks for all the great memories.

'And thanks for calling the kids after us!'

– Peter

CHAPTER 8

Peter first met Rala in January of 1994, when Patrick O'Reilly became *bagman* to the Irish team. Rala, a Dubliner, was about 20 years older than him, but they immediately clicked, and soon developed a strong relationship, though Rala did not find it very hard to make friends at any time during his rugby life.

It wasn't long before Rala and Dixie, his partner became an extension of our family. Our daughter, Jane as a toddler called them *La La* and *Dixie*, as the *Teletubbies* kids TV show was a favourite of hers. Rala is the ultimate gentleman, and is complimented beautifully by Dixie, who is incredibly great fun, and is generous to a fault. Even though our guest room is called "Rala's Room" and he comes and goes as he pleases, Dixie still loads him down with expensive gifts for each of us.

'Hi Anna/Claw heading down to farm tomorrow,' he has texted in recent years. That means Rala is coming to visit us.

On one occasion I texted back to say I'd be working in my clinic – next to our home – and told him to let himself into the house.

'I'll see you later,' I texted back.

At work that day I was wondering where my next client – who was new – had gone, as I had buzzed her in at the gate to our house. When I went looking for the woman I eventually found her on my couch, with Rala sitting opposite her, and the two of them deep in conversation about Inishbofin!

That's how it is for Rala and everyone he meets.

In Ireland camp Rala would ensure that Peter was always on time for the morning sessions. He'd arrive at Peter's bedroom door, half an hour before the team were due to meet, with a tray loaded with a bowl of porridge – specifically made with milk – and a pot of tea for the two of them, accompanied by 20 *Benson & Hedges* also for the two of them!

For a long time this was their secret, until Fester and Hendo (Rob Henderson) got wind of it, at which point driven by jealousy they started calling Rala, 'Claw's Butler'. What they didn't know in those days was that, in return for this breakfast service, Peter would drive the big van to training for Rala, because Rala was nervous of driving the van. He loved Rala's stories, and the laid back relaxed way they would just hang out together. Peter always found intense rugby talk particularly boring, so Rala's room was a homely retreat.

Rala has been very good to us always ever since, and when Luke was small he would include him in jobs around the various hotels, to keep him entertained. In the team hotel he once took Luke and Jane to the swimming pool to give us a break. Their mutual love of a cigarette is just one of the reasons why they are the best of buddies, but their relationship went deeper than that – they have a great respect for one another, and Peter always ensured that the rest of the lads didn't mess Rala around.

That was a law that everyone knew Peter had laid down!

Messing, as everyone knows, is an art form within rugby teams, where groups of boys have way too much time on their hands.

Peter and Gaillimh were the biggest boys of all and always had to get up to some divilment. A simple car journey from Dublin to Limerick was often a life-threatening experience – if any player dared to get into a car when Peter was behind the wheel. Not many wanted to make that journey. A long list of teammates, craic or no craic, simply refused to travel with Peter, as they felt the price their nervous system would have to pay was just too high.

Peter is an incredible driver, but as with everything he does he has nerves of steel. For those who were able for such a drive, there was the added dilemma of having to stay fully alert. Paco Fitzgerald was in the back seat of the car one Sunday morning reading the sports section of a newspaper when flames started leaping around him. An idle mind had set fire to the paper as they were driving, though it was not our car. I believe the burn marks were on the roof of Philip Danaher's Mazda 323.

Boys and big toys were always a dangerous combination. They liked to play bumpers, as people do in an amusement park, with other people's cars

One morning John Hayes was in front of Peter in his IRFU Ford Mondeo, and he had stopped at the traffic lights at Dennehy's Cross in Cork. Peter was driving his own jeep and he couldn't resist giving John a tip from behind. Of course John bravely replied, by reversing and tipping him back.

Mistake! One of John's bigger mistakes, in fact, as Peter put on the four-wheel drive and started pushing Hayes beyond the red light, and into the oncoming traffic. Peter still can't decide which was funnier – Hayes' face with mad panic spread all over it, or Killian Keane's roaring in the seat next to Peter.

'STOP… CLAW…

'STOP, STOP…

'YOU'LL KILL HIM!'

There were only two professors of messing. Peter and Gaillimh, and when they commenced with one another everyone else was happy to be far from the thoughts of both men.

For a while Gaillimh was training with white jocks under his shorts.

Back in The Berkeley Court he was filling the laundry bag to send downstairs to be cleaned, when Peter copped the state of the white jocks.

'You cannot send those to the laundry… what about the poor unfortunate who has to wash them?' he announced.

'They'll be grand... they'll be grand,' Gaillimh assured him, as he tied the bag and waited until housekeeping collected it. He then collapsed onto his bed laughing.

'What have you done now... you dirty b******?' asked Peter.

'I put your name on the laundry bag,' said Gaillimh.

But that was only one battle won by Gaillimh in a long war, and he would lose this particular war. When Ireland changed gear sponsors to Nike, Peter forecast that 'Gaillimh's fat a*** won't fit into Nike shorts!'

And Nike, indeed, were not a good fit for this Kerryman. The night before the first game of the Championship against Scotland, when the Nike gear was to make its debut, Gaillimh was very artistically drawing a Nike swoosh onto his old shorts with a black marker.

In the dressingroom the next day, after the team talk and just before the game, everyone was getting psyched up – and banging their heads against walls, or whatever took their fancy.

Peter, as usual, was ultra cool. Usually at this exact time when everyone else was getting wound up tighter and tighter, he'd disappear to the loo for his pre-match smoke. This day, however, Peter and Nick Popplewell were beside themselves trying to hold in the giggles and they were not going anywhere fast.

Gaillimh was standing in front of the pair of them.

He kept looking at them.

And they were not taking their eyes off him.

'What are ye up to... ye f******?'

At the same time Gaillimh was doing his best to work up his own deep pre-match psyche up, but the tears were running down the other lads' faces.

Finally, Poppy pointed to Gaillimh's shorts. There, in black, was a swoosh alright, but Nike was no more.

Instead there was a... Mike

And, below Mike was... Loves Joan.

In January, although the historic run of defeats had been stemmed, few were hopeful of Ireland getting a result in the Parc des Princes in Paris. In a decade, the best result we'd had against the French was a 15-all draw in 1985 and the string of eight consecutive losses to them also had a place in the record books. It was 22 years since we'd won there.

Peter was back in the company of Louis Armary, who was joined in the front row by Jean Marie Gonzalez and Phillipe Gallart on the tight side, but himself and Terry Kingston and Poppy were now rated as good as any front row in the Northern Hemisphere, but the three of them had to work their socks off in the loose just as much as the scrum as the French pummelled our line in the second half.

Ireland had refused to surrender. With eight minutes left it was 23-15 to them, with our points coming from Eric Elwood. By the finish, however, the French had four tries. Peter and all of the lads just played themselves to a standstill, and had nothing left by the very end when the scoreline read 35-15, with Phillipe Saint-Andre putting the last delicate touch to a French move which had their usual array of dazzling running and passing.

This was the game in which Noisy Murphy feared that Peter might not leave the field alive. And while Peter never had the same thought, he had no trouble telling anyone who asked him that it was the toughest and most physical game of rugby he had ever played in his life. A cut at the top of his nose, next to his left eye, had stitches in it and he had another four stitches inserted in his head.

He felt, at times, that he had been fighting the battle on his own out there – and he was adamant that if there had been a greater number of Munster men on the pitch with him he would not have sustained half of his injuries!

He had no memory who hit him, either time. That's because the French were lining up and hitting Peter, and when he left the field to get his second round of stitches, and reappeared from the dressingroom, the scoreboard was a surprise when he saw 35-15 staring down at him. But back into the battle he went. There were mean blows from both sides, and lots of boot was used as well. Again from both directions, and Peter had not one word of complaint at the end of it all.

The writing had been on the wall beforehand.

'Their two prop forwards, Nick Popplewell and Peter Clohessy are superb players,' French coach, Pierre Berbizier informed reporters two days before the game. 'They would run through a wall to reach the ball... if the wall had the courage to stand up to them.'

No surprise then that they targeted Peter especially during the game. 'I don't know how I got the cuts,' said Peter, '... but I wasn't aware of anything nasty.'

Nobody was too worried about what had gone on out there on the field. When Noisy was asked, in the post-match interviews, would he have anything to say about the physical side of the game, he shrugged his shoulders.

'I will take a look at them on the video... when I have time,' he replied.

Irish teams were able to take their beatings, that is the truest thing our opponents could say about us. We didn't cry to anybody afterwards. But we were losing so many games in the final 10 or 20 minutes of games.

Ireland had fitness issues, to say the least.

The IRFU, despite its shortcomings in dealing with women as equals, did always pay for wives and partners to go to the away games. This was my first trip to Paris, and I hated it! The prices were beyond ridiculous, the food far too different for my tastes – although in fairness, we were getting set-menus with no choice, and I struggled to recognize what I was eating, mainly through my own limitations of having zero French in my repertoire.

We were based in a hotel beside Gare Saint Lazare. Meanwhile the lads were in a palace in Versailles, until the night of the game when we moved to their new team hotel, The Hilton close to the Eiffel Tower. Joan Galwey and I got a lovely room with a balcony. Joan can turn her hand at anything, and I remember on the Friday night, her sitting up late finishing off the dress that she had made for the Saturday night!

In Paris, after the match the team dinner was still stag only, while we ate in a restaurant some distance away. The plan then was to meet the lads in Kitty O'Shea's pub later on though, Peter ably assisted by Gaillimh, had already started the serious business of anaesthetizing his wounds with copious amounts of pints. They were in the James Joyce pub.

It dawned on one of them, at some stage, that they were making a night of it in the wrong pub! They left the James Joyce, and jumped into a taxi, and without a word of French started babbling that they needed to get to Kitty

O'Sheas fast. Neither man could understand why the taxi driver was refusing to take them… anywhere!

The incoherent conversation went to and fro, and the boys were getting rightly annoyed that this 'French b*****' wouldn't take them. He wanted them out of his taxi immediately, it seemed.

'Typical… f****** French, rude f******!'

They got out of the taxi.

As did the taxi driver, who pointed furiously down the road. But the pair of boys were not going to be taken for eejits – so they grabbed the keys from the ignition, and ran down the road twenty yards… and dumped them into a plant holder.

The holder was next door to Kitty O'Sheas!

There was no real chance of any of our party getting in real trouble in Paris, as I think the French knew our ways. The Gendarmerie would accompany the team for the duration of its stay in Paris, and it was unbelievable to see how these guys operated. The outriders on motorbikes would flank the team bus and they would kick, or use their batons to hit, unsuspecting cars that were merely stuck in the traffic, but were in the way of the bus. A couple of these same boys were always stationed outside Kitty's smoking, still waiting to protect the Irish boys should they need it.

They also had other uses. I remember watching from the window of the team bus as Gabriel Fulcher's wife, Gill took a lift to an official function – in her beautiful sequenced black dress – on the back of the motorbike of one of the outriders.

Peter, like everyone else on the Irish team, still trained primarily with his club – even provincial team training hadn't really emerged at that stage. So fitness was the one thing that repeatedly caught out Ireland in the early nineties, and too many teams we were meeting were already engaged in far more serious preparation. Some were semi-professional in their thinking and lifestyles, if not fully professional.

Scorelines tended to rise against us in the last 10 or 20 minutes as our lads suffered. The levelling of the *fitness* playing field has been very evident in the last 10 years, and there is generally little difference anymore in this department between the major rugby playing nations. The main difference between winning and losing is psychological.

To be fair to the IRFU they recognized this in the nineties. At many training camps that Peter attended the team management also brought in some professionals to work with the psychological aspect of the game. One of these experts was an army man, a Captain, who recounted how he and his crew were on UN duty in a jeep when they accidently drove into an ambush.

The only way out was to turn around, so the four of them lifted up the jeep, turned it around, and put it back on the ground. They made their escape. When they told colleagues back in camp what had happened, the captain said nobody could understand how they had the strength to do such a thing as lift the jeep clean off the ground. To prove it, the officers went outside and sure enough not one group of men could lift the same jeep. A man's intention to succeed, the Captain stated, can often bestow super-human strength.

Any questions, the Captain asked?

Peter had listened carefully to the story.

He raised his hand, and the Captain nodded at him.

'Was there no reverse gear in the jeep?' asked Peter.

Ireland's decorated cyclist, Sean Kelly who was the toughest competitor of all on a bike in the eighties and early nineties, was also brought in by Pat Whelan to talk to the team.

'This man needs no introduction,' opened Pat.

'Hi ya... STEPHEN!' shouted Peter.

A quick wit and irreverence is what made Peter such good fun to be around in Ireland camp. With long tedious days and nights in hotels, and as many losses as defeats around the corner, it was needed.

Three weeks after Paris, a Neil Jenkins try made the difference at Lansdowne Road as Wales edged out a win, 17-15 and had a dose of luck on their side as well when a penalty kick from Eric Elwood cracked back off the upright near the end. We then had to head to Twickenham with two losses out of two at the team's back. The mood was gloomy with the Championship halfway through and the spirit that was raised the previous spring was struggling to re-surface. The team was not in a great place in January and February, and there was a tour of Australia awaiting Ireland in the summer.

The trip to London meant that Peter and Gaillimh would be rooming together. The boys were not given a choice of room partner, but it soon became evident in the Irish camp that Gaillimh and Peter were the only two that could stick each other's habits. In fairness to Gaillimh, as a non-smoker, he never complained about their room being filled with fumes!

After Gaillimh, Paul O'Connell tried to last a whole night with Peter once or twice. He insisted that one night with the Claw meant that he lost a whole year off his life. Keith Wood had complaints about Peter too – like the morning Fester woke gasping for a drink, reached to the centre bed-locker... picked up the open can of Coke... and took a massive gulp. Fester nearly choked to death that morning.

Peter had decided during the night that the can was his personal ashtray and he had made a serious job of half filling it with butts.

The captain of the team is the only player who is given his own room. But, in the later stages of Peter's International career, he was also given his own private room, whether the team management liked it or not! He was on great terms with the staff of The Berkeley Court and The Glenview Hotel in the Glen of the Downs in Wicklow, and he would ring ahead and request his own bedroom suite by number! This was very handy for the kids and I, as we didn't have to book our own hotel rooms anymore.

For Paul O'Connell's first Ireland cap, he was put rooming with Peter – a fellow Young Munster man, presumably, would be ideal moral support for young Paul, the team management reckoned.

Paul was always a complete professional from day one, and he took his training, fitness and diet very seriously, and he was intrigued to learn from the legend that was the Claw. He had lots of notes in his head by the end of that night.

'The Claw did everything a professional sports person shouldn't do,' Paul maintains. 'He ate McDonalds... ordered room service at midnight, and fell asleep with the TV blaring. He woke regularly during the night to smoke in the bed.

'On one of those occasions,' Paul continues, 'he woke me from my sleep and started talking to me.

'He said... "Do you want to feel the power of love?"

'What the f***?' thought Paul.

'Here is the hardest man in world rugby waking me at three o'clock in the morning and asking me... "If I want to feel the power of love?"

'Turns out, during his smoke, Claw was watching the Shopping Channel... and there was a CD for sale called *The Power of Love*... and, as he was buying one for himself, he wanted to know if I'd like a copy too?'

Ireland went to Twickenham and wrecked England's hopes 13-12 and the Championship then ended with a 6-6 draw with the Scots in Lansdowne Road. It was Scotland's only point the whole spring. We could have won it, we could have lost. We were not good. It was typical of the Irish rugby team at that point in time, as after an emotional high and a huge performance, there regularly were lows.

It was not a memorable Championship save for one game, and there was still the trouble of the Aussie tour to come in June. Our high, however, was as high as they can come! Twickenham, that Saturday afternoon in February, sustained everybody who cared about the Irish rugby team for a long time. It had been 12 years since we'd got a sniff of a win in their home, which was rebuilt into one of the most formidable stadiums in the world of rugby.

Peter was facing Jason Leonard, Brian Moore and Victor Ubogu. Leonard was in the early days of a spectacular and long career. Ubogu was a huge man with phenomenal muscle mass and because of his African heritage he was receiving a lot of attention from the English press. And Moore was the enforcer on that team. Moore liked to live up to supporters' views of him as a real pitbull. When he wrote his autobiography he titled it *Beware of the Dog*. He did not bite, but he talked a lot on the field.

Peter did not mind him being *mouthy*! He had so few teeth, it was very hard to understand what he was saying in the first place, and the only time Peter spoke to him during the game, their conversation was extremely short!

'What the f*** are you trying to say?' Peter asked him up close at an early scrum in Twickers.

It was a front row war, and like Poppy and Terry, Peter had the sleeves raggedly cut out of his jersey with a scissors. It was going to be a day for hard work, and rolled up sleeves would not have sufficed.

England were red hot favourites, and the boys loved to hear that. They were told they were no-hopers. They took that insult on board and took full advantage of it – and they also had another motivation, a very special one, as Kyran Bracken the English scrum-half who had been born in Skerries was being presented as the poster boy of English rugby. Bracken got special mention all of his own during the preceding week, and in the Irish dressingroom before the game.

Noisy Murphy informed the lads that Bracken had refused to play for Ireland. Noisy said that he had called him… and Kyran had flat refused, without a second's hesitation, to play for the country he was born in! Noisy kept stoking that fire in the belly of the team.

Years later, Peter played with Kyran Bracken for the Barbarians, and asked him about that phone call?

'What call…?' replied Kyran.

'I never spoke to Noel Murphy in my life…!'

England, remember, had beaten the mighty All Blacks in the same ground just three months before. But our pack were heroes, every last man. But the man who made Twickers his own that afternoon was Simon Geoghegan who had been through a tough time with injuries, and the foolishness of selection committees.

Two gifted moments of his won the game for Ireland. Firstly he got on the end of a fantastic cross-field movement, when Ireland moved the ball from the base of the scrum on the right side, and Philip Danaher and Richard Wallace set up the chance for Simon. He still had two men to beat, but he made swift work of them, shimmying inside and outside again, and making fast work of Tony Underwood in particular. His try lit up the stadium.

Then, in the second half, Jon Callard kicked a ball deep into our half, and Simon gathered it. He beat one tackle, smacked it downfield, and raced like a hare after it. He caught Rob Andrew and smothered him, and it should have been a penalty for them, but the French referee, a Monsieur Thomas, was obviously excited by what he was seeing as well.

It was *electrifying*!

We got the penalty, and Eric Elwood slotted it over. We won by one point, but we were worth every ounce of that single point.

The next morning we didn't wake in time for breakfast, so we ambled into brunch at the Chelsea Harbour Hotel. The bill for brunch was £110 sterling! We never did thank the IRFU for paying the tab.

At the airport, later that day, my sister Aileen had come out to meet us. I had sterling from home that I wanted to pass on to her for her new car.

I would only see Aileen once more after that – again at Heathrow airport, while I waited for my connection for my flight out to Australia to meet up with the Irish tour that summer.

Aileen and I walked to the car park so she could proudly show me her new car. They were our final moments together.

At work in the bank, a few days before I was due to leave for my 'once in a lifetime' trip to Australia I was overcome. And it wasn't about leaving my 11 month old son behind as I went to the far side of the world.

Mam had agreed to move into our house and mind Luke for us. When I think of it now, I am in admiration of what that must have taken out of her. She had a triple heart by-pass just three years earlier, and had buried Dad in '92, but, as always, she did it with complete love and without the tiniest complaint. I'm pretty sure that I will never be that selfless, and gracious about child minding!

So, really, I had no worries at all about leaving Luke, but that particular day at work I suddenly burst into tears. I was with my good friends, Monica Quigley and Mary Coffey, and they reassured me that my emotions were getting the better of me because I was about to leave my little boy and go so far away.

But I knew in my heart that wasn't it.

At the same time, I couldn't put my finger on what it was that was making me so upset. It was totally out of character for me to be emotional. Later, I would realize, that at some level I had tapped into the tragedy that was soon to unfold in our lives, but I shoved it to the back of my mind.

Shoulders back and undeterred, I headed for Oz to meet up with Peter and the Irish team.

It was June.

Ireland were in the home of the World champions, and also a place that boasted two of the strongest provincial teams in the World, Queensland and New South Wales. It was true to say that Ireland bit off more than we could chew, as the tour was as heavy as something the Lions might have signed off on, and it was also clear that even though the game of rugby was still amateur, this was in theory only, and in the Southern Hemisphere the game was barely hanging onto its amateur beliefs. The top Aussies were all full-time rugby players.

Poppy was unavailable for the tour and so the front row, which had gained such a strong reputation, was also going to be broken up. The good news was that Keith Wood was about to commence his spectacular career in the Irish No.2 jersey, a jersey which had been well served by Terry for so long, but Fester's time had arrived.

The tour started off so well. Too good, as Ireland beat Western Australia 64-8 and all sorts of records took a tumble. The journalists were left reciting elements of the famous tour to Australia in 1979, when Ollie Campbell and Tony Ward, two of the greatest out-halves of all time, went head-to-head for the Irish No.10.

Ollie and Wardie had scored 19 points each in single games in that tour, which was a record, and Eric kicked eight conversions and a penalty goal to equal them in that game against WA. Sixty-four was also the highest points total ever achieved by an Irish touring side against national or provincial opposition. Nine tries, although neither Simon nor Jim Staples on the opposite wing touched down – it was all down the middle at the WACA that particular evening.

With Poppy not around, Peter also had the pleasure of the company of Paco Fitzgerald. Paco and Peter were two happy Munsters' men with Fester in the middle of the front row in the opening game of the tour. It was a piece of history for Young Munster having two of their own playing for Ireland together, and on the field Peter and Paco had the same understanding they always had.

But it was all up hill from there for the team!

I had gone out to follow the tour with my dear travel buddy, Peter's Dad Noel, having left our one year old, Luke at home with my Mam, who was my rock in those days. I had gone because I always wanted to see Australia, and I reckoned we might probably never get out there again – though how wrong I was going to be on that, and I could have no idea how important Australia would prove to be in resurrecting Peter's rugby career two years later!

When the Irish management team heard that Claw's wife was following the tour he was duly called aside and told that when he was on tour... *he was on tour*!

They were not at all happy that a wife would be around the place! I duly took the royal hump with this, of course, as I had never interfered with Peter's ability to play. In fairness he was always very amicable before games, and never got wound up like some of the players, so my seeing him the night before a game or the morning of a match never distracted him.

My attitude has always been that if the players were in a public forum, that wasn't stag – guys only – then it was perfectly acceptable for me to be there. If Peter was ok with that?

And he was.

I had the most wonderful trip, because our older travel group of Mickey and Muireann Ryan, Johnny and Joan Griffin, and Daddy Noel were great company, plus many of Peter's friends from his teenage years were living in Australia, like Snap, and Billy and Liz Meehan, and Pat Kilbridge who joined us at every opportunity.

We arrived in Brisbane, and the first Test match was the following day. Ireland were playing at Ballymore, and little did I know at that time that this would become our new home quite soon.

There had been five losses since the opening win over Western Australia, and New South Wales had put 55 points on the board in the Concord Oval in Sydney, after which Gerry Murphy said he could not think of one good thing to say about his own team. We are capable of playing 50,000 times better than that, stated the coach to the waiting media. But we were not much better when an Australian XV hit Ireland for 59 points two weeks later. Against Queensland, who were the reigning Super 10 champions and had 10 Wallabies on their team, it had actually been tight, and Ireland put in a great performance, but still went down 29-26. Michael Lynagh kicked the winning penalty goal in the sixth minute of injury time.

For Peter, the game turned a bit personal, as some of the Aussies who'd been beaten in Musgrave Park two years earlier, obviously decided to keep an eye out for him. Garrick Morgan, their second row who had been sent off with Gaillimh in the melee near the end of the game in Cork, had a few words with Peter, and he was always happy to reply! Every game had its moments, and earlier in the tour Gaillimh had to get 13 stitches inserted to a head wound, thanks to the boys from ACT.

Queensland coach, John Connolly was impressed with us, however – but we did not know that when he was emphasizing that Ireland had a few 'top quality players' he was including Peter in that group. Connolly had taken note of Peter and their paths would soon cross again.

Mind you, it was a good job that John Connolly wasn't privy to the social habits of the visiting team.

For many years afterwards, I would hear Peter and the other players refer to that time in Australia as the *last great amateur* tour – the only two nights that Peter and most of the squad didn't drink were the evenings before the Test matches. In one of the team's hotels after one game they actually drank the bar dry!

At the end of the tour, as was acceptable to the IRFU, some players changed their return flights for a little holiday. Peter and I wanted to break the journey home, so we arranged to fly to Singapore for a couple of nights. Peter had sent his kit home with the team as we had planned to so some shopping there.

What we failed to factor in was that the general stature of the Asian community did not easily accommodate a prop forward. We could not find a single shirt or t-shirt to fit Peter anywhere in Singapore.

The humidity in the city was so high we were drenched in seconds every time we ventured outdoors. This meant that Peter actually wore the same stripy polo shirt for three days in this humidity.

There was no rushing or pushing when it came time for someone to sit beside him on the flight home, not that Peter noticed anything – he was in First Class, paid for by the IRFU. He did try to negotiate with the cabin manager for me to be upgraded to sit in the seat beside him, but the steward was having none of it.

That poor steward.

You'll earn your wages today, Peter decided.

Every time the steward went to the galley Peter pressed the call bell, and he duly drank his way home from Singapore to London. When we landed my loving husband then took off on a speedy wobble of a walk that lasted about 20 yards before I could catch him.

'He's sorry now... he didn't upgrade you, love!'

We lost the first Test match in Brisbane to Australia 33-13.

That night, after the game, Peter had come to my hotel to stay over, but after the warning from management I wanted to make sure no one knew about it – so I didn't even tell Daddy Noel. As far as he was aware Peter had just joined us for breakfast the next morning.

That day we moved to Surfers Paradise, a town on Queensland's Gold Coast, where we were to spend a few glorious days. For us it was summer at a balmy 20 degrees, but for the locals it was winter, and they marvelled at us two paddies, Daddy Noel and I, on the beach sunbathing as they strolled around with their puffa jackets and scarves.

Daddy Noel took off for swim, and came back refreshed and delighted with himself, and rolling his shoulders back he looked at me with a great smile on his face.

"F*** it... that *SPECIFIC* ocean is great!'

He was a fantastic travel companion, and we had many special laughs together. Each day he would ask me, 'Where are we today?' even though we were in the same town as the previous day!

The day we went to Warner Brothers Movie World theme park, I was thrilled to embrace my inner child with all my favourite cartoon characters, as Daddy Noel spent the day checking out the structure of all the buildings! It was a repeat of when I brought him to Sydney Opera House for the first time and, as I marvelled at the amazing beauty of the setting, Daddy Noel simply knocked his fist against a couple of walls, and then reported back to me.

'I know how they built that,' he stated with a satisfied expression.

The second Test was an improvement, 32-18 – and Peter broke through to score his first try for Ireland which was a special moment for his private band of supporters in the stands at the Sydney Football Stadium. In fact when Ireland left the field they were cheered by nearly everyone who made up the 40,000 in the stadium.

We had kept our very best performance to the last.

A surprise win was a possibility but the French referee, Joel Dumas messed up twice with decisions. One cost us a try, and the other had let Australia in for a crucial early try. The Aussies were 21-6 in front by the 30th minute and they were tearing big holes in our defence. They didn't need extra help from the ref. In the fourth minute Conor O'Shea had made a brave catch under a high kick from Lynagh and he was engulfed by yellow jerseys, but two of those jerseys went over the top. It should have been our penalty, instead they got the ball and Daniel Herbert got a try in his first game for his country.

It was 21-13 at half-time. Late in the half Niall Woods made a great run out of our defence with a real zip in his stride and the play was carried deep into the Aussie half. We won a ruck. Fester drove forward and we recycled the ball. It came back to Peter who was 15 yards out from their line.

He took on two of their number. He looked like he had been stopped, but he drove forward again and got the ball down. O'Shea converted.

I'm sure the Australians looking on could not understand where the Ireland team, which was playing with such fire and brimstone, and lots of intelligence and skill, had been for the preceding few weeks?

But we conceded two early penalty goals when the teams came back out for the second half. Ireland never gave up. We had a try by Eric disallowed, but Neil Francis, who had an amazing tour, finished off our evening with a great try. We could have done no more against the greatest team in the game.

The tour had ended with a blood-stirring game.

It was one long party on that tour, off the field at any rate. When the Irish team management invited me to the final Gala Dinner in Sydney I stoutly refused, despite Peter wanting me to go. I was still smarting from their *warning* not to see Peter during the tour.

Thankfully all of that IRFU behaviour changed dramatically when Warren Gatland came on the scene as Irish coach, and his wife, Trudi was especially pro-active in involving us ladies. She single-handedly broke down so many barriers.

The day after we returned from Australia, my life changed forever.

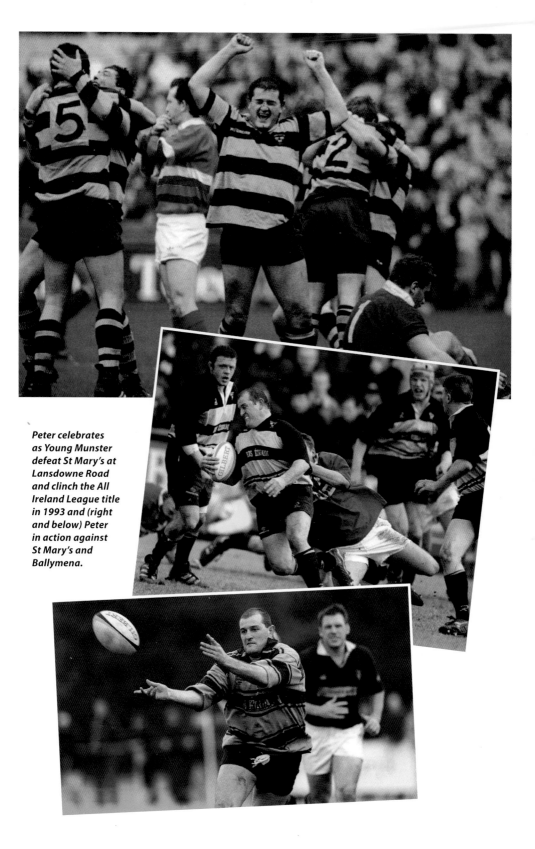

Peter celebrates as Young Munster defeat St Mary's at Lansdowne Road and clinch the All Ireland League title in 1993 and (right and below) Peter in action against St Mary's and Ballymena.

The Galweys, Mick and Joan, with Peter and myself at The Berkeley Court Hotel in Dublin during the early Ireland days in 1993 and (below) the girls were kept apart from their partners on the evening of games, but Joan Galwey, Eimear Danaher, myself, Rachel Francis, and Rachel Popplewell still make sure to enjoy ourselves.

Daddy Noel, Geraldine Quinlivan and myself enjoy the night at Anthony Foley's testimonial dinner and (below) early days on tour in Australia when Peter and I got to meet up with some of our oldest friends, Snap, Pat Kilbridge and Billy Meehan.

Rala, our Harry and Dixie on one of their visits to 'the farm' and (below) a proud Daddy Noel poses with Peter.

Harry's Christening with Luke, Eimear, Jane and Ray Ryan and (below) Luke, Harry and Jane.

The early days... and the final days! Peter with a very young Gaillimh and Pat Murray after an "Ireland A" game in Scotland and (below) Peter waves goodbye to the Irish supporters in Lansdowne Road after his final game in the old ground for Ireland in 2002.

Daddy Noel and myself on our memorable tour of Australia in 1994 (when he workd out how the Sydney Opera House had been built!) and (below) Daddy Noel, Meg, myself and Luke in the Stade de France for Peter's last game in the city in 2002.

The Clohessys: Peter, Daddy Noel, Meg and Ger, and (front row) Noel jnr, Dee, Mags and Des.

Our wedding day with (Back: from left) my brother Howard, and my uncles, Lawrence and Gena, and (Front) my sister Aileen, my Mam (Helena Gibson-Steel) my Dad (Harry Gibson-Steel) and my Nana Helena Gannon.

Our first and only ski trip as a family with Luke and Jane and (below) with the Brennans in sunny Toulouse.

With Mick and Joan Galwey, and Philip Danaher, on the famous grass at Wembley Stadium after Ireland had defeated Wales in London as the Millennium Stadium was being built in Cardiff.

The Munster crew led by Gaillimh and Keith Wood help Peter celebrate his 30th birthday with a large cake which they are about to insist he eats, head first and (below) typical horseplay between Peter and his great friend, Fester.

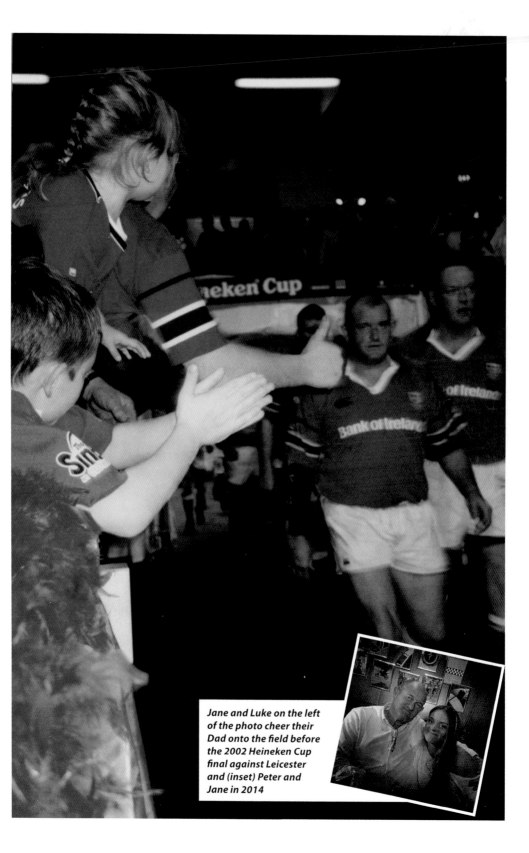

Jane and Luke on the left of the photo cheer their Dad onto the field before the 2002 Heineken Cup final against Leicester and (inset) Peter and Jane in 2014

Peter and myself, with Jane, Paul Coffey and Ray Ryan on TV 3's Celebrity Family Fortunes in 2013.

Peter returned to his love of horse-riding as soon as he hung up his rugby boots and (below) he finds retirement to his liking in Hawaii.

Peter a few days after setting himself on fire after his last game for Ireland and a fortnight before the 2002 Heineken Cup semi-final and (above) with Eddie Jordan and our late friend John Stronach from Scotland.

The boys, Peter, Trevor Brennan and John Hayes with their boys Josh Brennan and Bill Hayes, and our Harry.

'Ray.
'My oldest teammate and friend, you were there with me from the start... and through thick and thin.
'You are still my first SOS call.
'Thanks.

— Peter

CHAPTER 9

We collected Luke from my Mam on our first day back in Ireland and headed down to Kilkee to visit Peter's family. When we returned home on the Sunday evening I was told that my only sister Aileen, who was a psychology student in London, was dead.

Aileen was only 24 years old and had been murdered in her apartment.

Ray Ryan had been trying to contact us all day. The local Gardai, unable to locate us, had asked Ray to get a message to Peter. Finally, Ray had called us when we got in and told Peter to phone the Gardai immediately.

Peter made the phone call.

They told him that the two of us needed to call down to the station without delay, but they would not tell Peter why?

Peter got cross in the conversation, and insisted on being told there and then over the phone what they had to say!

Our world immediately spun into turmoil, as I gathered Mam and Howard, my brother to tell them the hardest thing I would ever have to tell them. That Aileen was gone.

My sister had the ability to light up a room with her personality. She was always smiling and laughing. In many ways, she was way ahead of her time. She was incredibly conscientious and respectful of every living thing. At the age of 12, in the late seventies, she announced to my mother that she was a vegetarian. Aileen even refused to use anything made of leather.

She would pick up stray kittens. She refused to set mouse traps in her London apartment and, instead, to my horror, she put her waste paper bins on their sides and placed cheese inside, in the hope of catching them that way.

She loved the freedom and the sense of excitement that living in London brought, and she embraced the multicultural city with an open heart. She could not abide narrow-minded thinking or discrimination of any sort.

In many ways, it was Aileen's caring and open heart that led to her life being cut short, and with that the world lost a shining light.

Our dear Nana was living in London at the time with our bachelor uncles who we were very close to. After contacting them, we arranged to fly to London the next day. I will be eternally gratefully to my friend Majella, who took that week off work to mind Luke for us, as we had no idea what was ahead of us over there.

We also have to say a big thank you to Dick Healy and our dear friend, the late Tom McInerney, who organised for Aer Lingus to look after us so well on that journey. Things like that make all the difference when your world has fallen apart.

We all arrived at the Metropolitan police station close to where Aileen lived in North London, and there a media circus began – one of the police officers recognised Peter and went to the press. Though Jane Murphy, who was a detective on the case, could not have been kinder, in fact we became firm friends subsequently. Dave Crompton was the Detective Inspector in charge, and he too was very kind, however I also learned a valuable lesson that first day.

Dave suggested that it would not be a good idea for Mam to identify Aileen, and he suggested that Peter should do this on behalf of the family. In fairness to Peter he had no problem stepping up, as he always did to support me, but my concern was when would Mam get to see Aileen?

Dave said not to worry that she would see her daughter, but in her current state it wouldn't be a good idea, he advised.

When you are in such a tragic and overwhelming situation for the first time, you automatically listen to those in authority, who have experience. Unfortunately I did so that day, and it is a huge regret. What happened next was absurd, because the murderer had injured himself when the police came to arrest him, and he was in hospital.

The authorities couldn't do a post mortem on Aileen until he was fit enough to give a statement to his solicitor. This meant that we had no idea how many days or weeks it would be before we could bring Aileen home.

All of us flew back home, and left Aileen in the mortuary – without Mam having seen her darling daughter.

Back in Limerick, Mam became very anxious about this, so I suggested that we fly back to London. I got advice from our family undertaker, and asked him to check with the London coroner as to whether we should still wait to see Aileen when she was brought home? Even though we still had no indication as to when that might be?

After checking I was assured that the embalming process would preserve Aileen's body well enough for Mam to see her. Yet again, I learned a valuable lesson – trust your instincts all the time with difficult decisions.

Two weeks later Aileen was finally released to come home to her family. We had the removal organised for that evening, with the funeral Mass the next day, but out of the blue I got a call at midday from our undertakers to say that Aileen's coffin could not be opened. They advised that no one should see Aileen and explained it would be a picture that we wouldn't be able to erase from our minds.

To my last day, I will remember the awful feeling, and absolute heartbreak that I was about to cause my already poor heartbroken Mam, when I would tell her that she couldn't see her daughter one last time!

That day, when Aileen arrived home, I was agonizing as to whether any of us should see her, but I decided that the only person whose judgment I trusted at this stage was Peter's. So, yet again, he didn't hesitate about my request.

He bravely went alone to the undertakers to see Aileen.

When he came out he gave me the devastating news that there was no point in any of us saying our final goodbyes.

'You won't know her,' said Peter.

With a very heavy heart I went home to tell my poor mother. I deeply regret not challenging the Inspector's authority in London a few weeks earlier. It was one of the hardest lessons I have ever learned. To add insult to total heartache, the following January as we sat in the Old Bailey in London, the prosecuting barrister held up photographs of Aileen as they found her… on her sofa with a thin line of blood trickling from her mouth after being strangled.

A photograph for all of us to see.

The behaviour of some sections of the media through all of this anguish for our family was remarkable.

In 1994 Ireland was a very different place, and there were very few murders it seemed, so a violent death was front page news if one occurred. And, in this instance, Aileen was the sister-in-law of an International rugby player. That meant front page news, in Ireland and England.

Of course we had no issue with the story being published. In my case I was used to reading about family in the papers, however it was extra heartache that my family, especially Mam and my 90 year old Nana, could have done without.

Family just did not seem to matter to some journalists. Neither did some of them care about accuracy and truthfulness. The *Irish Independent* had printed an article about Aileen that had many inaccurate details in it, amongst which it was written that Aileen was a nurse and that her boyfriend had killed her.

I understand one hundred per cent that complete and total accuracy might not matter to some in the media, but when it is such a personal and emotionally traumatic event for a whole family every little detail becomes vitally important.

I took the decision to call the *Irish Independent*, to offer them the correct facts and any other information they may like to know. My attitude was that if they were going to print any story about Aileen's death, they would surely want to be accurate in doing so. I also knew that I was leaving myself wide open and that they could possibly get information that perhaps I shouldn't share, but I was willing to take that chance to have the truth told at least.

What happened next was astonishing. I was in Peter's parents' home making the phone call to one of the editors on the news desk in the *Independent* – and I asked a friend to listen in on the extension line. So she would remember what I had said, as I may not.

I introduced myself and said that there were details of their story that were wrong and I was happy to be interviewed and give them any information they may want.

The person tore into me.

He started shouting abuse down the phone to me. I was shocked to the core, but somehow I remained calm, and I reiterated that I was merely offering to assist them by providing correct information. He continued to rant and rave.

Finally, he hung up the phone on me.

My friend came running into the kitchen to me, in floods of tears. She could not believe what she had just heard. She looked at me, and could not understand how calm I was – I'm not sure either, except perhaps that after living through such extreme shock this was one more unreal event in my life.

I came away from the tragic experience believing in my heart that newspapers have scant regard for the truth. In fact, I rarely read them anymore, except for the sports pages while Peter played for Munster and Ireland.

There was still a long road for my family to travel.

The following January the trial of Aileen's murderer was set for the Old Bailey. And this time we took Luke, now 19 months old with us, as we weren't sure how long the trial might take. This is when Eimear Farrell made a welcome entry into our family, at the age of 15 – Mary, her Mam, allowed her to take time out of school to come with us.

As Nana and our uncles were still living in Hayes in London, we booked into the Holiday Inn at Heathrow to be near them. That first day at court

I hoped against hope that the trial would go unnoticed by the press. I had Majella on alert in Ireland to check the papers and fax them to me if there were any reports.

Incredibly, I was to quickly discover that as family of a victim of a murder we had no special rights to seats in the courtroom – we had to queue with everyone else and hope that we would get a seat in the public gallery. And there were always queues.

In London there are members of the public who bring their flasks and sandwiches, and spend their days watching and listening to court cases! However, in fairness to these Londoners, as they got to know us they would hold a place for us in the queue at lunchtime.

After day one in court we returned exhausted to the hotel.

There were no faxes.

'Great', I thought.

I imagined we would be able to avoid more media scrutiny.

Day two was the same, thank God.

Day three was horrific in court, and we had to listen to the murderer's counsel argue that it was somehow Aileen's fault that she was murdered. Absurd and disgusting, but that story is for another day, and another book perhaps. It was a massive learning curve for all of my family to hear how the truth can be manipulated and how a whole different story can be presented by legal minds. We returned dejected to our hotel, to find that Luke was very sick.

Eimear reported that he was a bit off all day. At that time in London there were warnings about an outbreak of meningitis. We quickly decided to call a doctor. But as I opened our bedroom door, I found it difficult to push – there was a huge stack of faxes put under the door. Majella had done her job well, and sent all of the Irish newspaper reports.

My heart sank and, meanwhile, my head was spinning with concern for Luke. The doctor arrived and prescribed penicillin for Luke, but warned Peter and myself that he couldn't be sure that it wasn't meningitis, and he told us to be vigilant… that if a rash appeared we weren't to delay in calling him.

As I sifted through the papers, my heart sank deeper and deeper still as I read the newspaper reports. The sensationalism was profound. How were

Mam and Nana going to cope with this, I feared?

Within twenty minutes Luke was screaming the hotel down, and had developed a rash all over. This was one moment in my life when I really thought I couldn't take any more, that this couldn't be happening, not now! The only thing that seemed to pacify Luke a little was when I walked up and down the corridor outside our room with him in my arms.

The doctor was soon back and in our room, ringing the hospital. It was around 8.0 p.m. Suddenly, a German lady who was a guest in one of the rooms, came out and proceeded to shout at me because of Luke's crying.

I apologized, and explained that we were on our way to the hospital, however she continued undeterred. At that moment I thought I was going to just jump out of the 20th floor window! I went back into the bedroom and Luke cried even louder... and Peter shouted at me to walk him in the corridor.

When I explained that I couldn't because of the German lady, he went bananas. The doctor got quite frightened and hurried up doing what he was doing – anything, so that he could get away from these Irish nut-cases! Thankfully, when we arrived at Harefield Hospital we met a lovely Australian paediatrician who diagnosed that Luke was allergic to the penicillin, hence the rash, and what he had was a severe ear infection, probably caught in the hotel swimming pool.

Even as a fifteen year old girl, Eimear Farrell proved to be an invaluable support to us. In the hotel she was sharing a room with Mam, and that night in the middle of all the drama with Luke there was a knock at their bedroom door. Eimear opened the door to find a young reporter standing there.

He asked for my mother.

Eimear lied and said Mam wasn't there. But he then started asking Eimear questions, to which she replied 'no comment'.

Mam was amazed that someone so young could have such strong sense, and when she asked Eimear how did she know what to say to the reporter, Eimear just smiled.

'That's what they say on the telly!'

Aileen's murderer was sentenced to life, but he was eligible for parole by May of 2002. A couple of months before that he went missing from the open wing of Hollesley Bay prison in Suffolk. He went on the run and fled to Germany, where he killed a man before being returned to prison with a second life sentence. This time the judge said that he must serve at least 25 years.

We had all returned to our lives after the first sentencing with hearts that were still broken with grief. To my Mam's eternal credit, how she minded Luke for us, alone many times while I worked full time in the bank, and followed Peter's rugby life, I will never know. But she did it with all her heart.

And in many ways Luke was her saving grace.

For her, especially, there was to come more gut-wrenching invasion of her life and the life of her lost daughter. A few weeks later, to our horror, a "journalist psychologist" wrote a full page broadsheet article – analysing the *ins and outs* of why the murderer killed Aileen, even though the writer wasn't in court and had no knowledge whatsoever about Aileen. With the training and experience I now have as a therapist for the past 15 years, I would consider this quite wrong, but at the time I saw it as it was, just the media doing what they do best, trying to sell papers but causing unnecessary pain along the way. I don't hold any anger or resentment though, as I believe what goes around comes around, and we all carry responsibility for our actions eventually.

I also don't wish to paint all journalists or newspapers with the same brush. I have met many who do have integrity. The dilemma seems to be finding the balance between maintaining integrity and dealing in sensationalism. The simplest solution is if we, as consumers, start demanding integrity from our chosen media. If we do so, then they will have to provide it because we are buying their product.

We actually have all the power. We can tell them how honest and decent they need to be if they wish to stay in the business of selling news.

During the time that we were waiting for Aileen to be returned home, Nana and my uncles came home. Uncle Gus was terminally ill with cancer at the time – Aileen had been taking care of his affairs for him in London, and he had accepted that he had nearly run out of time. He was on chemotherapy, and also was diabetic.

Each day Daddy Noel would collect my four uncles and he would take them into Austin Quinlivan's pub to pass a few hours. The first day that Gus was going in, I called Geraldine Quinlivan to let her know he was on chemo and if he was having a drink to swap the mixer for soda water, because of the diabetes.

Unlike my other uncles who lived in Limerick with us for many years, Gus had spent most of his adult life in London, so he had never been to Austin's. As soon as he walked in the door, Geraldine looked at him.

'You sit up there on that stool… and don't you dare die in my pub!'

It was the start of many days of very valuable *therapy* during that awful time, *therapy* that Daddy Noel, Geraldine and Austin provided, and these things you never forget. Little things. Like the day after we had been told about Aileen.

Daddy Noel arrived to our house, quietly left £1,000 in cash on the counter, and left without saying anything to anybody.

Our lives would never be quite normal again.

But rugby life helped.

It always does.

Anthony "Slurpy" Foley.

'You served a hard apprenticeship with Gaillimh and me... despite the fact that your Mam, Sheila told you when you started to stay away from the two of us.

'I, for one, am glad you didn't listen to her!'

                                             – Peter

CHAPTER 10

In The Berkeley Court, in November of '94 after we had beaten the United States in a close enough game at Lansdowne Road – eleven points was all that was in it at the end – the talk quickly turned to the selection of the Barbarians team that would meet the touring South Africans the next month.

After the match, Kevin Flynn who was a committee member of the BaaBaas at the time, told Peter on the quiet that he had been selected at tight head, with Fester as hooker, and Poppy at loose head. This was a big compliment to the Irish front row and their ability.

Peter had told me this news before the official dinner, so when we stood at the bar in the function room afterwards it was with a highly raised eyebrow that I overheard another BaaBaas committee member speaking to Peter.

'Now, Peter... I will do my best to get you selected for the BaaBaas!'

This was typical of the politics and gamesmanship that existed within the inner sanctums of rugby in those days. As usual Peter said nothing, shrugged his shoulders, and never thought of it again.

The BaaBaas went on to beat South Africa 23-15 at Lansdowne Road – the game and the entire weekend was a big deal, as for political reasons South

Africa had not played at the oldest International HQ in world rugby for 25 years. It was also the first time that the Barbarians had played a touring side in Lansdowne Road.

South Africa were a top team at the time, and they were preparing to host the World Cup the following summer when Nelson Mandela would supervise one of his country's proudest months. Peter loved the home support and was adamant the crowd made the *vital* difference that day, as they totally got behind the BaaBaas. Francois Pienaar captained the visitors, while Robert Jones led the BaaBaas team that included many greats, such as Phillipe Saint-Andre, and of course our own special front row.

In the sixties the Baa-Baas had also beaten the South Africans, and boasted an all-Irish front row of Gordon Wood, Ronnie Dawson and Syd Millar.

How fitting it was that Fester should follow in his father's footsteps.

Peter, at the end of the year, had also been selected for the BaaBaas against Wales and France. As I needed to do an emotional trip to London, to tend to some of Aileen's affairs, it was a good opportunity to go there first and have Peter for support.

Peter and I flew to London a couple of days before.

Daddy Noel, Meg and two of our all-time favourite people, Austin and Geraldine were taking the ferry to Wales, and I would travel back with them after the game in Bath – as Peter had to fly on to Paris with the team. Ray Ryan had posed an interesting question to us all one time!

'If you had one last bus journey to take in this life... who would you want on the bus with you?'

First choice for all of us was Geraldine Quinlivan!

Geraldine was the best character ever for making fun, and she wouldn't do so quietly. In her loud and very best Limerick accent she had us in stitches at the game in Bath. We were seated at the try-line, and Bath is unusual in that the seats are lower than the pitch, so when you sit you are almost eye level with the pitch. The supporters in Bath of course are very posh and reserved.

Simon Geoghegan, who was Geraldine's hero on the Irish team, was playing for Bath against 'her Peter'. Every time Simon got the ball to race up the wing, Geraldine was up and out of her seat blocking everyone's view and roaring.

'Go back Simon... GO BACK!

'You're not supposed to score against us!'

The locals didn't really see the funny side, as indeed they didn't that evening either. Simon had recommended a jazz club for us to have dinner, while Peter was at the team dinner. It was a very posh and lovely venue looking onto water. There were long rows of tables that everyone shared. We didn't get off to a great start.

When the set menu of fish arrived to a well oiled and starving Irish crew, Daddy Noel could not believe his eyes.

'Ah love... get us another one of those,' he asked.

'I'll never have enough in that!'

The other guests at our table were just getting over that little blip, when the music started. Clearly the regulars were there to listen to the music, but Meg and Geraldine had different ideas, and they began a sing-a-long, which was bad enough. No one else was amused, especially the musician, but when they started heckling him to play songs they knew, it did look as though we would be asked to leave – before we were run out of the place by the angry audience!

The following day we said our good-byes. Peter went on to France and the rest of us took off to Fishguard for the ferry. As we were on the outskirts of one of the towns, Geraldine let a roar out of her.

'I've seen it all now... !

'LOOK...' she shouted, pointing to a sign.

'Imagine inviting people to park... and have... A RIDE!'

We were laughing so much, I had to stop the car and get out the camera and take a photo, and of course Meg and Geraldine weren't going to be left out, so the two of them swung off the pole for me specially as I took their photo.

The Seacat that day was a very rough journey, and a few minutes out of port we were already rocking. Meg, Geraldine and myself were outside on seats beside the lifeboats as the waves started coming over the railings, but

Meg and Geraldine burst into song.

Geraldine then roared at Austin.

'Bring out the duty free… this lifeboat is ours and by f*** the duty free is coming with us.'

Soon almost everyone was getting sick, except for Geraldine who was keeping an eye on everyone, and Daddy Noel who was still inside eating all the sandwiches that they had brought for the journey! At some point Geraldine was wondering where Austin had gone, so she searched inside. He wasn't with Daddy Noel, so she went to check the other deck, and sure enough there was Austin.

He was very seasick, and terrified he would fall overboard with the waves, so he had tied himself to the ships railings with his jumper!

Once we had at last docked in Rosslare, the captain spoke over the PA system. 'Thank you, ladies and gentlemen… we hope you had a pleasant journey?'

Top of her voice, Geraldine let out a shout.

'The cheek of that f*****, after the journey we just suffered.'

As we were heading to the car deck, one of the stewards thanked us for travelling with them. He also said he looked forward to having us on board again. Austin gave him a look.

'Unless you learn how to fly boss…' Austin said, 'I guarantee you'll never see me again!'

Driving off the ferry there was a big long line of cars queuing to board. Meg hung herself out the back window of our car, and started waving her arms at the queue.

'GO BACK…

'GO BACK… DON'T DO IT!' she shouted.

It was one of the best trips ever.

There were many learning curves in the mid-90s.

Peter broke away from the family building business and started his own courier company. Rugby was still amateur, but the pressures and travel demands were increasing with every passing year.

In the summer of 1995 Ireland were heading to the World Cup in South Africa but Peter made the decision that he would not be with the team.

He was working around the clock, in between training and playing for Ireland and Young Munster – not to mention the personal and deeply emotional stress that was our home life. So it was for these good reasons that he decided to make himself unavailable for the 1995 World Cup.

He was still in start-up mode with his new business, but his decision caused consternation within the IRFU, and it was suggested that they would organize for me to get leave from my bank job, so that I could run his business and he could travel to South Africa!

There were two reasons why I didn't agree.

One was that the bank had been very good to me always, but especially during the previous 10 months, giving me all the time off I needed after Aileen's death and the subsequent trial. I had just settled back into work, and how would my colleagues feel if I asked for more leave so that Peter Clohessy could play rugby?

More importantly, I knew absolutely nothing about the courier business.

Peter had actually decided in the spring of '95 that he wasn't going on the summer tour, but knew that if he announced it then, he wouldn't haven't been picked for the Five Nations. He wasn't alone in staying at home as Philip Danaher also had to say 'no thanks' due to his business commitments.

Peter's decision, however, opened the door for Paul Wallace and Gary Halpin to seek and nail down the tight head berths on the Irish squad in South Africa. Wally and Peter would also find themselves heading in opposite directions, two years later, when the Lions were starting their tour of the same country.

Peter broke the news to Noisy after the Welsh game.

He also had a word in Gary Halpin's ear.

'Well Gaza… you're in for South Africa,' said Peter.

'I'm not going.'

The pair of them were standing in our hotel bedroom in Cardiff.

Gary didn't believe him and he turned to me.

'Is he serious, Anna?'

'Absolutely Gary… hope you have a great trip!'

Although the game wasn't professional, the IRFU had started paying loss of earnings for time off work – with match fees and win bonuses.

The Union also paid expenses, and there was no shortage of money when it came to looking after the players in their hotels. In Paris, one evening after a match, a magnificent box tied with a big bow was delivered to the bedroom.

I couldn't wait to open it. I excitedly unwrapped the exquisite tissue paper but my excitement was short lived.

Inside was a freshly laundered set of training gear!

I clearly remember Noisy Murphy's equal excitement over the bill for that laundry. It was then that I discovered that, for several years, Mick Galwey had been bringing from home his week's worth of dirty laundry to The Berkeley Court and was getting it cleaned at great expense, thanks to the IRFU.

How well I hadn't known that?

All the glamorous hours I spent doing Peter's rugby laundry!

But the professional era was upon everyone in the game, whether they liked it or not! Ken Reid, the IRFU president, was one of those who was not shy about voicing his displeasure at such thing.

The change would have 'disastrous consequences' for the game in Ireland, Reid predicted, so incorrectly. He also said that during the World Cup he was going to let everyone in power, in every other country, know his feelings.

He was wasting his time.

Everything was about to change, and in a flick of a switch. For the likes of Peter and other International players the days of lining out for their clubs, and with their best friends from their childhood days, were almost at an end. They were ending fast, and they were to be enjoyed while they lasted – though, in May, Peter was in Munsters' colours as they went down 23-3 to Garryowen in another Munster Cup final front of 9,000 spectators at Thomond Park.

Gerry Murphy's time as Irish coach would end after the 1995 World Cup. And, after that, the national coach's job was, in many respects, handed from Billy to Jack… it passed hands too fast, as in successive seasons Murray Kidd, and then Brian Ashton, and finally Warren Gatland, took charge.

The game was moving into a whole new future, one of professionalism, and like many countries Ireland staggered forward to begin with.

The 1995 Five Nations was no better than the previous season for us. We managed one win, and that came in the last game against the Welsh in Cardiff.

England exacted revenge in the opening game, with a 20-8 victory and the only highlight for home supporters was Anthony Foley getting in for a try in his first game in a green jersey. Peter, and Poppy and Gaillimh, were praised in the newspapers for their work in the loose, but really there were only morsels of comfort for Irish fans after seeing England beaten twice on the trot in the previous two seasons. The 12-point win did not tell the full story of their superiority. It could have been an awful lot more.

Axel had reason to celebrate, but there were not too many other people all that happy. For myself and Peter, the trial of Aileen's murderer, which was commencing a couple of days after the England game, meant that our minds were elsewhere once games of rugby were over. There was the heartbreak of losing to the old enemy in a game of rugby, and then there was real life *tragedy*.

We had, sadly, come to understand the gulf in difference.

We lost badly to the Scots and the French, as England landed the Championship for themselves. The tournament did not augur well for the World Cup.

We managed to reach the quarter-finals in South Africa. We played well enough against New Zealand and Wales in our group games, and against the All Blacks Gary Halpin got in for a try. We scored three tries in total, which was amazing in itself against the mighty favourites for the tournament, but they got five with Jonah Lomu leading the charge with a pair of them. They won 43-19, but it was enough to give the team sufficient momentum to have a six-try win over Japan and then get back to Ellis Park in Johannesburg a third time to just about slip through against the Welsh. Three tries to two, and 24-23 to us, and watching it at home with Peter we could not have been happier for Gerry Murphy and the boys.

The big problem, however, was that Gerry Murphy did not have the strength in depth in his squad and the likes of Simon Geoghegan, Brendan Mullin, Nick Popplewell, Neil Francis, Paddy Johns, David Corkery and

Terry Kingston had to play in all three games, and then get ready for the quarter-final against the French in Durban a few days after. That ended 36-12. The team was flat, and tired and ready for home.

Paul Wallace only played in one of the games in the tournament, and when the team did get home he was presented in the media as Peter's No.1 challenger for the tight head jersey, and not Gary Halpin.

In those days we would spend our summers in Kilkee and one afternoon, as Keith Wood was recovering from a shoulder operation, himself and Anthony Foley decided to do a day trip to Kilkee to visit us in our mobile home.

It was one of the longest parties ever – it officially lasted three days – with the two boys still in the only clothes that they had landed in. In fact, on the third night, Peter was so *poisoned* that he couldn't make it to the pub, but I went with the lads anyway.

On day two, we had decided to go out to Doonaha beach, a few miles beyond Kilkee. The Danahers had arrived in their new jeep so Peter decided he would spin back to Kilkee and bring the jet ski for some craic, but the writing was on the wall that morning when the jet-ski trailer broke off from the jeep – and was headed directly for a parked car, complete with a newspaper-reading driver.

Peter had to crash the Danahers new jeep into the jet-ski trailer to stop it from crashing into the parked car.

When he arrived back at Doonaha, therefore, the jet ski was now in the back of the jeep. There is no slip at Doonaha – just some steep steps, and 30 feet of very rocky cliff. Peter, much to the absolute shock of all of us, drove the jeep down the rocky cliff and onto the beach.

By now we were starting to cause a bit of a storm on the family-packed *quiet* beach, as Boris Danaher – Philip and Eimear's beloved English sheepdog – was also on the family day out and when he met an "in heat" labrador, he decided to make a family of his own. That was the day I learned that when dog's mate they end up stuck back to back!

At this point, Fester, Slurpy (Anthony Foley), Peter and Philip were in the sea, and Boris and the stuck Labrador were running up and down the beach much to the disgust of many aghast families.

'She wont let him go... unless he pays her,' roared Philip from the water.

Once Boris gained his freedom again, he was then put on the jet-ski and taken for a spin. Families around us were now loudly complaining about the danger of the jet-ski in amongst the swimmers.

The boys decided enough was enough.

So they carried the jet ski on their shoulders – including Fester who still had a wound from his recent shoulder surgery – back across the beach! Then some reality struck. Getting the jeep down onto the beach was one thing, but getting it back up the rocky cliff was an entirely different challenge. My heart was in my mouth before anything else happened, but I guessed what was about to materialize in front of my eyes.

It took Peter several attempts but, by God, he wasn't going to let it get the better of him as he drove the jeep back up the cliff to safety.

The Galweys, the Danahers and ourselves also went to Kilkee for the weekend just as the World Cup had kicked off against the All Blacks. Gaillimh hadn't been selected in the party and, of course, Peter and Philip were sitting it out. This was also a time when mobile phones – and, therefore, a fast text message– were unheard of!

We were watching Ireland playing live in Richies pub in Kilkee when Jim Staples came a cropper. The game was not long over when the barman came up to us to say there was a phone call for Philip Danaher.

Philip went to the end of the bar to the phone, and came back to join us saying nothing!

He assumed the call was a set up by the lads, and he was not going to get caught in their tricky web. He was completely wrong. It transpired that Noisy Murphy had called his son, Kenny from South Africa and told him to find Danaher, and do so as quickly as possible!

Kenny took an educated guess.

He looked up the names of pubs in Kilkee, and found Philip in the sort of company he guessed he would be keeping. Kenny, who is also a professional prankster like Gaillimh and Peter, got Philip on the phone but, of course, Philip hung up double quick!

Noisy himself had to get on the phone to Richies Bar.

Philip came to us a second time, and told us that he was off to Limerick to pack his bags. He had missed out on the World Cup in 1991 and, at 29 years of age, he felt that he might not make it in '99.

One of Peter's summer drinking buddies was gone the next morning.

One evening, in November of that year, Peter had collected Luke from playschool, but when I arrived home I noticed Luke was wearing different clothes? And he was looking a little pale?

When I asked Peter, he said that Luke had got sick at school that day, but that he seemed fine now. Later that evening I got a call from Fiona, who is married to Noel, Peter's brother. Fiona asked me how Luke was?

Their son, Evan went to the same playschool, and Fiona said she was concerned about Evan as a lot of the kids were sick that day. I told her that Luke seemed to have come around and appeared fine. At 5.0 a.m. the next morning we got the dreadful call, to tell us that Evan had just passed away from meningitis.

This was an incredibly tough time for everyone, and I have no idea how Noel and Fiona managed to stay sane. Their second son, Noelie, who was five months old, was then admitted to the same hospital for observation, just in case. The death of a child has to be the worst grief in the world for any parent to bear. I found this unbelievably heart-wrenching, so I can't imagine what it was like for Noel and Fiona.

Having held myself together reasonably well over the previous 12 months of trauma, I was shocked at how I fell apart after Evan – perhaps it was the grief from Aileen's death, and the shock of the realization that Luke had clearly had a close call with the virus that day also, but, thank God, had somehow overcome it.

I became an absolute mess.

When Fester, Gaillimh and Philip Danaher called to see me at Peter's Mam's home, I couldn't rise above it.

It was also incredibly unfair to Meg, Peter's Mam, for me to be in this state at her house, but I couldn't face my own mother who was living with us at the time.

I couldn't handle looking at the pain in her eyes also.

Mam had known Evan as a regular visitor to our home when he came to play with Luke, and as a midwife she had helped Noel and Fiona in the early days when Evan was born.

It was all just too much.

'Quinny.

'Another man who served his apprenticeship with Gaillimh and me. You were always great company, but your Mam, Mary... she was even better craic.

'You were a great man to have on a team, but one tormenting b****** to play against! The most honoured man in French rugby, Fabian Pelous had an immaculate disciplinary record, but Quinny... you broke him.

'Pelous was so tormented he kicked you up the h***... and got yellow carded.'

— Peter

CHAPTER 11

We were all just muddling through our lives at times.

December of 1995 was a sad Christmas for both sides of our family, and it did not help that Peter was selected to go on the Irish tour to the United States over the holiday period. In order to build a distraction for all of us, I organised a New Year's Eve dinner party at home for Peter's family – most of my guests were well *oiled* by the time we rang Peter in Atlanta to wish him a Happy New Year!

It was a hard time to be separated from Peter.

Daddy Noel collected me from work in my car one Friday evening while Peter was still away. He was driving our car because he always enjoyed trying his children's cars when they were on holiday – of course, he always had his own transport, usually a choice of a few, but for some reason he enjoyed swapping when he got an opportunity. As I didn't need my car when I was at work, Daddy Noel dropped me off and picked me up again that Friday.

On the way home, on the Dublin Road, the guy behind us didn't realize that traffic had stopped, and ploughed into us, also sending my car into the three cars in front of us. I instantly felt my neck had done something weird, and before we got out of the car I said this to Daddy Noel.

And he felt the same. However, we agreed there and then not to mention it, as we didn't want anyone to think that we were on a claim mission! My heart went out to the poor man who crashed into us. His wife had just had a baby, and he was clearly distracted. We re-affirmed that we were all fine, except for our car. It was a crumpled wreck!

I called Peter to tell him our car was written off, and to assure him that we were all okay.

As usual he didn't say much.

'Are you okay?

'Is Daddy okay?

'Well then, that's grand,' he continued, '… how's the car?'

I was in shock, and full of energy at the same time that evening – I remember wanting to go out and try to find the bank crew who were on the usual Friday night session. The following day was an entirely different story, however.

It felt that I had been knocked down by a truck. Every part of me seemed to hurt. This was the beginning of a two-year journey of constant pain. I couldn't even carry a handbag!

Sitting wasn't an option either. It was kneel or stand, they were my two options in life. Working in the bank was out of the question, so my days as a housewife began. Because my Mam worked really hard as a mid-wife all her life, my image of *freedom* was staying at home all day and choosing whatever you wanted to do, whenever you wanted to do it?

Trying this out as a career path when you are in chronic pain, and your husband is away every second weekend following his passion and having great fun, is probably not the best time to arrive at a judgment. But being a full-time housewife nearly cracked me up! My doctor, Miriam Callanan was my saving grace over those two years, as I went to a gang of specialists.

Over the years to come this group of people would total 48 different doctors, specialists… and medical personnel doing scans!

There was no way, I decided, anyone without a medical degree was getting their hands on me!

In hindsight this was a very peculiar decision, as I recall both of my parents travelling to a Mr Heffernan, in Fethard in Tipperary, every time anyone put a disc out. My fear was practically phobic – so, instead of heeding the advice of many, I muddled on, with painkillers, muscle relaxers, regular physiotherapy, and a great many days and nights spent in absolute frustration with the constant thought that my body was letting me down.

Some of the specialists told me I would be this way forever, and to get used to it. Others told me it was degenerative – at 27 years of age… please, come on! And still others told me there was nothing wrong with me at all. That last observation was always the one that freaked me out most of all, because if there was nothing wrong, why was I having all this pain?

Was it really all in my head?

Add to this my programming from childhood, which had taught me a strong work ethic, and I really came close to losing my mind. I agonized about what my former colleagues in the bank may be thinking of me?

Turns out though, that car crash was one of the best things that ever happened to me.

In the second-half of 1995, the game of rugby had formally taken its giant step into a bold new future. The exact date when this step *commenced* was August 27. The International Rugby Football Board announced that we were amateur no more.

After three days of meetings in Paris, where Syd Millar, the IRFU President and Tom Kiernan were present on behalf of Ireland, the IRFB produced the white smoke. Contracts for the game's best players were the next piece of business!

While some people in the game here moaned that we were facing possible ruination, if not bankruptcy, others saw an opportunity for Ireland to really compete against the best in the world, finally!

The Leinster boys were the first to get wind of what this would mean to their pocket. In January '96 they found out that if they had played in all four Interprovincial matches the previous year and were involved in their three games in the European Cup – Leinster reached the semi-finals in the competition's inaugural year before losing to Cardiff, while Munster finished second behind Swansea in our group – they would each receive £3,500 from the IRFU.

There was a £400 appearance fee for anyone who played in an Interprovincial game. Anyone who took part in the European Cup got £600 per game. A semi-final appearance meant this was upped to £750 – so Peter could start working out what his first annual pay check as a professional rugby player might come to!

For provincial players in the Ireland squad, who had already played in that season's two Internationals, and made appearances in the four Five Nations Championship games in 1996, it looked like there would be minimum earnings of £27,300, whether Ireland won or lost.

But the IRFU small print also promised £500 per point gained in the Championship. There was no doubt about it, rugby was becoming all-business.

One week after coming home from Atlanta, 29 of Ireland's 30-man squad were due to sign their contracts following consultation with any legal advisers they wished to have on their side. Over a two-day squad camp in Dublin, *Day One* was for training, and *Day Two* was for contracts.

The odd man out was Munster's Eddie Halvey. He'd been out injured for a few months with a groin muscle injury, and he had not made it back for his comeback match, but Eddie was not exactly fretting. He'd also worked out a three-year deal with English first division club Saracens worth £50,000 per year. Once Eddie signed on the dotted line over there, the final national contract was going to be placed in front of Anthony "Axel" Foley.

The English clubs, clearly, were already raising the bar for the IRFU, if they wanted to keep their best players here in Ireland.

It was exciting.

The game had turned pro, Ireland had a new coach in Murray Kidd, a New

Zealander who had done good work with Garryowen, and a new manager in Pat Whelan. Munster were holding the reins of the national team. There was so much to look forward to, but most especially there was the opportunity for Peter and myself to start rebuilding our lives.

The game was on. Pat Whelan warned that all of the players had been given specific fitness targets. It is very clear to each player what he has to do, Pat warned. Some were being told to work on upper body strength, others needed to rapidly improve their aerobic fitness. We aim for shorter and sharper sessions, warned Kidd.

Peter was given the thumbs-up by Kidd and Whelan and was chosen over Paul Wallace to start against Scotland in the opening game of the Five Nations at Lansdowne Road. It was his 15th Irish cap.

This meant that Peter was about to replace the International caps record held by the legendary Tom Clifford, who was the most capped Young Munster player of all time. Tom Clifford had been a giant amongst men and Munsters' ground was named in his honour. He was also a fine hurler and he played League of Ireland for Limerick, but when he moved from wing forward to the front row – just like Peter's swap of positions – he began his legendary rugby career. Of course, nowadays, 15 caps seems like a small number, but this is really because there are so many more games now than there were in the 40s and 50s, and indeed in the 1990s.

Paul Wallace had held the tight head berth since the World Cup, and was in the front row for the autumn matches against Fiji and United States, so Pat Whelan had to field questions about Peter's reselection.

He has great experience at the highest level, said Pat, and he brings his own qualities of abrasiveness and work rate to the position. The team management, marching to a new era in the game, also took the decision to close off the team's final training sessions to the media, which did not go down all that well.

Ireland were beaten by Scotland in Lansdowne Road, 16-10, but Peter did mark his historic number of caps by going over for our only try.

There was a month's wait until our second game in the Championship, in the Parc des Princes. The French had also lost to the Scots, in Murrayfield, in the second round of games and, therefore, they were eager to get their season up and running – and say their goodbyes to their famous old ground!

We were not unhappy to see the back of the place. Ireland had never won a game in the Parc des Princes. We had not beaten France since 1986, and the last victory on French soil had been in the Stade Colombes in 1972.

For Peter, the goodbye to this particular French *Parc* was about to make headlines – headlines that would run and run... and run.

'First time we met, you were just out of school... and cock of the coop. Young Munster forwards brought you back down to earth.

'Turns out, though, you were right... you were cock of the coop for Munster and Ireland, and anyone else you played with! You were probably the best player I ever played with or against.

'Sorry Drico!'

– Peter

CHAPTER 12

Tonnes of ink was spilled onto newspapers to deal with Ireland's visit to Paris in '96. Though most of that ink was devoted to Peter. What happened in the Parc des Princes that afternoon left people divided, depending on whether someone wanted to support Peter, or wished to see him lynched!

"Is Peter Clohessy a muck savage who should never be allowed near a rugby pitch again?"

"Good Riddance to the Monster from Munster."

"Ban signals end for Clohessy."

These were just three newspaper headlines here in Ireland that were not unusual in the days that followed. Interestingly, the French media were in far less of a state of fury. After all, it was a rugby game that had just ended, and their big second row, Olivier Roumat wasn't injured at Peter's hand... or boot! In France they viewed the brutally tough game that had finished and the action taken by one Irishman against one of their own as part of the supreme physical contest. They had their prop Lascube, their hooker Mascato and their flanker Carminati heavily suspended in the nineties for various incidents in games.

The French were happy for the book to be thrown at an Irishman on this occasion, but they were not going to make anything more of it than that.

The book was thrown.

Peter was banned from the game for 26 weeks.

"The international career of Ireland tight head prop Peter Clohessy is almost certainly over," was the verdict of Ned Van Esbeck in *The Irish Times*.

The game had ended with another awful scoreline.

France 45, Ireland 10.

But for one single action of Peter's, it was just one of the very many forgettable days in the Parc des Princes that Irish teams and their supporters had to swallow. We were 12 points down by the 20th minute, but the French had not even played all that well in the opening quarter. We never got to grips with them, and any good ball we did win was handed over just as quickly. Peter had tried to run with the ball and gain some yards for the team but, like everyone else on the field, I could see that he was deeply frustrated.

David Humphreys kicked one penalty before half-time, but it was 24-3 at that stage, and it was obvious that there was no way back for Ireland. N'Tamack, Castel and Campan went over to total seven French tries by the very end. We did get a penalty try, and that was Ireland's first try in the wretched ground since 1980, but everyone with Irish blood felt down and out when the final whistle was blown by England's Ed Morrison.

Going into the game, Peter was clearly influenced by his last experience of playing in Paris in '94, when he was cut open by the French in several places. He was determined that there would not be a repeat performance from them!

He viewed attack as the best form of defence.

And he honestly felt that every French player was the enemy, if that was what it took to ensure that he came out on top in the battle.

The crowd was especially loud and intimidating once the game began. That's why Peter decided to respond to them too, and gave them the middle finger! Parc des Princes was a cauldron of noise, and a whole different proposition to the Stade de France in later years.

In one ruck, Peter had made the decision to rake one of the French players. He did not know who it was at his feet, but a microsecond later as his foot descended he changed his mind. He made contact with Roumat's head, but there was no downward pressure, and that's why the Frenchman was not injured.

That February, I was still out of work sick. But I wanted to go to the game and, therefore, I decided that if I could make it to Paris, then I should try to go back to work also. So, I'd duly arranged to be back in the bank the Monday after the match, just to see... perhaps I could work?

I did pick my time... didn't I?

During the game there had been lots of the usual needling that I'd expected between Peter and most of the French players, but there was nothing that seemed out of the ordinary to me, though, afterwards, for some reason I felt very uneasy.

In one of the corporate rooms in the stadium, as the match was being replayed on television, I mentioned to Kristy Johns, Paddy's wife, that I wasn't happy. I needed to watch the game again, and this time more closely on the screen. Intuition is a sharp device, I guess!

The team joined us from their dressingroom, and I anxiously asked Peter if anything had happened out there that I had missed?

'No...

'What are you talking about...?' was his easy response.

Peter was as relaxed as he had ever been after a game. So I decided it was just me being over-anxious. We got back to the team hotel, and were getting into the lift to go to our room and get changed for our respective male and female dinners, when Neil Francis joined us.

'I think there could be some trouble coming your way, Claw,' Franno said, as the lift doors closed.

Franno mentioned something about RTE showing some incident in the game at home. When we got into our room we tried to decide who would be the best person to call back in Ireland, to ask what RTE was showing? Most of our friends we knew for sure were in local pubs watching whatever it was and, in the absence of mobile phones, that meant our choice was either to ring my house, or Peter's house.

We opted for Peter's.

Cian, our teenage nephew, answered the phone.

'What are they saying on telly… about the game?' Peter asked.

'They're showing you standing on a French player's head… !' Cian responded, adding that RTE was playing it, over and over again.

Cian then offered to put Daddy Noel on the phone.

'No… thanks!' replied Peter.

He hung up!

RTE showed the incident over 50 times directly after the match.

In the 24 hours that followed, Peter was cited for foul play. Furthermore the French victim, Olivier Roumat, whose head Peter was accused of standing on, had no injury or mark on him whatsoever. Neither was Roumat complaining!

But, apart from the information we had from Cian the evening of the game we had no idea what was going on back home. We were separated for dinner as usual, and I was like a cat on a hot tin roof – I couldn't eat and I certainly didn't want to be there. All I wanted was to meet Peter and find out what on earth was going on?

But in typical chauvinistic IRFU style, I was the last person they decided to say anything to. As arranged after dinner, we went to Kitty O'Sheas pub to meet our husbands and partners, but there was no sign of Peter there.

Terry Kingston had to tell me that they had taken him from the dinner, off to a tribunal hearing. I was left waiting with the team and wives and partners in Kitty's until closing time.

There was still no sign of Peter.

Our party arrived back to the Hilton Hotel at around 2.30 a.m.

No Peter, once again.

But I did have a shoulder to rest on in Peter's team-mate, Maurice Field.

He was infuriated that the IRFU had totally neglected to let me know what was happening? Maurice finally had enough and he rang Murray Kidd and told him that I was in reception in our hotel and that I had no idea where Peter had gone?

Kidd explained that Pat Whelan, as team manager had accompanied Peter to the tribunal which had been hastily called. Shortly afterwards, Peter arrived back at the hotel. He explained that he had been given a choice to go to a tribunal that night, or fly back to France on the Monday?

Peter chose to get it over and done with – without even knowing what the hullabaloo was all about. After all, the French coach, Jean Claude Skrela said immediately after the game that he had no intention of citing Peter for the action against Roumat. Skrela had seen it clearly and knew that no damage was done to his man.

Skrela, like most rugby people in his country, also knew of Peter's special relationship with the French. It was just two years, after all, since Peter had to leave the same field injured, and showed up at the dinner that evening with stitches inserted in three different parts of his head.

There was no question of Peter complaining at that time, or anybody on the French or Irish side of the fence threatening to cite any member of the home team! Now, all of a sudden, Peter found everyone in citing mood.

He had been called into a room to find a large disciplinary committee. There were three officials from the IRFU (president Syd Millar, Tom Kiernan and Billy Lavery) and a similar number from the French side. Both sides were intent on citing him on the video evidence. Also there in the room was the match referee, Ed Morrison and the match commissioner, Alan Hosie of Scotland. Eight men in total. It was all done so fast, and it was more than a little one-sided, to put it mildly.

Back in our hotel bedroom we found a heap of messages under the door, as Peter's frantic family had been trying to contact us all evening. The footage was still being played 'round the clock. No wonder they were all going berserk at home.

All Peter and I knew for sure was that Oliver Roumat was not injured, as Peter had been chatting to him at their meal before he was led to the tribunal. It so happened that Roumat did leave the field during the game – he had suffered an eye injury in another incident entirely. People watching had that sight of Roumat in their heads, and it also did not help Peter's cause any that the referee had warned him, on the intervention by a touch judge, after an incident with the French hooker, Jean-Michel Gonzales. The hooker had also left the field injured.

The next morning we left Paris for Dublin – and, on arrival, we were due to go to the small internal transfer lounge to wait for our flight to Shannon.

Apparently the disciplinary committee was to make its decision that day. Hosie, the match commissioner, was going to make the final judgment on the matter, and it had been arranged that the IRFU secretary, Philip Browne would phone him when he landed in Dublin. Again, quite extraordinarily, the entire press corps was somehow in that internal transfer lounge awaiting us when we got there!

There and then, in front of the assembled journalists and radio commentators, Peter was informed of his punishment. The IRFU were happy for the press to see Peter being told of his 26 weeks ban, and they were also happy for the press to report on how Peter responded to the news.

As we had disembarked the Paris flight my good friend, Clodagh Kingston discovered that she had left her diamond necklace back at the hotel in Paris. She was very upset and crying. I quickly realised that these same journalists on 'Claw watch' might easily mistake an upset Clodagh as Peter Clohessy's wife.

I had no choice but to talk very sternly to my dear pal and ask her to dry up her tears, in order to avoid more press sensationalism. I didn't want them reporting that Claw's wife had broken down upon hearing the news! Clodagh and I often laugh about that now, particularly as she got the necklace back the following week when she was in Paris on business.

But there were no smiles in Dublin airport that afternoon!

As we stood in the transfer lounge, Peter was called aside to be told the judgment of the disciplinary committee. I stood with Clodagh, but Terry Kingston had heard the news before me.

He walked over.

'How long did he get?' I asked.

Terry said he would tell me, once we left the transfer lounge. He was afraid that I would react badly in front of the press.

I assured him that I wouldn't.

'Twenty-six weeks, Anna,' he replied instantly.

'That's not too bad,' I said and breathed a sigh of relief.

Unlike today, when PR men are out front at all times, Peter was left to explain himself to the press. The IRFU had nothing to say on his behalf. Luckily, Terry Kingston was calm and decisive, and before Peter could open his mouth – and say God only knows what – the Irish hooker got out a pen and paper and wrote a statement on Peter's behalf.

"I did not deliberately stamp on Roumat,' it stressed. 'In fact I was not aware of any problem until a few hours after the match and the Ireland manager, Pat Whelan told me there was a problem. I could not even remember the incident clearly."

Peter also told the media that he was being held back by two French forwards at the time. "I hope my explanation will be accepted."

On the Saturday in Paris, Murray Kidd had said, 'Don't worry Peter, we'll stand by you all the way.' On Sunday in Dublin, when the sentence was announced, the Irish coach spoke to Peter again.

'See you next year, Claw,'

The flight to Shannon was turbulent. Literally, we were on one of those small Fokker 50s, and the pilot was having trouble landing it. The aircraft was all over the shop. After the second attempt to land, he announced that he would try once more... but that if he failed we would be going to Cork instead.

Richie Wallace was sitting directly in front of us.

As he was trained as a pilot, I tapped Richie on the shoulder to ask if he thought the pilot would be able to land the thing? But Peter lost the plot when he heard me.

'What the f *** would he know about it!' blasted Peter.

'I don't give a s*** if I never play rugby again,' he continued.

'... just get me on the ground!'

It was one in less than a handful of times that I have ever seen Peter afraid. On the way home we stopped at Philip Danaher's house, to finally see for ourselves what all the fuss was about?

And as planned, I went back to my job in the bank the next day. My back and neck were as bad as ever, and I couldn't sit at my desk. But stubborn as I am, I knelt at my desk until tea break, when I went to the staff room. And there on the table was a copy of *The Irish Times*.

The entire top half of the front page had a photograph of Peter on the pitch in France. He was saluting the crowd with his middle finger! At this point I surrendered to my back, neck and life stress, and as I went home I didn't realize that I had just finished the last day of my banking career.

The media frenzy that followed was, once again, another first for a player of any sport in Ireland. But "the story" was also International news. The ban had been handed down by the International Rugby Board, but such was the attention that there was now a possibility that the IRFU was going to take further disciplinary action.

Peter was advised to seek legal help.

Philip Danaher and Brendan Mullin, in particular, were a great support, as they understood how the politics of the IRFU inner sanctum operated. They recommended enlisting the help of a particular solicitor, Seamus Connolly of Moran and Ryan Solicitors, who was incredibly helpful – more than that, as Seamus didn't even charge Peter for his work at the time.

As neither of us had a word of French, we also sought out the help of Maria Hackett, the travel agent who has organised so many trips for us over the years. A native of France, Maria didn't hesitate to help.

Peter wanted to talk to Olivier Roumat.

Maria got the number for him, and Peter phoned Oliver to apologise for any hurt he may have caused, though he knew that the Frenchman was not injured. The *conversation* turned out to be pricelessly funny, because Peter actually got through to Roumat's housemate.

Peter was speaking English and the other guy had no idea what he was talking about. And he kept replying in French. Peter was shaking his head as he listened.

Their efforts quickly led to the two of them cracking up in laughter on the phone together and for the next five minutes that's all they did. However, it was important that Peter could state that he had apologised to Oliver Roumat – so we sought the help of Maria again. She made contact with Oliver a second time, and delivered the apology to him on Peter's behalf in a language he could understand.

Oliver went on record as saying there was nothing to apologise for!

Neither did he subsequently, not even once, complain about Peter.

The 26 weeks ban meant that Peter couldn't play rugby again until November of 1996, not that this particularly bothered him. He had decided he was going to hang up his boots, at 30 years of age.

The IRFU had cancelled his playing contract, and also fined him his £3,000 match fee. Worse, there was a sizable queue of people racing to the highest moral ground they could find, so that they could condemn Peter from such a height. It included Willie John McBride, who is best remembered for his "99 Call" during the Lions tour of South Africa in the seventies, which demanded that all of the Lions team should immediately get their retaliation in first against the home team and resulted in one of the most violent matches in the history of the game as every Lions player started striking out at his opponent. "There are enough injuries in the game which happen by accident," stated McBride in one newspaper, condemning Peter forcibly. "We can do without things which cause injuries in this fashion."

I found that a curious change of perspective.

But he was not alone. Others, including former Irish coach, Jimmy Davidson called for a life ban to be imposed on Peter. Everything else was forgotten. The brutal history of front row battles between Ireland and France! The manner in which the French had repeatedly targeted Peter! And, most of all, the fact that Olivier Roumat did not have one scar on his head as a result of Peter's boot landing on his head.

While my life would certainly have become much easier if I didn't have to put up with Peter's absences due to rugby – and Luke would have had a Dad who wasn't away so much – I was very well aware that a rugby career has a short shelf life. It can end at any moment with a serious injury. Even injury-free, the longest someone can get to is about 35 years of age – unless you are Buddha Healy of course!

Believing that we have one good run at life and we should have no regrets, and also wishing not to have to suffer listening to Peter when he got older lamenting the fact that his rugby career ended prematurely, I tackled his decision head on. I convinced him not to throw in the towel.

Not too long afterwards, we were in Coleraine, at my good friend Eliz McCrory's house. Peter had a mobile phone at this stage, a block by today's standards, and he got a call from John Connolly.

Connolly had coached Old Belvedere for a period the season before. He was a hooker in his own playing days, and had clearly taken note of Peter during the Irish tour down under. And as someone with the nickname "Knuckles" gained it has been said during his time as a nightclub bouncer in Darwin – though Connolly also suggested it had attached itself during his rugby days in Swansea – he obviously liked Peter's strength and passion on the field. He now asked Peter if he would be interested in playing a season with the Queensland Reds?

Connolly was one of the foremost coaches in the game, and his Reds were incredibly successful, winning the Super Six Championship in 1992 and later the Super 10 Championship, which included the best teams from Australia, New Zealand and South Africa, in 1994 and '95. Peter would be playing with and against the greatest players in world rugby.

He told me about the call.

But Peter was treating it as a bit of a joke… so I asked why not?

'Don't be ridiculous… !'

'What about the courier business?' he asked.

Instantly I told him we were going!

Again, I got the *don't be stupid* look!

'If you go to Queensland and play Super 12's… you'll be picked for the Lions tour next year!' I informed him.

The British and Irish Lions were touring South Africa in 1997.

We agreed.

For the first time, Peter was now a truly professional rugby player.

The Super 12 had replaced the Super 10 in 1996, when the Reds were knocked out at the semi-final stage. Connolly wanted Peter on board for the following season, which would run from February to May, 1997. Queensland paid him $100,000 for one season, which meant that we could pay someone at home to run the business and Peter's only job was to play rugby in one of the most beautiful locations in the world.

Connolly informed Peter that he was going to move his International tight head prop, Dan Crowley to the loose side, so that Peter could step into his usual position.

And, as he did his job, I could enjoy my new life there as well.

It was a dream come true.

Giles Warrington.

'The only time in my life that I trained voluntarily, you were my personal trainer... and not alone that, but you did it completely free of charge.

'Thank you Giles, for teaching me about fitness.'

— Peter

CHAPTER 13

Peter had signed for Queensland before his suspension was up. So, even though we weren't heading down under until January of '97, he was eligible to play rugby again in November.

Interestingly, while John Connolly was very anxious to have him play again as soon as possible, it was a different story at home here in Ireland. And it was a big surprise when Munster came looking for him at the last minute to play in their game against Australia at the very end of the month.

The Aussies were on tour again, and Paul McCarthy and Ian Murray were injured, so it seemed that Munster coach, Jerry Holland and their manager, the late Colm Tucker felt they didn't have any other option but to ask Peter to play.

Munster, of course, then had to go and ask permission from Queensland to release Peter to play in the game. When Peter ran onto the pitch at Thomond Park at half-time the crowd welcomed him back with a big cheer. So, there he was, in his only game in Ireland in a new season, playing against his new teammates, Ben Tune, Jason Little, and Toutai Kefu. Australia hammered Munster that day 55-19. It was retribution for the defeat in 1992.

It was in that Australian game, unfortunately, coming back from his spell on the sidelines that Peter injured his back. Peter had also moved from Young Munster to Garryowen during the summer, though he would never play for them as it turned out. He wasn't enjoying his rugby and felt a change of club might give him a fresh perspective.

His injury would niggle at him all season in Queensland and, subsequently, it would have a say on his Lions' career as well.

One week later, Peter linked up with his new team. Queensland were on a tour of Britain in preparation for their new season, and his first game in a new and equally famous red jersey was against Pontypridd.

Peter and I, with Luke, drove to Cardiff to link up with the Queensland tour – and we doubled the journey as an opportunity to pick up a new speedboat that Peter had bought. The day before the game he was formally introduced to his new teammates. The senior squad members were on duty with Australia, so there was mainly a bunch of younger players in Pontypridd. But they were especially welcoming.

After the game, the Queensland boys decided they should have an induction for Peter, so they began a series of drinking games to ensure that their Irish recruit was fully tested regarding his durability off the pitch.

I was waiting in our hotel room.

When Peter arrived in, he swayed in the doorway. Then he slurred an explanation of what had transpired.

'They tried their best… lovie,' he said slowly, but proudly.

'But… I was the last man standing!'

Word was sent from the Queensland dressingroom quite quickly to the senior players who had yet to meet Peter.

'Whatever you do… don't take on CLOEY in the drinking department!'

For the one and only time in his life, Peter had voluntarily been training for several weeks before meeting up with the Reds. This began with Giles Warrington in the University of Limerick who agreed to take Peter on, and get him the fittest he ever was in his life. All for Queensland… and, possibly, The Lions!

Giles' deal was simple.

He would commit one hundred per cent, but if Peter failed to show up for a session, even one no show, the deal was off. And Giles delivered. Peter was the fittest he had ever been, and we took off to Queensland for six months confident in the knowledge that he would not let John Connolly, or himself, down.

My Mam, Luke, Peter and I arrived to 30 degrees of Queensland sunshine a few days before my 30th birthday.

Bliss!

We settled in to our brand new two-bedroom apartment, and Peter set off to his first pre-season training session the following morning. Queensland were coming back after their off-season break. Peter, therefore, quite rightly thought that with his new fitness levels he would hold his own with the Aussies, who had been fully professional in everything but name for a couple of years before us.

He was wrong, wrong… and wrong again.

That first evening, when he came home from the first Reds' workout, I thought he was going to collapse at any minute. He actually fell asleep into his dinner!

When he awoke, he looked at me with those eyes that said… *This is all your fault!*

It did take a couple of weeks, but he began to settle into his new training regime, and we loved our new lifestyle – training, sitting by the pool or going to the beach, and back home for barbies! It was perfect. The whole experience for Peter, and the rest of us, was so exciting, but there was nobody to compare notes with as no other International player from Europe had ever gone to play Super 12s, due to the Aussie season running parallel with the Five Nations.

It was a piece of history for the game, and for Peter it was the best career re-invention ever.

Brisbane was a wonderful base for us to explore Australia.

Our apartment was in Alderley, a northern suburb of the city, which was a perfect location. In a five-minute walk we had the choice of two 50-metre swimming pools, a fantastic playschool for Luke, and a local shopping centre, while the train station was on our doorstep.

The Queensland team were very welcoming, John Eales, locally known as "Nobody", because *nobody is perfect*, was indeed the perfect gentleman. He was a World Cup winner in 1991 and would captain his country to victory in '99 also, but he was not just a lock forward, he was a playmaker for the Reds and Australia, just like any back, and he also kicked penalties and conversions. There was nobody like "Nobody" in Australia.

He became a good friend to Peter, as did other Australian legends like Tim Horan and Jason Little, and Glen Panaho, Garrick Morgan, and Kefu, who was learning to play guitar at the time. On an early trip to Darwin, to play Northern Territories, Kefu was rooming with Peter and his practicing was driving Peter nuts.

'Kefu... for f*** sake, will you stop at that s***!'

'I'll stop playing,' Toutai replied, '... if you stop smoking?

'I feel like I've swallowed razor blades!'

Damien Mendez, the team's fitness coach it so happened, who would end up working with Munster for a couple of seasons afterwards, was Peter's drinking buddy! Peter had not decided to do a complete lifestyle u-turn.

Mam had come with us for the six months. There was no way I would have separated her from Luke for that length of time, as he was her lifeline after Aileen died. Then, shortly afterwards, Meg arrived for six weeks, followed by Daddy Noel a couple of weeks later – and Jane Murphy's trip overlapped with Meg and Noel's for a couple of days, so our *two-bed* was getting a bit cramped. I had to hire a people carrier to get us around.

Peter, of course, was on the move. The Reds travelled to New Zealand and South Africa for their Super 12 games, and when he was away I would plan trips to explore as much of Queensland as we could.

Occasionally there were day-trips, or often we would head off for a few nights. The day-trips especially were great. I would pack up a full picnic with the icebox filled with whatever we had in the fridge. At every beach there are public barbies, showers, and picnic tables. So we would hang out on the beach, cook our dinner, shower and head home.

We would no sooner be home, than I would have the map out planning our trip for the next day. Poor Meg was exhausted just watching me!

I have always loved travel and exploring new places, so this was heaven to me. On the other hand, Peter couldn't have cared less about travel. In those days he was happier in Kilkee surrounded by his family and friends. We have often returned from a two-week sun holiday, and the following day Peter will invariably ask me... 'Where were we again?'

The internet was a new phenomenon that Australia was actively embracing in the nineties, but I was still much happier pouring over the accommodation brochures when choosing our next destination.

The Reds, meanwhile, got off to a disappointing start to the season. It was an amazing occasion for all of us watching in Ballymore that evening, March 1 – to see Peter in that red jersey. Queensland had been more *maroon*, but turned *red* with every passing season, and by 1997 they were looking more and more like Munster.

They faced the ACT Brumbies and although Tim Horan went over for two tries in front of the home crowd of 15,000, they were 10-7 down at half-time, and lost 24-19. It was the worst possible start.

For Peter, it was also an immediate education. The game was faster than in Ireland, the pitches were much firmer, and teams did not commit as many forwards to rucks. The mauling game, which was such a part and parcel of the game at home, was also far less evident.

As all of the matches were played in the cool of the evening, the atmosphere in Ballymore was party-like, but for Peter, every single game in a Reds' shirt from that evening on was like playing in an International. Except, the team did not socialize after the game. That was another *big* difference.

Instead, it was straight back to the drawing-board, and right into the serious preparation for the next game! Peter loved playing with so many world-class players. ACT had sat back a bit near the end, allowing the Reds in for their tries. And that, at least, earned a bonus point, as in Australia they were already using that points system – if you lost by less than seven, you were awarded one point, and if you scored more than four tries you got a bonus point.

John Connolly was happy enough with the opening performance. And he told Peter that he did well, as he had to learn so much on his first outing, and he was also propping against Patricio Noriega, an Argentinian with a big reputation down under.

Queensland then had a road-trip to South Africa and New Zealand. It was a shock for Peter, to have to continually travel so far for *club* games, and one three-week road-trip with the Reds was as all-consuming as an Irish tour abroad!

At one point, Knuckles brought them all to a police academy for one training session – which was an improvement on the previous year, when the Reds had been taken to an army camp in a rainforest to shape up, and the players had to hike 24 kilometres through bush carrying a wooden pole!

One week after the ACT defeat, in Pretoria, in Loftus Versfeld, they lost 14-3 to Northern Transvaal. John Eales kicked an opening penalty, but two tries from their scrum-half, Joost Van der Westhuizen decisively settled the game. Six days later, the team moved onto Bloemfontein. This was a real battle, three tries apiece. Dan Crowley, Jason Little and Shane Draham scored for the Reds, but they lost again 35-24.

The team was just not firing.

Back closer to home, in Waikato, the Chiefs were well on top in the second-half and won 31-6. But Peter got the Man of the Match award, which happened to fall on his 31st birthday. But the month ended with a fifth defeat, and the most resounding one of all – the Blues in Auckland tore into the Reds and scored six tries in front of a big home crowd of over 30,000. It ended 49-26. The Blues would end up impressive Super 12 champions.

It was not until round six of the season that the Reds finally landed a win, seeing off the Otago Highlanders 37-24 in Ballymore. The season, therefore, was really over before it got up and running. There were three wins and two more defeats in the second-half of the Super 12, which did include a ten-point win over their fierce rivals, the Waratahs, in Sydney, but the Queensland Reds finished three from the bottom on the table, just ahead of the Chiefs and the Highlanders.

Before the season had kicked off, Peter and I left Luke with Mam in Brisbane, and we flew to Cairns – Peter's teammates got a great kick listening to many of his pronunciations. Cairns to them was "Canes".

The small city is over 1,000 miles from Brisbane, and is a must for tourists because of its tropical climate, as well as being the perfect location from which to explore the Great Barrier Reef.

I knew I had *arrived* in life, as we sat on a catamaran and sailed out to the reef. Tony Edwards called me as we were heading out over the water and it was a secret joy to listen to his detailed weather report – a cold, wet, miserable January night – from back home.

The next day Peter decided that he wanted to try white-water rafting.

I had my doubts, and I didn't think it was a good idea for me to go with him as I was still *carrying* my back and neck injury, and the photos on the leaflet Peter had in his hand looked challenging.

I decided I would follow on the bus tour. However, when we got to the starting point, I was itching to try it and I spotted a Japanese man, who must have been 80 if he was a day, joining the training group. I reckoned I'd be safe enough. We took off down a gorge – all I could think of was that Meryl Streep movie, *The River Wild* where she takes her whole family down a nasty river and gets into a tangle with a pair of troublemakers. Okay, maybe the waters weren't quite that terrifying!

But our boat did flip over.

For about one minute Peter was panicking, as he couldn't find me anywhere. I was trapped under the upside-down dingy.

I couldn't get out, because the other passengers were in the water hanging onto the ropes around the dingy, pulling it down on top of me. Somehow, I was totally relaxed under the boat. It didn't faze me for some reason, or perhaps I'm just slow to realize when I'm in some big trouble!

Peter then popped up in the water beside me.

When we got through the rapids, we were in lovely calm waters surrounded on either side by steep cliffs. It was only then that we felt the intense January sun. It seemed like there was no air. It was melting hot. So our group decided there was only one thing for it… to jump into the water.

I wasn't at all impressed with the dirty brown colour of the water – a result, apparently, of the rains a few days before – so I suffered the heat and stayed in the dingy. It was at this point that the tour guide started talking about crocodiles.

'There's one that lives at the bottom of this river!'

'What do you mean?' I blurted in reply.

'… bottom… of…

'THIS RIVER?

'Is there a barrier across the bottom… or something?

'Can he come up… HERE?'

I was in a state with all of my questions.

I was eyeing Peter in the water at the same time.

'He can swim up… if he wants,' the guide finally responded, giving me his best *ignorant tourist thinks there could be a net keeping a crocodile at the bottom of the river* look.

The Australians, I quickly discovered, are incredibly laid back about their dangerous wildlife. Same with their surfers, who don't seem to have a care in the world about sharks. Or the fact that redback spiders, indigenous to Australia, are tiny but can kill you with one bite.

I remember panicking about those spiders initially, particularly as Luke was a typical three year old wanting to explore all the time. I had warned him that if he saw any bug, he was not to touch it.

'Call me or Nana… straight away.'

It's funny though, how we all get used to these aspects of a different life in a different country. By the time we were leaving Australia, there was a web of redbacks right beside our front door, and we didn't even bother to move it!

Noosa was by far our favourite place.

It was only a couple of hours north of the city and we scooted up there as often as we could. A beautiful beach and a fabulous choice of restaurants, all on amazing Hastings Street – surrounded by a magnificent national park. I couldn't wait to bring our youngest children, Jane and Harry there in 2013, when we were on the Lions' tour, and they loved it as much as Luke had 16 years previously.

On one trip to Noosa, there was Mam, Daddy Noel, Meg, Jane Murphy, Peter and I, all being led by the three and a half year old Luke, in single file down that main street – and we were all joined together with Luke's three meter long plastic yellow chain. All of us singing *Heigh Ho... Heigh Ho* much to the surprise of the crowded street!

We loved the great freedom of living abroad.

We were released from the usual *have to's*, of having to attend this or that party, or event or funeral and, instead, it was a time that was just about us. After everything we had gone through, we wanted that as a family. We needed it. It was also a most special and re-energising time in our lives as a couple.

The IRFU may not have been supportive of Peter, but the Lions' management knew talent when they saw it. England's Fran Cotton, who was Lions manager, and the coaching pair of Ian McGeechan and Jim Telfer, had no hesitation. Cotton had received videos of Queensland games specially so that he could keep tabs on Peter's form during the Super 12.

Peter was selected for the Lions 1997 South African tour!

The news came directly to our home in Brisbane, by fax. He was in a 35-man party that was dominated by the Triple Crown winners, England, but he had good company in Keith Wood, Jeremy Davidson and 21 yea old Eric Miller.

'We knew the criteria for selection, and we followed it, getting the right type of player for the game we want to play,' explained McGeechan. 'All the selections were made irrespective of where they came from, club or country.'

Or continent, in Peter's case!

He had broken new ground by becoming the first player to be picked to play for the Lions, during a season in which he had not played for his country. We were both thrilled at his selection.

Of course, I was quick to say, 'I told you so!'

This meant that his Queensland season was about to come to a premature ending. I must admit, I was upset to be leaving our new, perfect lifestyle before schedule. Before we knew it, we were packing up and heading home – for Peter to re-pack, and fly to London to begin life as a Lion. His back injury had been improving.

He could now walk without collapsing!

One day, on the beautiful beach at Noosa, a wind caught our big sun umbrella and it was flying down the sand threatening to kill some poor sunbather. Peter took off after it, but his leg kept giving way. He kept falling down. He had no power in it.

By the time we were on the way home, he could actually run again. What he didn't realize, until the first Lions' training session in London, which took place at the London-Irish grounds in Sunbury, was that he couldn't run backwards! Each time he tried to run backwards he was still collapsing!

This was the beginning, and end, of his Lions' career.

There were some fringe benefits to his brief few days with the Lions, like all the free gear and promotional presents – and the Lions were tops when it came to handing out freebies to the players! They had massive amounts of gear, all of it monogrammed. But as Peter was packing to come home, the Lions' management asked for the gear back!

This seemed like an awful waste to Peter because there wasn't another player with the initials PC on the squad.

What would they want to do with it? he thought.

Peter, being Peter, decided that since he had travelled half way around the world to get to London, the least he deserved was to take home the gear. So he did, the whole lot of it! Though, afterwards, he could never wear it.

He felt it wouldn't be right.

But at least our family got all those Adidas towels!

With Peter's withdrawal from the Lions squad the door was opened for Paul Wallace to take his place. They shared an interesting but silent moment together at Heathrow Airport.

On the travelator that services the Aer Lingus gates, disembarking passengers move side by side with the embarking travellers – separated only by a full-length clear glass from ceiling to floor.

Peter and Paul looked at one another through the glass. All they could do was nod a quick salute to one another.

For Paul, his career was about to seriously take off. He won his place on the Test team and did as much as anybody, in a pack led by England's Martin

Johnson, but inspired by sensational displays from Fester, to impressively defeat the reigning world champs on their own soil. They won the first two Tests, the second 18-15 thanks to a Jerry Guscott dropped goal – and claimed the series 2-1. It turned out to be the last occasion for a Lions team to come out on top until the 2013 tour of Australia.

But for Peter there was not even one ounce of begrudgery. His career, too, was on the upswing. The Lions selection, even though he did not get to leave London, was a validation, and told everyone at home that Peter Clohessy was one of the best tight heads in the world, and that he could not be ignored by any coach or group of selectors.

Peter's career, despite his bad back, had never been in a better place.

'I am devastated,' Peter commented in a statement to the media when he had to pull out of the tour. And he was initially, as his injury had shown huge improvement and he was certain that he would be in full health by the time the tour commenced in South Africa.

When he got home, however, Peter actually wasn't disappointed at all. He said he didn't fancy six weeks in South Africa. He'd been there with Queensland for their Super 12 games, and he was in no hurry back anytime soon, he announced.

CHAPTER 14

There was a further bonus to being a Lion, even for a few days!

The IRFU was now grading the value of contracts – the highest being £50,000 for Lions' players.

Yippee… jackpot!

I was sitting in La Picolla restaurant with my school friend Sarah – the same Sarah I had matched with my husband 14 years previously – when Peter rang with the news. For the first time in his life, in Ireland, Peter was fully employed by someone else – until then he was accustomed to being the boss, as he always had his own business.

However, all during his professional career he continued to run a variety of businesses, though the lifestyle that went with rugby changed dramatically with the arrival of professionalism. There was daily training, and many more matches. Soon, there was the introduction of the Heineken Cup, and with the game becoming a very serious business the social scene was not what it once was.

Allelujah, for that at least!

The downside was that, come rugby season, Peter was travelling for 30 weeks, which meant that it was a full-time job just keeping up with him.

During the Six Nations Championship – after Italy had come on board – if he wanted to see Luke and Jane, I would have to bring them to wherever he was based in some hotel or other. Our life meant lots of packing, planning, planes, trains, automobiles, and hotel rooms – which, as anyone with small kids know, are like prison cells to young children!

My trusted partner on these trips was Eimear who, by now, was my children's other mother. She was the ideal travel companion, and she passed many hours in those dreaded hotel rooms entertaining my kids while I went to the match, and afterwards the dinner. It may have sounded a glamorous step up in our lives but the reality was something entirely different. The first thing you learn is how to fulfill all family social obligations on your own!

Non-rugby friends' weddings were rarely attended by us as a couple unless they were in the small window, in summertime, and I quickly learned to either stay at home, or go alone. While we did make many good friends within rugby, the lack of time available for any other sort of socialising meant that we generally lost touch with other friends who weren't in that circle.

I'm happy to say that when Peter finally retired most of our old friends forgave us for our absenteeism and are now back in our lives.

The move to Australia was very significant for many reasons, and it was interesting that on his return the public and media perception of Peter had changed dramatically. He was now no longer cast as a *bad boy*, but was valued for the immense contributor that he was on the pitch.

Peter was now a total pro!

He had learned his trade – how to be professional – in Queensland, so it was an easy transition for him. He still had his courier business, which he was managing to run, but being paid to play demanded much more time away from Limerick, so it became increasingly difficult to keep a hands-on approach to his business affairs. He juggled both until the summer of '99 – at which point he sold the courier business to Limerick Express Couriers.

For the next two years he was able to concentrate on rugby alone, which was a first for him. During that time I would often bring up the subject of, 'What will you do when you retire from rugby?'

'I've no idea,' was his usual reply.

But, true to form, he wasn't particularly worried about it either. On the other hand, I was very aware that a rugby player's career could end abruptly at any stage, and as I was no longer working in the bank I considered this an important question. It was two years later that Peter thought opening a bar would be the way to go.

He had seen a new building at Howley's Quay in Limerick, and thought this might be a good location for a bar. The asking price was massive at the time, and even with my previous banking experience I couldn't guess how much repayments would be on a mortgage that size, so I rang a good friend of ours who had an investment business. Yet again in our lives synchronicity was at play, as our friend had been approached by a group of investors who wanted to buy that building, and open a pub, but they wanted someone local to be involved!

So Peter Clohessy's bar at Howley's Quay was opened in 2001. Peter was wondering what to call the nightclub, which was also planned for the premises, so I rang Joan Galwey, who did not have to think too long at all on our behalf.

The Sin Bin was born.

When we moved to Brisbane in '96, I registered with a GP there, and because she was a medical doctor who was also trained in acupuncture I *let her* put needles in me. I couldn't believe the pain relief.

The real breakthrough came one day in Brisbane when I wandered into an exhibition in the South Bank centre. There were two signs. One read Reflexology, and the other Aromatherapy. I did not really know what they were, but thought they sounded like a nice treat, so I ambled into the Reflexology booth.

What happened next literally changed the path of my life. The reflexologist didn't ask me one question, not even my name, and yet from examining my foot she could tell me exactly what was wrong in my body, from my sprained sacroiliac joint right down to my sinus issues. Back in the apartment that evening, I pulled at my feet and toes, but no way could I recreate the pain that the therapist had caused me during the session.

When we came home later that year I found a really good reflexologist in Diane Hannagen, and I went to her once or twice a week for a couple of months. She completely sorted my neck and back. This started my interest in the world of complementary and alternative medicine and, now, 18 years later, Diane is a director and Head of Education at the Holistic Centre of Excellence, which I founded four years ago. I am passionate about my work, and wake up every day excited to learn what my clients and students will teach me.

It's a far cry from the broken girl I was after my car crash.

Murray Kidd was no longer Ireland coach. And his successor, Brian Ashton, who was a highly thought of English coach who had met with lots of success with Bath, was also under pressure.

It was a frantic time for the game of rugby in Ireland, and while Peter had been enjoying himself in Queensland, second-guessing seemed to be top of everyone's agenda here at home. After Peter's last game for Ireland, against the French, Kidd led the team to a convincing win over Wales at home, but we lost just as heavily to England, and Ireland propped up the 1996 Five Nations table, with Wales a nose ahead on points difference. The Wooden Spoon was all ours.

In the first week of 1997 Ireland had a winter training camp in The Algarve, but then lost 37-29 to Italy in a preparation game for the fresh Championship. That left Kidd's record at six losses out of seven Internationals. There was also a battering by the Barbarians, 70-38. The axe was coming down quickly on Murray Kidd's Irish coaching career. He resigned, after a six-hour meeting with IRFU officials, less than a fortnight before the start of the '97 Championship.

Neither was any time lost by the IRFU in grabbing Ashton. He was contacted on a Tuesday, was in Dublin on Wednesday, and his role was cemented down by Thursday. Ashton had to gear up for the French immediately but had Mike Brewer, the former All-Black, still helping out as his forwards' coach.

Ashton pointed the finger of blame at his pack when the French defence refused to give Ireland any real scoring opportunities. We lost 32-15. All our points came from Eric Elwood's kicking. The front row was solid, however, and Poppy, Fester and Paul Wallace could not have been blamed for the shoddy performance. The French performance was equally unimpressive, and their discipline came apart midway through. They had their two locks yellow carded, Olivier Merle and Hugues Miorin. Miorin got his for stamping – but, in addition, one of their props, Franck Tournaire was caught kicking our replacement hooker, Alan Clarke in the face.

It was a completely different administering of justice to 12 months earlier when Peter was in the dock. This time the IRFU and the French federation met on the Saturday night of the game, and viewed the video evidence of the incidents – whereupon our officials decided to leave it entirely to the French to sort out their own man!

Tournaire got a one-match ban. It was as incredible as it was unbelievable, but there was no great fuss in the Irish or foreign media.

Peter had watched the French game on TV in Australia, but the special treatment of Tournaire wasn't a worry or a concern for him – he was looking after his own career in Queensland. In fact, nobody in our family took much notice.

The Five Nations seemed so far away from our lives.

We beat Wales by one point in Cardiff, got hammered 46-6 by the English at Lansdowne Road, and there was a second hammering, this time 38-10 by the Scots in Murrayfield. The Wooden Spoon was Ireland's again.

Peter was back in the Irish squad that summer. Ashton didn't pick him for the warm up matches, however he was left with no choice in December, when Paul Wallace was ruled out for the Italian game. Yet again there was an unprecedented and distasteful decision made by the RTE newsroom, when they chose to show in slow motion, on the six o'clock and nine o'clock news, the Olivier Roumat incident in Paris – which had happened 22 months previously!

It was his 17th cap for Ireland.

The game in the country was at a worrying low.

Peter didn't find Brain Ashton much help with the pack. He found him quiet generally. He was a backs' coach, first and foremost, but Peter did find it strange to have an Englishman in charge of Ireland. It did not sit right with him.

Would England ever ask an Irishman to coach them? he wondered.

Ashton's short reign was just about over anyhow. Peter was back in the replacements for the opening Five Nations game against Scotland in Lansdowne Road. Wallace was first choice on the tight side, with Reggie Corrigan and Fester making up the front row. We lost by a single point, 17-16. It wasn't our worst display against the Scots, but Ashton was clearly furious once the final whistle sounded. He pointed his finger primarily at our out-half, David Humphreys.

'I don't know whose game plan that was,' he stated, alluding to the amount of possession Ireland had kicked away in the final 20 minutes, '… but it was nothing to do with me!'

However, the IRFU were staring hard at Ashton and, for the second season in a row, Ireland got a new coach mid-stride.

He was not Irish!

That was the bad news. The good news was that he knew the Irish game, he had coached here on and off for almost a decade and, the really good news for Peter, was that he was someone who knew all about the front row. He'd been capped 17 times for the All Blacks.

Peter liked Warren Gatland from day one!

The Heineken Cup did not appear to be particularly Munster's cup of tea at the very beginning. For the first three years, after the competition was unveiled for the 1995-96 season, we did not pop our heads out of the group.

In Year One we lost out on points difference to Swansea and Castres. In Year Two we won two and lost two in a group containing Toulouse, Cardiff, Wasps and Milan (there were no home and away games at that time). And in Year Three we finished bottom of the pile against Harlequins, Cardiff and Bourgoin.

We did win our very first Heineken Cup match, however, beating Swansea 17-13 on a Wednesday afternoon in November in Thomond Park. The game was played in the middle of the day because there were no floodlights up to the job of an evening kick-off in the famous old ground. Still, about 6,000 people turned up for the novelty of a *European* game. Not that anybody in the ground was fully aware of the significance of the late try by our captain, Pat Murray, who took a pop pass from Paul Burke, and broke a tackle before getting the ball down.

Munster may not have taken Europe by storm in those opening three years, but we did whip up one whenever anyone came to Limerick! We could not be beaten at Thomond and, thanks to Murray's try, the team's unbeaten record in the ground lasted until 2007 when Leicester ended the proud run. It was no harm really that an English team finally brought Munster to their knees in front of their own people, because we had slain so many of the "great" English clubs, and even in those early lean years of the Heineken Cup we were able to send Wasps and Harlequins – two teams which formed the spine of the brilliant English team – home with more than a sore ear!

That first win over Swansea was poor enough, and certainly not the stuff of legend, but it was the first all-important win. And, afterwards, as we did back in the good old days, Peter and most of the guys went out on the town with the referee, Ed Morrison – even though he was on the receiving end of serious flack earlier in the afternoon, he and Tony Spreadbury, were tremendously good fun off the pitch!

Our second match in Europe was against Castres.

First, we had to find the place!

None of the Munster players had a clue where it was.

Ah... days without Google!

I got out my *Lonely Planet* French guidebook to try to locate the town. One of the best things about the Heineken Cup over the years was that it opened up France to thousands of us, and made us very adept at independent means of travel. Ever since, Munster supporters have found the most amazing routes and travel methods to get to games.

When Peter did get to Castres, he was not to forget it for some time. He was genuinely shocked at how openly hostile the crowd was at that first away Heineken Cup game. And the hostility presented itself before the game even began.

Munster were booed coming onto the pitch, and booed again as the players' names were announced on the public address system. The noise level at times during place kicks was unbelievable, and certainly not anything that the players had ever experienced before.

It was so intimidating that Peter and Gaillimh insisted afterwards that Kenny Smith had missed a vital kick at goal... because he slipped in his own s****!

Munster lost 19-12

When Munster played Cardiff in Musgrave Park, I collected my Uncle Gena (Eugene) from Nana's house in town, where I had grown up, and along with Eimear and Luke we headed to Cork. We stopped for something to eat in Merchants Quay first, and we were rushing back to the car to get to the game on time.

When we got to the car poor Gena was panting.

'These fags are killing me,' he exclaimed.

We lost the game, when Cardiff scored a late try – and marked Munster's first Heineken Cup defeat on Irish soil. Luke ran on to the pitch after the game, and somehow managed to get lost. He was very upset when he finally found us, but Gena was always great with Luke and he managed to console him.

A couple of nights later our phone rang at around 2.0 a.m.

It was Nana, who was 96 at the time, to say that Gena had collapsed. I told her to call an ambulance immediately.

I woke up Peter and my Mam, who at the time was living with us in Annacotty. Peter didn't hesitate when I suggested that he was the one to take Mam into the city, and I would stay home with the sleeping Luke.

By the time they got into Nana's, two of the ambulance crew had a defibrillator out to work on the unconscious Gena.

Poor Gena was gone.

But, the next obstacle was to get Gena, who was a big man, down a few flights of winding stairs. Mam stayed in the sitting room consoling her heart broken Mam and Uncle Laurence.

Munster were playing Bourgoin in France that weekend, so Peter wasn't around for Gena's funeral. Luke was devastated as Gena and himself had a very special relationship, and it was his first time to experience grief.

Again I navigated those few days alone.

‘Brian O'Brien.

'One of my first memories of you was when you were manager of the Munster team... and you got onto the team bus and started doing somersaults out of the baggage racks!

'Over the years you became a trusted friend... a great man to listen and then offer wise advice. Little did we know that when you sang Stand Up And Fight in the dressingroom after an early Munster match, that it would become our team anthem.

'But it's appropriate... you were always a great man to stand up and fight for what was right.'

– Peter

CHAPTER 15

Our third Heineken Cup experience was eventful, at least. There were big scores. We lost to Harlequins at The Stoop 48-40. There was emotion and controversy. Keith Wood led Harlequins onto Thomond Park and we won 23-16, and Fester did not get a welcoming reception from his home town.

Most of the talk from The Stoop was centred on an incident between Gaillimh and Fester. Gaillimh landed a punch on his old buddy.

Fester had to leave the pitch.

Peter did not take much notice of the pair of them. He was sick of losing games with Munster. He knew we had shown them too much respect, especially in the opening quarter. Harlequins were very good, but giving them 20 points early on was unpardonable in Peter's head.

No team was that good – and no team should ever be 20 points better than Munster. It was a game he chose not to forget in a hurry.

Peter was psyched up for the return game. All of the guys were. Add in the home crowd, who were baying for revenge, and Fester was certain to be the centre of attention! Everyone seemed to be shouting abuse at him. It was too much. After the game he was not himself.

'Your cranky…!' Peter laughed.

But, typical of the selective amnesia that is sports, Keith Wood became a true hero for Munster all over again when he was back in a red shirt two years later.

In France, against Bourgoin, we lost 21-6. Once again, Peter and Co. had no idea what part of France they were going to, and for those of us who did not travel out we got our taste of the intimidating atmosphere listening to Len Dineen's commentary on our radio.

At one point late in the game Bourgoin had a penalty. They formed a wall – a wall Peter decided to charge!

Peter was at full speed coming to the wall when, suddenly, it opened up. And coming through in the opposite direction was a massive Bourgoin forward, also head down and in fourth gear. It was quite a crash. A complete wreckage, in truth, and Peter genuinely thought his leg was broken.

He was lying on the ground in agony.

Gaillimh stood guard over him.

Finally, Gaillimh looked down at Peter.

'You're all right Claw… the fire brigade is here!' he announced.

Peter craned his head up to see a bunch of French men of all ages, in long white coats, and wearing big white wellies, running in his direction with a stretcher.

Gaillimh burst out laughing.

Peter had no choice but to join him in laughter.

In the ambulance, the crew was insisting on taking Peter to the hospital, and he was adamantly refusing.

'I'm flying home…

'… HOME!' he tried to inform them.

Len Dineen had no more news on 'Claw's state!'

I decided never to miss a Munster game again.

Killian Keane wore the red No.10 in Bourgoin.

In the background, in Munster, there was a young kid trying to make a name for himself, and break into the big time, but Ronan O'Gara was safely tucked up in the stand that particular day.

Killian, or simply KK to our family, was Peter's brave travel buddy for many years, which was an interesting partnership. KK is a rock of sense, a pure gentleman – and dressed like a gentleman always. He was the fashionista of the team for years, but he was also naturally witty and funny.

Within the Munster squad, KK was also the ultimate source of technical information and the nitty gritty on the opposition – in fact, when he retired from playing, Declan Kidney used to send KK off to study Munster's opponents.

When he later worked with Keith Wood in a PR business, KK landed Peter an advertising contract with Nicorette, which seemed reasonable to start with as Peter was off the fags at the time. The contract included Peter judging a Nicorette competition for the *Best Giver Upper*.

Three months after the campaign had started, there were six finalists remaining. By which time Peter was well and truly back on the fags, and this caused KK a great level of distress.

The two of them were put up in The Shelbourne Hotel the night before the final selection and, of course, they went on the beer. The morning of the final, KK went to Peter's room to wake him, and the panic began – as the smell of cigarettes off Peter was wicked.

KK duly acquired a bottle of mouthwash.

Peter went to the meeting room.

The finalists made their way in front of the panel to tell their story about giving up the cigarettes. The first prize was a family trip to Disney World in Florida, so it was serious stuff. In fact, Nicorette had a special machine that the contestants had to blow into, which could read if they had smoked within the previous two weeks.

The first couple of finalists told their stories and blew into the machine as requested, and when they left one of the judges said that one had failed the "breathalyzer". The same thing happened with another finalist a few minutes later.

At this point the panel decided that there must be a problem with the machine. So one of the judges looked at Peter.

'Peter, you don't smoke anymore...' he said, '... why don't you test the machine.' He was being innocent enough in his request.

Peter had to think on his feet.

He looked out the window.

'That dirty b****** of a traffic warden... giving me a ticket...

'Back in a minute!'

He bolted out the door.

By the time he came back from moving the car that was never there – he had taken the train to Dublin – the judges had come to the decision that the machine was certainly faulty.

Peter hooked up with KK after the meeting.

KK was still pale.

He was considering having to repay the contract fee, but Peter talked him down in his usual practical and calm manner.

KK always knew that where the Claw was, there was usually action!

He says that's one of the reasons he always stuck close!

The IRFU had realized by now that they had a fight on their hands to hold onto the best Irish players all over the country. Too many were taking to England by air and by boat – history was repeating itself, as the English game was where some decent money was to be made.

In February of 1998, the IRFU rolled out their plans for the future. They were bold enough, as in addition to awarding players like Peter "Category One" contracts worth £50,000 each, the union here pledged to have 100 full-time rugby players in Ireland without delay.

The previous season each province was entitled to just six full-time players, all on a basic retainer of £25,000, plus 22 part-timers on £7,500 apiece. Peter and Eric Elwood had already been tied into three year "Category One" deals, but for so many other players the big decision was whether to jettison their day jobs and take the opportunity of a lifetime – and get paid for something they had always loved doing. There were no shortage of takers and the game in Ireland has never looked back!

They were going to have to work for their pay, however, as negotiations at this time were ongoing between the three Celtic Unions who intended forming their own league.

Warren Gatland, for one, could not be happier. He had told Peter and the guys that his plans were centred on a home-based International squad. Now he was getting what he wanted. The loss of up and coming players to the English game was finally stemmed.

The big step from an amateur state of mind to a wholly professional one was not going to be taken overnight. And it was not just that Munster could not get it right on the pitch in those opening three years of the Heineken Cup.

On one of those early pre-season tours of Italy, one of the hotel bedrooms had been totally wrecked. The team management of Colm Tucker and Jerry Holland instructed the boys themselves to find out who was responsible?

The bill for damages was quite significant and would have to be paid, stated Jerry and Colm. The pair of them left the meeting and asked the players to sort it out.

The culprit owned up, and no one would have guessed who it was! Peter arrived late to the meeting, and entered the room at the part where the players were collecting money between them to pay for the damages.

'Hold on a minute,' he asked in a loud voice.

'Are we sure one of us did this?'

Peter genuinely believed there should be some room for doubt – after all, how could something have happened that himself and Gaillimh weren't part of? But the culprit looked at Peter, and shamefully nodded his head.

The collection continued.

Everyone was learning, most of all the management team

Nobody had gone to *professional* school. Sure enough, on one occasion in those early days, the team arrived at their hotel in France to find that they had not been due until the following week. The management allowed the players to grab any rooms they wanted, and went looking for beds elsewhere in town.

The men in charge also worried about buses turning up at airports and hotels. In Wales, on another occasion, a driver arrived to bring the team to Llanelli, but turned out he was not certain where Llanelli actually was – and at times like these, when management was holding its breath, Peter and Gaillimh, supported by Alan Quinlan and Frankie Sheehan, would start shouting, 'SHAMBLES... SHAMBLES,'... just to test the nerves of the men who were supposed to be in charge.

Quinny and Peter had first met in a Munsters game against Shannon, in a game in which Peter accidently rucked Buddha Healy.

Buddha was playing for Shannon and he was also driving for Peter at the time in our courier business.

'Clohessy... you dirty b******,' shouted Quinny, '... you're even doing your own employees!'

Food had to be considered on trips abroad. The average diet of a man from Munster did not necessarily sit well with a man from France. The Munster guys did not like their beef very rare and bloody.

Getting home, double quick after games, was also something that grew into a necessity. The modern Irish rugby player was turning into a professional animal, and a feed of drink too often in his diary was not exactly what any coach was ordering.

Ear pieces took a couple of years before they became standard issue, and brought an end to coaches shouting crazily for things to be done in front of a hostile crowd.

Team meetings the evening before big games had to be toned down – though that took some time, and the team talk before the 2000 Heineken Cup final was one of those that went into over-drive and left the players unnecessarily drained. All of these little details needed tweaking. Even down to the little remote-controlled car that Declan Kidney decided should show up in the dressingroom before one game.

Declan saw that Saracens used a similar toy car to bring their kicking tee onto the field and he did not want his men distracted by such an inoffensive happening.

***

It all started to come together, slowly.

Year Four in the Heineken Cup picked up, and while we were lucky enough to have Padova in our group, we did take care of Neath and finished second behind Perpignan after four wins, one draw and one defeat. Munster were hitting the European quarter-finals for the first-time.

To get there, we had played all of our home matches in Musgrave Park, which was unusual, beating Padova, Neath, and Perpignan in Cork. We drew against Neath at The Knoll, beat Padova in their place, but lost to Perpignan away.

For the Perpignan match at Musgrave Park there had been a small ceremony to mark the 20th anniversary of Munster beating the All Blacks. Luke was asked to be mascot on the day, which was a wet and miserable one, but he did get to see his Daddy score an all-important try.

Ulster also won their way through to the last eight, topping their group that contained the deadly presence of Toulouse. But, for us, a taste of France in Colomiers was on the menu. If we had lost our last game in the group against Padova we would have been heading to Ulster instead, but given the fact that Munster had not won a game in Belfast in two decades maybe France was a smarter destination?

We were a band of the walking wounded as the day zeroed in on the team. Both of our wings were in trouble – Anthony Horgan had already been ruled out, and John Kelly was nursing a hamstring. Peter was in the best of health, but Des Clohessy was joined on the forwards' injury list by eight others! We were in trouble, no matter how Kidney tried to hide it – and Peter always told me how Declan Kidney was a master of hiding the bad news.

We had never won a Heineken Cup game in France – by now the team had defeats by Castres (12-9), Toulouse (60-19), Bourgoin (21-6) and Perpignan (41-24) tumbling around in its head. Colomiers were ranked right up there with that lot and had only been pipped by Perpignan in the semi-finals of the French Championship the previous year. On their home ground, in Stade Selery, which was really a suburb of Toulouse, they had won all eight of their European ties up to that point. Stade Selery was somewhat of a Thomond

Park at that time!

We did not play well. Worse still, *they* did not play very well either! We lost 23-9, and while Declan Kidney pointed to a five-week lay-off as one of the possible factors for a non-performance, the players saw other things.

Peter certainly saw the quarter-final as another learning curve – and he hoped a last, decisive such curve. The hosts were gouging in the scrum, which was actually unexpected by our guys. Equally, they did not expect to be spat upon by some of their opposite numbers.

He saw that to get to the very top in Europe, Munster and every last man on the team would have to think again about what was needed. Especially on the biggest days. The greatest teams were merciless.

Who would have thought that Munster ever dispensed mercy?

Never again, vowed Peter.

Of course, with professionalism, and the blossoming of "Club Munster", the players were suddenly being treated with celebrity status.

This again was new, certainly in Limerick, where up to that point there was no such nonsense, as the lads were just the lads who were club members – and there was no novelty as everyone had access to them after games in their clubhouses.

There was a natural self-regulation in that if a player got notions about himself he wouldn't be long being brought back into line by those around him.

This switch to celebrity status seemed to occur overnight, and the players were having to be protected from the public. They now had private team rooms for family after games, and roped off sections when they were out and about. The attention that they were receiving off the pitch was a big culture shock, especially to us partners. The guys of course generally enjoyed it, especially if they had won a game.

When I would regularly witness girls throwing themselves at the lads just because they wore blazers, I would often have a quiet word with them and say, 'Look girls, they just play rugby, they still have sweaty socks and smelly jocks like every other guy!'

But it was worse it was getting.

Now for a thick-skinned seasoned partner like me, it wasn't challenging, but there were occasions where I had to console some of the younger WAGS as the pressure of the female attention on their partners became too much for them.

Usually this would be when the lads were well on after a few pints and they wouldn't even notice that these girls were tactically pushing partners out of the way, so they could grab a player's attention. I remember one evening a girl shoving me to one side as she looked at me and said, 'Where's my Peter!'

Yet, I was still horrified one evening in Peter's bar when I stood with one of the players, and saw a girl hand him a piece of paper with her name and number on it. He tossed it on the ground.

'Do you know her?' I asked.

'No,' he replied.

'But were you chatting her up earlier on?'

'No... I've never seen her before!' he insisted.

I couldn't hide my horror that it had now come to this!

Marcus.

'Apologies for making you wait so long!

'Another gentleman, and although you were competing for the same position as me, we were always good friends... even if you did set me on fire!'

– Peter

CHAPTER 16

Young Munster were going well in the All-Ireland League in 1998, and went up north for the biggest game in Ballymena's history, with a play-off place up for grabs for the winners.

True to form Munsters had over 500 supporters with them on the long journey and they possibly outnumbered the home support. However, on the field Ballymena held all the advantages. They had nine members of the Ulster squad that would win the Heineken Cup title the following season, while Young Munster had one Munster man, Peter.

Munsters beat Ballymena 21-13, and Peter's brother Des partnered him in the front row that day after he had made the switch from wing forward to loose head prop.

Des went on to get his golden opportunity on the International stage that summer when he was called out to replace Reggie Corrigan on Ireland's South African tour. However, Des didn't have the same commitment to rugby as Peter did, and although he had the ability his career in green was short lived.

Warren Gatland made a big impact with people.

He had arrived in Ireland as part of the All Blacks tour squad in 1989 as understudy to the great Sean Fitzpatrick. It was during his brief stay here that Galwegians approached him with a view to becoming their player-coach

– and when they asked him if he had ever played prop, Gatty said... 'Of course... prop... sure thing!'

It was a white lie, but Gatland stepped up to every challenge that faced him in Irish rugby, with Galwegians and later when he became Connacht coach, and when the time came for him to lead Ireland on the sideline he knew our thinking, our personality, our insecurities and, most of all, our recurring fears.

There was something else about Warren Gatland that Peter always identified with – he saw Ireland as *family*.

Ireland was more to Gatty than just a game of rugby.

He was a pragmatist. He did not do bull****, as Peter regularly observed. Though in taking the reins of the Irish team from Brian Ashton, after that opening defeat to Scotland in the '98 Five Nations, the new coach was inheriting a scalded dog. Ireland would run straight into another three defeats in the Championship – and then they had a tour of South Africa with which to try to straighten things out.

'Only the best for the boys,' commented Pat Whelan.

The Irish team manager was standing in front of the Trianon Palace Hotel in Versailles, actually within the estate of King Louis XIV!

It had a cocktail bar named after Marie Antoinette – and the rich and famous had rested their heads in the opulent palace, including the Duchess of Windsor, President Eisenhower, and Marlene Dietrich – as well as Gatty, Pa and their team from Ireland the night before!

It was here also that the World War One treaty of Versailles was drawn up and handed to German messengers. These were changing times for the Irish team. It was like being on tour with the Reds back in Oz, reflected Peter. Good things were happening. The team no longer rested themselves for the 48 hours before a game, as they did in Ashton's brief tenure. Peter could live with that, because he knew it was right, even though he faced an intensive 30-minute workout with the team.

Also, Gatty had asked the IRFU to set up a *goodwill fax line*, so that supporters could stay in touch with the team – and there were already over 1,000 messages of support sent from home!

Not too many were headed "Peter Clohessy". Not because he was back to *bad boy* status, but due to the fact that Poppy, Gaillimh and Peter were all on the replacements bench for the game against the French in the Stade de France. Yes, they had a new home in France. The Parc des Princes was no more, thankfully.

A new dawn for an Irish team in Paris presented itself, however, we had another defeat to contend with. Peter, and his two *oldie* buddies did come on during the 80 minutes, and the French were given more than they bargained for, but it was still 18-16 at the end. The French had to pull the game out of the fire, for once, and for Ireland the rot stopped – in addition to a brave performance right to the end, we got a first try in Paris since Freddie McLennan's in 1980, when Denis Hickie galloped 50 yards and crossed the home line in the 35th minute.

Hickie, who was as fast as Simon Geoghegan, faster perhaps, had scored at the Arms Park and also Murrayfield in his debut season the year previously, so he was heading for a personal *Grand Slam* of away tries in Twickenham!

'The French are only human,' Gatty had told our guys over and over again in the build up. He promised his team that the French would make mistakes, and he asked that they pay for those mistakes. The All-Blacks saw every other International team as fragile as any human being! Gatty wanted to get that through to the Irish as well – the other crowd are not a bunch of robots!

Warren Gatland continued to do things his unique way, and even though we lost our two remaining games in the Championship – to Wales 30-21, and to England 35-17 – and propped up the table with no wins, and the dreaded spoon for the third year in succession, his way was uplifting for Peter.

He brought the Irish team *home* to Limerick for starters. Perhaps Pat Whelan and Donal Lenihan, who were now also part of the management team, had a word in his ear?

The team was based in The Castletroy Hotel and training in the NCTC for the remainder of the Championship after Paris, and Philip Danaher was added to the coaching ticket. Also, Gatty announced that he was not too bothered about getting over to England to check on the form of Irish players over there, which was a clear cut message to anybody who had signed on with English clubs.

Peter remained on the outside of the team looking in, however. He did come on against the Welsh, in the 54th minute, but the front row was a settled combination of Reggie Corrigan, Keith Wood and Paul Wallace. And Gatty seemed happy with them. And everyone was delighted for Denis Hickie who did indeed get his landmark try at Twickenham. Two of them just to be sure!

The good news was that Warren Gatland was finally given a full-time contract by the IRFU in April, despite the run of defeats. He had been on a caretaker role up to then, but the bad news was that a two-Test, seven game tour of South Africa was beginning at the end of May.

John Hayes came trundling onto the field and headed straight for Peter. Ireland were facing the Boland Cavaliers in the opening game of the tour, and Justin Fitzpatrick had gone down injured. Hayes got the call to come in!

Reggie Corrigan had been taken out of it when the game was 45 minutes in. Eager to get into everyone's good books, John had told the Irish management some weeks before that he could play at both sides of the scrum, but as he came on to the pitch he wanted to talk to Peter.

'Will you go loose head?' he asked in a bit of a panic.

'You're the one that said you could play loose head!' replied Peter.

'I never played there before!' continued John.

'Please Claw… will you go over?'

Peter could see the young man needed help.

'Ok…!

'I'll see what it's like!'

We conceded a pushover try shortly after, but the three lads up front quickly settled and with John revved up for his debut in green, and Peter getting to like his new role on the loose side, they finished the game in perfect working order.

Actually, Peter couldn't believe how much easier it was to play loose head, and he would always credit that switch with extending his rugby career by at least two seasons. It was, however, quite a remarkable change, as technically tight head and loose head are vastly different positions. The tight head anchors the scrum, and is a physically tougher ask.

Some in the media actually were moved to hail Peter as the 'Player of the Tour' and he was certainly enjoying his rugby at that time – perhaps it was the new lease of life that the move to Queensland had given him, or the obvious higher fitness level that professionalism had commanded of him. Or his motivation to regain an Irish jersey again.

During that tour Peter, for some reason only known to him, told Rob Henderson that I was pregnant.

I hadn't told anyone at home the news. The morning that we were all leaving South Africa we were hanging around the hotel in Pretoria, and the boys were giving it welly in the bar. Hendo suddenly appeared with a bottle of champagne, heading in my direction.

I quickly made an exit to the toilets.

But there was to be no escape. Eimear, who had come out with our group and was taking care of Luke – a group that also included Daddy Noel and his pals – was sent to get me, and with that our news was announced by Hendo to the entire squad. I was very embarrassed, and ran for the cover of Daddy Noel, but cameras were produced to record the moment.

I better tell Mam... before someone else does! I said to myself.

Two years earlier, in 1996, we had decided that it was time to take the only child status from Luke, and as Luke had obliged by being conceived promptly in '92, we didn't envisage there would be any delay – once we had our minds made up for number two.

Life lesson... number two million.

We are not in control of our lives, and the matter of whether we can have children or not! Despite things not happening immediately, we were not too concerned apart from a little anxiousness that the injuries from my car crash may be causing a problem. So, one year later when there was still no baby, I was referred to a professor in the Rotunda Hospital in Dublin for tests.

Before that we had to check Peter's sperm count.

Dr Mickey Griffin assured him it was no big deal, just deliver the sample in the envelope that Mickey had written Peter's details on to the office in St John's Hospital in Limerick within 30 minutes of taking the sample. All Peter was asked to do was hand in the envelope, and just walk away.

When Peter handed the envelope to the lady in St. John's she duly tore open the package, shredding the personal information on the front.

The information had to be repeated.

Verbally... there and then.

A red-faced Peter had to answer the following – name, address... and when was the sperm sample taken?

I informed him that it was the least he could do for our children! Following that test there were further investigations, the details of which would be classified as TMI (too much information). I then had a laparoscopy done, a simple procedure done under general anaesthetic where a camera is inserted through the belly button to view the inside of the womb, ovaries and anything else of importance. Afterwards the professor reported that he had found a lot of cysts, and that he had zapped them.

'What do you mean?' I asked.

Dr Peter Claw stepped in and decided to answer for the professor.

'He bursted them... !'

The professor didn't argue with his new sidekick and to this day I don't know what zapping a cyst means! They didn't seem to think that the cysts were part of the fertility issue, so I was scheduled to start some hormone treatment. However, I decided to wait until after the summer tour to South Africa.

South Africa was always on my bucket list. But by the time we were departing for South Africa I was 10 weeks pregnant with Jane.

Peter had been in the team because Paul Wallace had strained his groin, and Ireland defeated the Boland Cavaliers 48-35 in that opening game in Wellington. In the dressing-room afterwards, team captain Paddy Johns grouped the whole party, players and management together, and insisted on a rousing rendition of *Ireland's Call*. It was important to get a difficult tour off to a good start, even if the try count was a tight 6-5 to Ireland, as nobody was sure what lay ahead. Ireland had not toured South Africa since 1981.

But the mood in the camp was good. Peter liked the fact that the management trio were no older than himself, or not very much – Gatty was

34, Lenihan was 38, and Danaher was only 32!

He liked the style they imposed, especially as it was decided at the end of a long season to limit training to one spin per day. Gym work in the afternoons was optional, which meant that Peter saw all of his afternoons as being completely free. Himself and Rala could have some *him and me* time! Peter knew better than anyone in the Irish squad what was in store.

He'd played in South Africa twice with Queensland – he knew the pitches would be hard and the crowds hostile (the 10,000 in Boland had made their feelings known about the result alright!), and he knew that a warm day carried the heat. He also knew all of the South African teams like a game to be really pacy!

We were swept off our feet in the next three games, losing to the Eagles, Western Province and the Griquas within seven days, and in the last of those games we got a right beating, 52-13 from the home side.

It was with a sense of foreboding that we faced South Africa in the first Test in Vodacom Park, in Bloemfontein. We went down 37-13, and in the second Test in Loftus Versfeld in Pretoria we had nothing left to give on the field really, losing 33-0. The only reprieve had been a 26-18 win over the Leopards between the two Tests.

The team came home tired, but not dispirited.

The Warren Gatland era had commenced with five defeats in five Internationals, but for Peter there was absolute certainty that a corner had been turned. And that pretty soon, Ireland would be playing, as well as living, as professionals.

Daddy Noel had his good friend, "The Mayor" of Cape Town, John Quigley, and a couple of other lads with him. But the trip proved very challenging. For starters, security was a major issue, it simply wasn't safe for Eimear, myself and five year old Luke to walk around Cape Town. The only place where we felt safe was in the Victoria and Albert waterfront shopping centre – mind you, the Hard Rock Café at that V&A was bombed a couple of weeks afterwards.

Even the trip to Robben Island was challenging… but for different reasons. I was sea sick on the short journey to the island, my early pregnancy weeks being a contributing factor. So even though I was delighted to be visiting Nelson Mandela's cell, I was still very green and queasy, which is why I didn't notice what the guide was saying as we stood in the prison quarry and watched Luke play with a big pile of stones.

Eimear gave me a big nudge.

It was only then I tuned in to hear the guide say that the pile of stones was a memorial that had been started by Nelson Mandela and Bill Clinton!

Too late. The entire tour group was now watching Luke desecrate their sacred memorial. We may as well have spray-painted "The Claws Were Here!" I'm sure being pregnant probably added to the anxiety that I felt about our safety on that trip, but so too did the stories coming from Peter.

On this trip we both finally had mobile phones. Hello to technology, and a whopping phone bill of £1,200 when we got back home because of the roaming fees! So while we didn't actually see that much of each other on the trip, we clearly were talking a lot!

At that time in South Africa it was legal to carry weapons, so in some of the bars and restaurants they had cloakrooms where the customers would hand in their weapons as they came in – and collect them again as they were leaving. In a strange way, we felt safer in the bar's that had those cloakrooms.

Lucky for one member of the Irish team, it was one of these same *gun-free* premises that they were in when a South African female took exception to the behaviour of one Irish rugby player, which by all accounts was tame enough. She did not think so!

When she did retrieve her weapon she showed up at the team hotel looking for the same player.

God works in strange ways, and *someone* was looking down on the team and made sure that it was Rob Henderson who happened to meet this girl as she arrived at the hotel asking for the offending player.

Rob was certainly the only team member on that trip who had the sense and the ability to talk her down!

On the day of the first Test Daddy Noel was wearing an old Ireland training jersey belonging to Peter. The lads were tucking into the beers at the bar in the grounds. Daddy Noel was very proud that day as lots of supporters were coming up tapping him on the back, making comments about Peter.

He turned to me with a broad smile.

'Wow… isn't it amazing how many people know me?'

I waited 'til some time later to point out that the jersey had "CLOHESSY" written across the back of it! He was doubly proud the following week, as Des was called out to replace the injured Reggie Corrigan.

We did not fall in love with the Afrikaners. Indeed the majority of white supporters appeared to be particularly dogmatic and antagonistic. After one of the Test matches, the team had gone into the changing room, but somehow Trevor Brennan was still on the pitch.

A few rows behind me in the stand, which was close to the pitch, there was a South African supporter in a SA blazer. He started hurling abuse at Trevor.

I could feel my stomach begin to turn, but then I mistakenly calmed when I saw Trevor smiling back at the man.

It's ok, I said to myself.

I heard Trevor, very calmly, reply to this individual, 'Sorry… I can't hear you… come here!'

The man approached Trevor.

As Trevor came face to face with the guy he hit him swiftly, and turned and walked away. Donal Lenihan was also on the pitch, and I quickly called him over and warned him of the impending complaint that was sure to be lodged – or gun that might possibly be produced!

We stayed in a beautiful B&B on the beach in Wilderness, a seaside town on the southern cape, for a couple of nights. There were two ladies running it who seemed pleasant enough. Until John Quigley tipped one of the chambermaids, and then there was war.

The same women went berserk.

Tipping the staff would allow them to get above themselves, they warned us. When Peter had tipped the chambermaid in his hotel, a week earlier, she had started crying.

The contrast between the *haves* and *have not's* made it difficult not to feel guilty for being in the "wrong" category. Not the ideal emotion to be carrying around on a holiday.

‘Trevor.

'Playing against each other, we always fought.

'You had such a short fuse we could bank on four or five penalties just by rising you.

'But you're a man I always had great respect for... on and off the pitch. I still believe you should've been a Munster player.'

— Peter

CHAPTER 17

Partnering a professional rugby player does require massive resilience and stamina for lots of reasons. That autumn when Ireland were playing South Africa, Peter's brother Des got married on the Friday. As was often the case in those days, I went to the wedding on my own.

At this stage I was heavily pregnant, and it was a long day. Luke was a page boy, and I was constantly checking on him. The following morning I didn't even have shoes that would fit me, my feet were so swollen. I had to buy a pair of shoes two sizes bigger just to get me through another long day and night.

I then had a drive to Dublin to get to the game.

It was a busy autumn. South Africa were here, and there were two World Cup qualifying matches against Georgia and Romania to get through.

Peter had found a new lease of life as loose head. He was now playing there for Munster and Ireland, and was chosen there for the World Cup games, with Ross Nesdale and Paul Wallace completing the front row.

There was little trouble from either Georgia or Romania. We won the first game 70-0 with 10 tries, and coasted through the second, which was not as pretty, 53-35. Then came the South Africans.

At Lansdowne Road, Ireland proved a different proposition for the World champs! Peter was back on the tight side of the scrum in the absence of Paul Wallace, and himself and Fester carried good ball all afternoon long. Victor Costelloe was immense, and Dion O'Cuinneagain and Andy Ward were getting on every second ball. Our pack looked world class, and Nick Mallet, their coach observed as much after the game – admitting that if Ireland had the same quality out wide they would have been in trouble. It was unfair to our backs, because Kevin Maggs was brilliant in the middle of the field, but the pack was especially powerful for the full 80 minutes and no one *died* for a change.

Playing for the full 80 minutes needed to become a standard day's work, in Peter's book. We lost 27-13, but our performance was far better than the scoreline suggested. We left half-chances behind. Van der Westhuizen's hand trip denied a lightning fast O'Cuinneagain a promising one-on-one with Montgomery, Ward just could not hold onto Conor McGuinness' off-load, and Mal O'Kelly failed to locate Justin Bishop with a skip pass. Eric Elwood could only land three of his six kicks – whereas Percy Montgomery, from easier angles, was five from five.

The Africans, like all great teams, could win games that were not going their way, and that's what they did in the end. They rocked us with 17 points in five stunning minutes!

But we came back. We won the remainder of the game 7-3, and Fester scored one of his barnstorming tries that even brought Mallet to his feet. 'Look… Wood is the best hooker in the world, simple as that,' stated the South African coach, and he cuffed one of his own around the ear in the process. 'James Dalton may not like hearing that, but Wood blew through him, and if he (Dalton) wants to be the best in the world he can not let that happen.'

On December 26, myself and Peter went to Cork and booked into a hotel. The following afternoon I checked into the Bons Hospital, and Jane arrived safely by cesarean section the next day. Our good friend Clodagh Kingston had just checked out with their new arrival, whom they called Anna, the day before.

A few years later when the Kingstons had their second child, I remember chatting with Clodagh and when I asked what they were calling their son, she hesitated and said she didn't know.

It was a couple of weeks later that she admitted she was too embarrassed to tell me that they were calling him Peter. They did get an awful slagging from the rugby crew, and they were blessed when their third was Abigail – because if they had a boy they had picked Harry as the name, which it so happened was our dog's name at the time!

Mam brought Luke to Cork, to visit his new sister, and he stayed down with Peter for a couple of days. Peter went back for training, and returned the night before I was due to go home. The Cork contingent of Donal Lenihan, Kenny Murphy and Ken O'Connell were very concerned that Peter wasn't *lonely* in Cork, so they took him out on the p***!

The next morning I rang Peter in the Kingsley Hotel. When he answered it was clear he was still not sober, so I insisted that he get up and turn on the shower. Once I heard the shower running I relaxed knowing that it would wake him up, and he would be along shortly to collect myself and Jane.

When there was no sign of him after an hour, I rang the room again, but the phone was off the hook. I had no choice but to call the concierge at the hotel, and ask him to go and knock on the bedroom door.

In fairness he agreed. Peter finally answered the door, however he quickly thanked the concierge and closed it – as he realized that the shower was still running and, in fact, the bath was overflowing all over the place!

In the Five Nations in '99 we had France and England at home, and were on the road to Cardiff and Edinburgh. It was a Championship in which Ireland needed to step up and prove that they could live with all of our neighbours as a professional rugby outfit. There was no room for excuses. We had a real chance of taking one of the two big scalps and having a season to remember.

Like everyone else in the Gatland camp, Peter knew how hard they were working. An Irish team had never been fitter – fags or no fags in Peter's case!

And they knew that the skill level between all of the home nations was evens-stevens. Ulster, after all, were Heineken Cup champions, beating Colomiers in the final, and they had proved that an Irish team could take on the best in Europe, and win.

It was time for Ireland to get out from under the bottom of the pile.

David Humphreys, fresh from Ulster's victory, was holding down the No.10 shirt in his battle against Eric Elwood. There was a fight for lots of places on the team. Same in the pack, where O'Cuinneagain, making his first Five Nations start, and Eric Miller were battling hard.

Peter felt an Irish team was never as ready to take down France, and end 16 years of mostly bruising frustration. This time, in Lansdowne Road, the game produced the same fierce physical exchanges as before, and as the game wore on the French became dangerously indisciplined. There was plenty of eye-gouging going on in the scrum, which the match officials didn't see much of, but they had no excuse when Phillipe Benetton landed a right hook into the face of Keith Wood as Fester was lying on the ground, right in front of the touch judge, Jim Fleming of Scotland.

Ridiculously, it was Phillipe Bernat Salles, their winger who was mistakenly fingered by the Australian referee, Peter Marshall. He was shown a yellow card instead.

The French got out of jail, in every possible way. It was a nightmare afternoon for Humphreys, something that can happen to any out-half. A hero of Ulster's fairytale win a week earlier, he missed with four kickable penalties, the last coming one minute over the 80 minutes with the Grand Slam champions on the ropes.

The French led 10-9, but David's kick veered just right of the post. It was awful for him, and heartbreaking for the rest of the team. A win which was sure to propel Ireland forward, and win the respect of every other team – and stuff some fear into them as well – was taken from our grasp.

David had kicked three penalties, at the same time, and we were 9-0 in front with the game entering the final quarter. We had rucked and mauled the French all over the field, but Benneton got through for a try for them in the 63rd minute. We were still in the lead when the game entered the 80th minute, but Wally wandered offside. Thomas Castaignede kicked them one point in front. Then we had our last gasp chance to win the game back.

But David Humphreys went from zero back to hero, all over again, in our next game against the Welsh. He kicked three penalties, two conversions and two dropped goals in a game that was extra special because the Welsh had hired out Wembley Stadium as their home for the spring, while the Millennium Stadium was being built in Cardiff. The Tricolour fluttered on one of the Twin Towers overlooking the famous old football ground, and the Welsh Dragon was on the other.

It was quite an occasion. The crowd also made the most of the occasion, and we were still singing 10 minutes after the game had ended. Kevin Maggs and Fester had scored our tries, and we had held out to win 29-23. As we joined with U2 helping them with *In The Name Of Love*, down in the dressingroom Fester was giving his team a rendition of *Clare To Here*, but when he stopped the whole room went quiet – and Gatty and his players sat back and listened to the supporters singing their lungs out.

Discipline had been an issue in the previous few Internationals.

Gatty, as an All Black, knew that being physical and holding your discipline when it really mattered was a requisite of all the great rugby teams down through the years. There was a time to play, and there was a time to stop the other team playing – and his Irish team needed to know when each was necessary.

He had warned the lads, in the week before playing the Welsh, to keep their heads about them. They listened… Peter too.

Peter took a punch that day.

And it took a lot for him not to retaliate.

'I took a dig for you today… and it hurt!' he reported to his coach when they got back into the dressingroom.

There was a sense of positivity, and expectation, rising in the Irish camp, and most of the credit for that was down to Gatty. He was a players' man, and the players knew that they could trust him to stand by them.

Trudi, Gatty's wife, created a new role for a coach's wife – as she got to know all of the partners, and I dare say that it was her family values that influenced many new initiatives that happened during this time.

On New Year's Eve we had all been invited to The Glenview Hotel in Wicklow, while the boys were in camp, and another couple of times we were officially invited to dinners before the boys went on tour. Trudi shocked all of us at one of those first events, as we sat with our partners at an informal dinner in The Glenview.

She made a speech, first of all, which was unheard of!

Then she went on to say that each of the females should stand up and tell the room something that people didn't know about their partner.

One by one, women stood up around the room, and when it came to my turn I got to my feet said, 'I am Anna Gibson-Steel... married to Peter Clohessy, and really this question should be answered by Gaillimh...

'He spends more time with Peter than I do...'

Gatty and Trudi were the same age as many of the older players, so they had more in common than any other coach before then. From my perspective, it was the first time I felt truly welcomed.

Everyone on the field, and watching on in Lansdowne Road, was fired up for the visit of England two weeks later. After two of the strongest performances in years a Triple Crown was in sight, but that dream went by like a flash. That's how the game was for Peter. England were like a stone wall. Their defence was inch perfect. It was not that Ireland played badly, it was just that England were in control for the full 80 minutes, and even when David Humphreys kicked his fifth penalty to leave just five points between the teams, they still went down the other end and brushed up the scoreboard with a Tim Rodber try in injury time.

We had actually taken the lead just after half-time, but we then lost the run of ourselves – literally running from deep positions which were really hopeless. There was no calmness, no control... we just wanted to win!

That's not how you win a game boys, Gatty told them in the dressingroom afterwards.

Gatty wanted to give our visitors a torrid time of it up front in the first quarter, but instead, England bossed everything from the start. Our scrum was nothing like it had been against the French and Welsh, and the referee, Paddy O'Brien did not give Peter or Wally an inch to try to turn the tide in the front row.

The wind was well and truly out of the team's sails, all of a sudden. And instead of rounding off so much hard work and promise with a big performance in Edinburgh, we fell apart. The Scots ripped our defence apart. They got four tries, and left the boys with a 30-13 defeat, and completely dazed at how a season that was filled with so much promise halfway through had turned into a fast, downward spiral.

Little did Peter, or anyone else in and around the team, realize that there was help at hand. The newspapers were talking about a couple of young lads from UCD who were ready to step up to "Ireland A". They also suggested that the pair of them could learn a lot from being included in the tour of Australia in the summer.

Ciaran Scally was chosen at scrum-half for the warm-up against Italy in April, but his college team-mate, 19 year old Brian O'Driscoll, who was touted as a centre or out-half, was kept on the bench.

'We've been impressed with him for a long time,' stated Gatty, '... he looks to have a good future in Irish rugby. We don't want to hold him back, but at the same time, we don't want to drop him in at the deep end either.'

The coach said that O'Driscoll straightens his line brilliantly. He said the boy has a low centre of gravity. And he said that he was bloody hard to stop when he had the ball in his hand.

At the same time, Gatty didn't want the boy to come to any harm!

The weekend in Edinburgh, that March, was one of the best and one of the *last* great drinking trips for me. It was my first weekend escape after having Jane.

I remember the freedom of not having a baby with me, and did I make the most of it! On the Friday night before the game I had booked into a nice B&B in Grosvenor Square – no need to spend wildly, I thought, since the next night I would be in the beautiful Balmoral Hotel with Peter. It was also the first weekend that Fester was introducing his new girlfriend, Nicola Vernal to all of us, and he asked would I take care of her for the weekend?

I had given Fester the details of the B&B where Nicola could call to meet me on the Saturday morning. Fester said she would be getting into Edinburgh *early* that morning.

Meg, Daddy Noel, Auntie Majella and John, Mags and Nick (Peter's sister and husband), and our family friend, Mike Cunningham had all booked into a hotel on Princes Street that was above Marks & Spencers – a perfect location, in the centre of the city. It was a favourite with rugby supporters – and the staff there were all well versed in the various escapades.

That Friday evening was one of the best ever. The sing-song was unbelievable, and then there was pitch and toss – organised by Mike Cunningham – where the men put a 10 pence coin in their belly button, slapped their bellies hard on both sides, and whichever 10 pence went the furthest distance was a winner.

I didn't compete in that game!

He also organised some greyhound racing, and provided the commentary and a betting service! The *greyhounds* were Irish rugby supporters on all fours racing across the lobby. The sing-song finished as the buffet breakfast was being set up at 6.30 a.m.

I duly hailed a taxi outside the door of the hotel, and asked the driver to take me to the B&B, though from his chat it suddenly became obvious to me that I didn't paint a pretty picture – what would a girl on her own be doing, leaving one hotel at 6.30 a.m. and heading for a B&B?

I decided it was best *not* to try to salvage my character... what was the point! I got out at the B&B and had to waken the owners and ask them to let me in? That made it two Scots in a row who were not impressed with me!

I collapsed into a coma.

There was no way I could possibly have heard Nicola knocking on my door at 8.0 a.m. But, in fairness to her, she went for a walk around the city and came back an hour and a half later – this time getting the still extremely unimpressed B&B owner to open my bedroom door.

I couldn't speak, however!

All I could manage was a wave to her to take a seat. In the shower, I prayed for the stamina to be able to *take care* of Fester's girl.

Having not had a drop to drink for the previous year, conversation was a struggle for me. My hangover was excruciating. I also had hardly one night's sleep in three months, so between the two I was on my knees all day.

We stopped at the Balmoral before the game to collect my match tickets and to assure Fester that I was indeed looking after Nicola. Fester was well aware of the "bitchiness" that existed between some of the partners – my role was to save Nicola from any of that rubbish.

When I met Peter at the hotel he thought it was hysterical to see me so hungover, and he immediately and *proudly* showed me off to Gaillimh.

I was so distracted that I got on the official partners' bus with Nicola, but only realized half way to the stadium that I had forgotten my ticket. I rang back to the hotel and Peter got the ticket.

I did my best to protect Nicola from the girls, some of whom were notorious for gossiping on the bus journey, but in my incapacitated state I let a few comments slip through. Nicola was well able though to take care of herself!

But her suggestion that potatoes for lunch should aid my recovery was ill-founded and I spent most of the afternoon in the invalid toilet. The game was a blur, but at the final whistle I realized that my nightmare hangover was gone. I was thrilled, as we gathered inside and waited for the boys to come from the changing room.

I couldn't hide my elation at feeling better, but this met with much disapproval from the other girls.

I was beaming... and Ireland had been beaten!

ROG.

'A pure gentleman, you cost me dearly in cards!

'But, even if you did skin me, thank you for always showing great respect to my family all through your brilliant days with Munster and Ireland.'

— Peter

CHAPTER 18

'Claw is the Law!'

It was Ronan O'Gara who first stated this to be the case within the Ireland team squad.

At this point in Peter's career he was treated with absolute respect by the players and also the team management, and this allowed him certain latitude that was reserved... just for him really.

Players and management would seek his advice.

But that did not mean that Peter Clohessy was running the show. Ireland by now had a nutritionist on board. And, quickly, there was a blanket ban on room service in hotels. The acquirement, therefore, of late night snacks became a challenge, but one that Peter rose to admirably.

In any of the Irish hotels this was an easy assignment, as Peter was on a first name basis with most of the staff in every single establishment.

This was not the case in the Balmoral Hotel in Scotland. When Peter rang room service the night before the game and asked the man to bring him a packet of cigarettes the porter refused. There is no room service for the Irish team, the poor man explained.

Peter corrected him. He explained that he fully realised that there was a ban on any food being served to the room, but that he would like some cigarettes.

'But smoking is bad for you!' the porter foolishly replied.

'I'm 33 f******* years of age,' Peter shouted, '... and I'll decide whether I smoke or not!'

He was a very brave porter.

'I'm sorry sir... but I'm not bringing them up to you.'

Peter blew his lid.

He dialled the team doc's room, Donal O'Shaughnessy.

'Shocks,' stated an agitated Peter, 'You'd better tell that p**** to bring me fags immediately...

'Or, I'll go down... and tear his head off!'

The cigarettes were delivered.

But, mostly, *Peter's Law* held.

Mike McGurn, the new fitness coach whom Eddie O'Sullivan was to bring on board, had gained quite a reputation in Britain where he prepared the St Helen's rugby league team to a treble of Challenge Cup, Super League and World Club titles. Mike was brought in to guide everyone to an even higher level of physical fitness.

In his first week on the job, after a morning training session, Mike sat down in front of Peter as he was having some lunch.

'Now Peter... we're down in the gym for 2.30 p.m.,' began Mike...

'I won't be going to the gym!' Peter interrupted.

'It's only something light,' continued Mike.

'I won't be going to the gym,' Peter repeated.

'Look... it will only be for a little while...!'

Mike was not letting up.

He was not sure if Peter was just taking the p***.

He found out that was not so.

'You're not f****** listening to me,' barked Peter.

'I don't do gym!'

Mike took off to Brian O'Brien, who was the team manager, and sought some extra advice on how to get around Claw?

'I'm not sure if Claw is taking the p*** out of me or not, but... he says he's not doing the gym?'

'That's right' says Briano, '… Claw doesn't!'

The respect that Peter had earned from his coaches, management team, and teammates afforded him this unique place.

After Warren Gatland's exit as national coach, Peter also got on really well with Eddie O'Sullivan, who also valued Peter's opinion. So it was a bit of a culture shock to Peter when Declan Kidney came along to Munster.

The difficulty, in Peter's opinion, was that Declan treated the lads like students, and he assumed a traditional teacher mode. And Peter, who never enjoyed that style of leadership when he was at school, was certainly not going to enjoy it in his 30s! Peter felt sympathy for ROG and Stringer.

'F*** it lads… ye were rightly stung,' he insisted. 'Ye haven't escaped him since school!'

At this stage the age gap was widening between teammates – ROG and Stringer had been ball boys at one of Peter's first Munster games! It was interesting because ROG in particular used to connect with Luke a lot. He was always very good to him, and the lads enjoyed being able to put Luke up to stuff that they thought would bother Peter. Not that this ever worked, given Peter's laid-back style of parental control! The younger lads were always very respectful towards me also, probably because they put me in the same category as their mothers!

When Donncha O'Callaghan arrived on the scene with Munster, he immediately gained the official label of "Team Messer" and retired Gaillimh and Peter from their roles. Donncha's older brother, Ultan had played with Peter years earlier, and again Ultan was great craic.

Donncha, however, took the pranking to greater heights – sometimes 30,000 feet. On flights he was always seated in Row 1. Every second person who went to the loo at the front of the aircraft would find Donncha waiting for them at the door as they came out – as if he was next in line to use the toilet.

He'd open the door, and shout…

'Oh, my God… the smell…

'WHAT HAPPENED IN HERE!'

The other person, meanwhile, scuttled back to their seat red-faced.

In fairness to Quinny, I heard him stopping Donncha from doing this to me. Clearly at my age, old enough to be their mother they might have thought, I deserved a little more respect.

Plus, there was always Peter... the master of revenge!

Though Gaillimh and Peter never actually retired from this department or exited the centre stage for good.

The team was a family affair, and all on the team were privy to all the goings-on. So when Gaillimh swallowed his front false tooth, as he was having lunch in Tipperary with Quinny and a few more lads before heading to Galway for a training session, everyone had to be alerted!

Most of the lads of course were weak with laughter when they realized what had happened. They also decided they should help, naturally – and it was collectively agreed that making Gaillimh sick was the answer to this particular problem, so they readily volunteered to help in the process.

The manic effort did not bear fruit.

Gaillimh rang the team doc, who advised that he should stop in Limerick to get an X-ray to make sure the plate wasn't stuck in his oesophagus. The X-ray confirmed that it was safe to proceed, and that he would pass the tooth over the coming days.

Naturally, as Peter was rooming with Gaillimh in that camp, he was able to observe from a safe distance as Gaillimh searched for the tooth on several occasions daily.

The morning of the game, finally, Gaillimh *found* the tooth. And Peter was down at breakfast when Gaillimh landed in, with his full complement of teeth.

'You dirty b******... I can't believe that you put that back into your mouth,' stated Peter.

'What do you want me to do... stick it back up my h*** again?' Gaillimh replied. At the end of the game, Gaillimh made a bee-line for as many of the players' wives and partners as he could find.

And, always needing to have the last word... he kissed them all.

Returning to Australia with Ireland for the summer tour of '99, which was also a warm up for the World Cup that autumn, was extra special for Peter.

There were many press interviews at the time, most commenting on how he would be playing against many of his former Queensland teammates. Dan Crowley was the Australian prop, and he had played in the famous game against Munster in '92, as well as playing with Peter for Queensland in '97.

'He is a dead-set dinosaur,' Dan fondly told the Aussie press in reference to Peter, '... from rugby's old school.'

'When "CLOEY" (as the boys on the Reds team used to call Peter) arrived in Queensland, we became firm friends. We all got on with him because he's that type of guy... he would fit in anywhere, but everyone over here liked him.'

Peter had arrived in Queensland as a tight head, allowing Dan to move to the loose side. But by the time Peter was back, on Ireland's summer tour in '99 he was playing loose – so in fact, Dan and Peter never did get to scrummage against one other.

Peter had a tour of Australia, and the World Cup in front of him – but he still found time to get to Buenos Aires to play for a World XV, and score a try in a celebration game in which the visitors lost 49-31 to Argentina. He was actually in the form of his life, and enjoying every last minute of his career.

Even though every game was a fresh challenge at his age – and even though he was meeting all sorts of new faces coming into the Munster and Irish teams. Mike Mullins, for starters – Peter had not played with many guys who had dyed-blonde hair, were tattooed and ear-ringed, and played the guitar! But Mullins had retraced his roots and was now a teammate at Young Munster, and also with Peter in the Irish dressingroom.

Peter was notorious for not knowing very many of his teammates by first name. He does not have a head for names, even if he is seeing the same face day after day.

'Peter called me "Hey You",' insists Gordon D'Arcy for the first few years that he played for Ireland.

It was only a four-game tour of Australia, beginning against New South Wales Country XV and then New South Wales itself, before two Test matches. Fester was back in charge as captain.

We had won our opener, 43-6, but then went down 39-24 to NSW. Gatty wasn't happy at all.

The lads were on the training field at Southport School in Brisbane, which was famous in Ireland as the location where Tony Ward had been told in 1979 that he was being replaced by Ollie Campbell for the Test games ahead.

The school found fame a second time with the Irish.

There had been four inches of overnight rain. But Gatty was still fuming inside at how submissive Ireland had been against New South Wales. The workout lasted a full two and a half hours. At the end of it all Fester was on his knees and stayed put for a full five minutes. Another man had his head in a wheelie-bin. It was not Peter, who was adamant that he would not go down in the history books by collapsing.

The session had started with bleep tests – with everyone running different distances against the "bleep". Then the serious stuff began. On the dead-goal area on the next pitch, Gatty wanted sets of five scrums.

After eight such sets, Fester asked everyone if they were knackered?

'If you're not… then now's the time to start working!' he shouted.

Peter was feeling it more than anybody. He was in for every scrum, as Paul Wallace was protecting his damaged shoulder and was told to run a mini-marathon around the pitches, shirtless, while all of the work was going on with the scrummaging machine. When the machine was driven nearly 20 yards infield, a boorish local grounds-man sought to intervene.

He was told to get lost.

The scrums stopped after the tenth set.

Ireland were hammered in the first Test at Ballymore, 46-10.

With Brian O'Driscoll suddenly giving Ireland new options beyond the pack, Gatty and Donal Lenihan had set about opening up Ireland's style of play. But after the biggest defeat ever by Australia over an Irish side, they came in for a torrent of abuse. The team also felt beaten up. The scoreline may not have reflected a battle, but the Irish dressingroom certainly resembled the left-overs from such a happening.

Rod McQueen, the Aussie coach, said he was 'disappointed with a few of the off-the-ball incidents', but insisted nobody would be cited by the home team. No quarter had been given. Peter had rucked Ben Tune, his old Reds' teammate, off one ball and he had to be replaced. Though Gatty was also annoyed with Peter because the referee had reversed a penalty decision when informed what had happened. He suggested in the after-match press briefing that he would drop any Irish player who had been indisciplined, but he also saw that the Irish scrum had been very strong under the fiercest of pressure.

The half-time lead in the first Test had only been 10 points to the home team. It was after that, that Australia went through the gears and left Ireland rooted to the spot.

The team headed to Perth for Round Two.

They were 6-3 up after 30 minutes, when Peter scored his third try for Ireland – breaking through Daniel Herbert's tackle after a move involving Kevin Maggs, Dion O'Cuinneagain, O'Driscoll and Trevor Brennan. Peter had also become Limerick's most capped player, winning his 30th cap and passing Fester's late father, Gordon. He was flying, and Ireland looked a completely different team to a week earlier.

We led 11-9 at half-time, and added another penalty from David Humphreys straight after the break. In the dressingroom at half-time, Gatty had warned his boys that the game would turn on one moment, one mistake. They needed to be strong and disciplined.

One turnover could decide this, he repeatedly warned them.

'The game was there for us... for the taking,' Gatty admitted when it was all over. 'We had them on the ropes in the second-half, but we then made a crucial turnover. Silly things lose games.'

Ireland outscored the home team three tries to two, with Kevin Maggs and Justin Bishop also going over, but it was 32-26 to them on the board high in the sky in the Subiaco Oval. We had let them tot up a tenth straight win against us – and the chance of making them second-guess themselves, and second-guess Ireland, before meeting a few months later in the World Cup was gone.

We warmed up, fatefully, against Argentina for the World Cup.

It was Peter's first and last World Cup. He had Fester and Wally with him in the front row. Paddy Johns and Jeremy Davidson were powerful locks, and that day against the Argies Trevor Brennan, Andy Ward and Dion O'Cuinneagain were in the back row. Ireland had strength and pace in the pack, and they had Brian O'Driscoll breathing new life into the rest of the team.

Matt Mostyn scored three tries, and we had a huge 32-3 lead early in the second-half – and then we let the Argentinians get ideas about themselves. Instead of a rout, it was 32-24 at the end.

Nobody knew the full price that would soon be paid for that half-victory!

Fester led the way against the United States in our opening game of the World Cup. Lansdowne Road was only over half full, but those who turned up saw the US destroyed 53-8. Fester got four tries. We also finished Group E with a big score, putting 44 points on Romania. But the group was all about ourselves and Australia – and the question that Gatty said we had left unanswered in Sydney in the second of our summer Tests.

On Irish soil, did we believe that we could finally stop them?

In Sydney we had shown that we were up to the job. But the Aussies had put themselves in the mood for another World Cup win by taking the scalp of the All Blacks in the meantime.

The fastest route to the final means beating Australia, Gatty announced publicly. However, his plan was something different – the plan was to beat Romania, beat Argentina and get an easier route to the quarter-finals. So Gatty didn't put out his best team against the Aussies!

The team was gung-ho. We had waited four months, for October 10, but on the day Ben Tune and Tim Horan crossed for tries. The Aussies coasted home in the end to a 23-3 win. Ireland then defeated Romania, with Peter back in at tight head.

However, the morning of the game against the Romanians, Peter was getting out of the shower when he slipped a disc.

He was told he would have to rest for a week.

We faced a play-off in Lens, against Argentina!

He watched as Ireland prepared for Argentina, in a play-off for a spot in the quarter-finals, but he was confident he would be back to take his place against the French in the last eight at Lansdowne Road.

Nobody seemed to doubt that it would be Ireland and France!

But a handful of us still made the trip to Lens, which was awkward enough – we flew to London, but Virgin had cancelled our next flight. There was much flapping about to get us onto another flight that would see us get to the ground in time for the Wednesday evening kick-off.

It was chilly in the stadium that evening, and the place was only half full. There was something ominous about the whole atmosphere.

Gatty brought in seven fresh players to face Argentina. Reggie Corrigan came in at loose head instead of Peter – and made it a total of 30 players who had been used during the tournament. It was shrewd planning and use of players – as long as Ireland actually beat Argentina!

For Gatty, the game was personal. He was facing his old team boss, Alex Wylie as the former All Black coach was now with Argentina. Gatty had one eye on Wylie, and one eye on the French four days later. The Irish management said they were totally focused on the job at hand in Lens, but with so little time in the turnaround for the quarter-final at Lansdowne Road, it would have been impossible not to have divided attention.

In the Stade Felix Bollaert that evening everything went so exactly right – and then everything went completely wrong!

As he sat in the stand, Peter felt disgusted as he could see 10 minutes into the second-half that we were in trouble. And everyone was gutted in the dressingroom afterwards.

We were in front until the 75th minute. Ireland had most of the possession and territory. But we could not kill off the Argies, and suddenly when they took the lead we panicked. There was still six additional minutes added by the referee but our heads, inexplicably, after looking so controlled, were gone.

We tried 15-man lineout mauls, but could not get over their line. We threw everything at that line, but the Pumas blocked charge after charge – though they were helped by the fact that so much of our work was being done by players in green having their heads down as they raced for the line.

They threw in a few professional fouls to really frustrate and panic us further, but Australian referee, Stuart Dickinson refused to award us a penalty try which would have been entirely justified.

It should never have to come to such an ending.

The ruck count was 62-40 in our favour, but we lost the game 28-24. We had no tries, and that's why we lost – David Humphreys was close to impeccable with his kicking, shooting seven penalties from seven, but he also shaved the post with two dropped goal attempts and hit the upright with another.

Wally had been off the field with a blood injury when we earned our only five-metres scrum of the evening, 12 minutes from the finish, when we were 24-18 ahead, and could have finished them off. Seven minutes from the end Matt Mostyn saved a certain try when he came in off his wing and snuffed out a two-man overlap. But at the next set piece wide on the right their replacement out-half Felipe Contepomi floated a long pass out to Gonzalo Camardon. His pass in front of Diego Albanese gave their left winger time to get in at the corner.

Gatty had lost his own battle with Grizzly Wylie.

In Ireland, he would also find out before too long that Lens was a defeat that some people could never forgive.

That evening, in the team hotel, there was nothing else for it but to drown our sorrows. The Munster players took up camp in the reception of the hotel, which was an atrium with the bedrooms circling around it overhead. They duly drank the bar dry – and ended up drinking some shocking green liquor, as Tom Tierney entertained the party with his childhood song *We Are The Greeners*, a tribal song that the teenagers who came from the Fair Green sang!

Apparently, my laughing was tormenting Trevor Brennan so much that at 3.0 a.m. he got out of bed and came down to join us.

CHAPTER 19

Bordeaux, May 6, 2000.

It was a coming of age for Munster and all of the team's incredible army of supporters. It had been a long time coming. But on that Saturday, in the warmth of a perfectly early summer's day in the south of France, Munster announced that they were ready to be the greatest team in Europe.

It was like something we had never experienced before, none of us! But over 3,000 Munster supporters found their way to the French city. And the stories of how people got there were on the fringe of folklore by the time we all got back home.

Two lads had come on motorbikes.

Others got to Paris and took the high-speed TGV down.

Some flew to Spain and drove up.

The determination of the fans was almost equal to the team's fierce desire to be No.1. But the supporters demonstrated their passion in a family way with the locals – we took over Bordeaux with sing-songs and banter, and the French totally accepted our Irishness.

The morning of the match was a scorcher. My sun cream was passed around the stand, and was near empty when it found its way back to me. One man near us got a phone call from home – they had spotted him on the telly – and rang him to tell him he was sunburnt!

The Toulouse supporters, as usual, were loud and noisy with their travelling brass bands, but Munster had learned by now how to deal with the intimidation, and in the pre-match activity the team purposely went to do their warm up in front of the French fans – they booed and jeered our boys, and our boys lapped it up!

In the searing heat it was Munster who proved the fitter team. The three years of professionalism was finally paying off. Keith Wood had left Harlequins and rejoined Munster, along with new signings John Langford and Mike Mullins, and the team was complete, and ready for lift-off.

Langford had joined Munster the summer before. He'd played a few times for Australia and had three years in the Super 12 with the ACT Brumbies behind him when he decided to come to Ireland and try it here. He hailed from Wagga Wagga, halfway between Sydney and Melbourne, which was strong Aussie Rules and Rugby League territory. He was 31 years old, and after having had John Eales standing in his way back home on the national stage, he wanted a fresh challenge. He was first pointed in the direction of Leinster, however.

Luckily, Mal O'Kelly decided to come home from England and start back with Leinster, and John was told, 'we don't want you!'

John and his wife, Nicole settled into their home in Limerick, and made life long friends with Munster players and supporters.

John and Gaillimh were a force to be reckoned with in the second row. Even for those waiting in the queue to get the chance of wearing a red jersey for good. For Donncha O'Callaghan, and Paul O'Connell and Mick O'Driscoll, the pair looked immovable.

'Langford... back here every year!' Donncha would loudly moan in the dressingroom. 'You'd think he'd give one of the young lads a chance, wouldn't you!'

Peter and Terry Kingston celebrate the game-winning try in the famous 22-19 win over Australia in Musgrave Park and (below) a young-looking Munster pack including Gaillimh, John "Paco" Fitzgerald, Peter and Terry weigh up a different opposition during the early 90s.

The Irish front row of Peter, Terry Kingston and Nick Popplewell pack down against England in 1994 (top) and (inset) Peter with a full head of hair in his earliest Ireland days. Peter acts as scrum-half and gets the ball away against France in 1995.

Peter and Poppy in the Parc des Princes in 1996 when Ireland suffered a heavy defeat.

Peter hits the deck in that infamous clash in Paris that would lead to his 26 weeks suspension.

Paul Wallace, Keith Wood and Peter clear their lungs before the World Cup clash with the United States at Lansdowne Road in 1999 and (below) Mick Galwey, team manager Brian O'Brien and Peter chat with a Vatican Guard during Ireland's visit to Rome for the Six Nations Championship in 2001.

Richard Hill of England fails to stop Peter as he charges forward in the 20-14 win over the 'old enemy' at Lansdowne Road in the Six Nations game delayed until the autumn of 2001 due to Foot and Mouth.

A proud Peter with team mascot, Luke leads out the Irish team at Lansdowne Road in 2002 as he celebrates his 50th cap for this country and (below) Luke keeps an eye on Gaillimh and his Dad during the singing of the national anthem.

An emotional Fester takes it all in after Ireland had defeated England, while Peter surveys the dressingroom and (middle) Peter charges through the Italian defence. Eddie O'Sullivan and the Irish team listen to Peter's few words on the evening of his 50th cap for Ireland.

Peter gets up close to the All-Blacks at Lansdowne Road in 2001 (above) and he sits all alone in the Ireland dressingroom after his last game for Ireland against the French in the Stade de France.

Peter breaks through the Perpignan line in 1998, in the early days of Munster's adventures in the Heineken Cup and (below) crashes over for his try.

The Munster team that defeated Stade Francais 27-10 in the quarter-final of the Heineken Cup at Thomond Park in 2000 and (below) Peter and John "The Bull" Hayes catch their breath in the dressingroom after the 31-25 semi-final win the same year over Toulouse in the south of France.

Peter sizes up the Stade Francais pack during the quarter-final of the 2000 Heineken Cup at Thomond Park, which Munster won 27-10 on their way to the final in Twickenham.

Keith Wood, Gaillimh and Peter celebrate another European victory.

Ronan O'Gara celebrates Munster's famous six-point victory on French soil over Toulouse in the 2000 Heineken Cup semi-final and (right) Peter tackles Pat Lam of Northampton with some help from Peter Stringer in the 2000 final in Twickers that we lost by a single point.

John Langford and Peter take the long walk off the field in Twickers after the defeat by Northampton.

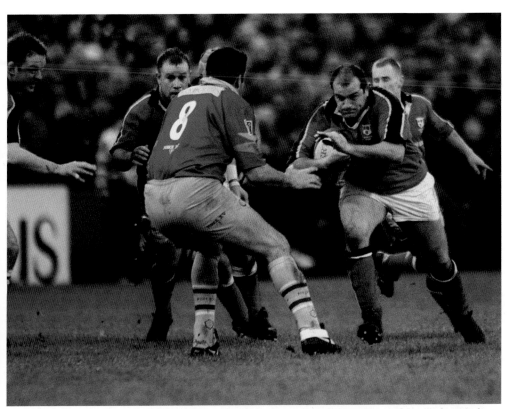

Munster and Castres became arch-rivals in the Heineken Cup, and here Peter takes on Thierry Labrousse in the 2001 campaign which ended with another disappointing one point defeat, this time by Stade Francais in the semi-final.

Peter breaks through the Harlequins defence in 2001.

Peter and Rob Henderson thank the Munster faithful who travelled to the south of France to witness the 25-17 Heineken Cup semi-final victory over Castres and (below) Peter celebrates with Gaillimh and Frankie Sheehan.

Peter breaks through the Castres defence a year earlier in 2001.

John Hayes, Frankie Sheehan and Peter prepare for an early scrum against Leicester in the 2002 Heineken Cup final at the Millennium Stadium in Cardiff and (below) Peter leaves the field for the last time close to the end of the 2002 Heineken Cup final in the Millennium Stadium.

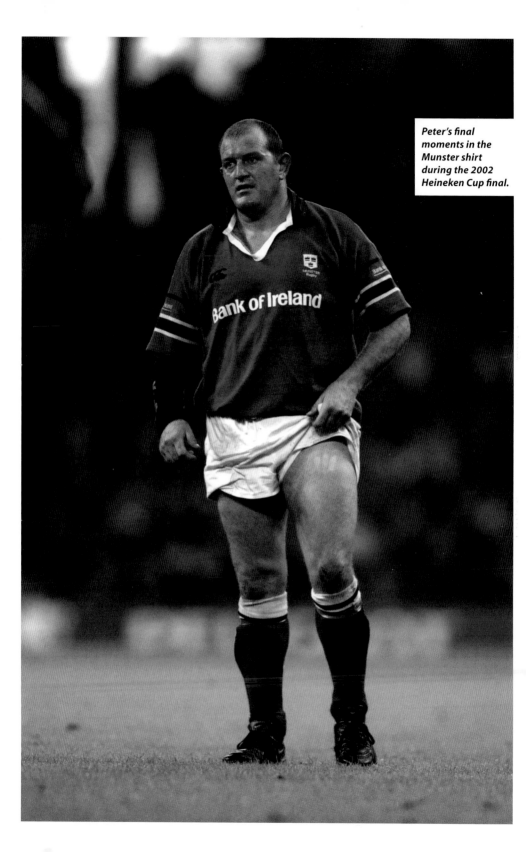

Peter's final moments in the Munster shirt during the 2002 Heineken Cup final.

John gave us huge options in the lineout as he was a natural jumper and a great asset to Munster. He became one of the boys very quickly. Just after he arrived, there was a team session in Kilkee. They left the pier on a few boats and they headed out to Donegal Point – where they had to jump overboard and swim home! Then they had to run five miles back to the pier! Peter's legs were bleeding from the friction of his rugby shorts when he got back home that night.

But, Langford found it harder to believe that, after the training, everyone went on the beer.

Even when Munster lost Fester at half-time in Bordeaux, the team didn't drop their pace, apart from John Hayes taking his time – apparently 17 seconds, on someone's watch, to get up from a tackle. But, The Bull rose in time to receive a pass from Dominic Crotty and went through their scrum-half to score a special try.

It was indeed our special day.

The Six Nations Championship began with Ireland having an awful lot to prove in the spring of 2000. Italy had joined in, so *Five* had become *Six*.

The Irish provinces were doing well, but the national team still had the monkey of the World Cup to shake off its back. Things did not start well. We played England in Twickenham and got slaughtered. It was a shocking match. Ireland did not turn up on the day and that evening in Jury's Hotel in Kensington, the Irish fans were venomous. They were spitting fire at the lads.

It was tough for Peter and the rest. Of course they knew they had to take the rough with the smooth when it came to their careers, but no team goes onto a pitch with the intention of playing badly. An angry supporter right in someone's face is also a difficult moment, especially when the player actually feels twice as disappointed, and four or five times more angry with himself, than the angry supporter!

We didn't know it at the time, but Clive Woodward had England on a fast and direct route to becoming world champions in 2003. They simply went through us for a short cut. It was 23-5 at half-time, and they were headed for a half century, and a record win over Ireland.

Our scrum did not have a good day. Peter, Fester and Wally got the brunt of it from Leonard, Greening and Vickery, but there was no stopping England anywhere on the field. Within three minutes of the restart Neil Back went over for the fourth of their six tries. At that stage, we finally began to stem the flow. And Gaillimh was called into the action to lend some old-hand support. He went over for a try, which meant that England's 32-point winning margin actually fell short of their 46-6 victory three years earlier. That was a small comfort.

Coming on top of our World Cup exit, the pressure was on the coach. But Gatty did not show it to the players. Instead he was relishing the future, he insisted, and decided to throw two new lads in for their first caps a fortnight later against Scotland. Ronan O'Gara and Peter Stringer were in for their Championship debuts – as was John Hayes, so the numbers from Munster were beginning to pile up.

Everyone, old and new, realized it was a make or break game. The front row led the way. Hayes, Keith Wood and Peter played out of their skins. The media had questioned whether The Bull could really scrummage? That foolishness was blown out of the water by him, as was the notion that Gaillimh's best days were long over. If we were in danger of heading into the history books for all the wrong reasons in Twickenham, Ireland was looking to be in history's good books this time. After 47 minutes we were on course for our biggest ever score in the Championship – eclipsing our 30-17 win over the Welsh four years before – and it looked like we might even better the country's biggest ever win, 24-0 over France in 1913. But the Scots denied us that by getting over for two tries late in the game.

ROG, however, of all people, and for a man who owned the rights to the word *confidence*, was nervy on his first big day, and was replaced by David Humphreys – but only after ROG had struck one touchline conversion, and had demonstrated definite glimpses of his brilliantly precise use of the boot. Stringer had some good moments too, but was equally uncertain beside him during the first 40 minutes. To be 13-10 in front at the end of the first-half was really some achievement, since the tension could have been cut with a knife. We were 10-0 down early on, but proceeded to score five of the very best tries, including one from another new boy, Shane Horgan.

It was obvious that there was a new breed of more ambitious Irish rugby players on display in Lansdowne Road that afternoon.

Ireland won 44-22. Kieron Dawson looked a world-beater in the back row, someone with amazing speed to the breakdown, and "Axel" Foley and Simon Easterby were quite phenomenal for the full 80 minutes.

The record victory for Ireland was not long coming – and the Italians were on the receiving end on their first Championship visit to Lansdowne Road.

The mix in the Irish team was something new.

There was the strong flow of Munster blood, more of it than anyone had experienced in a long time in a set of green jerseys. There was also the freshness and excellence of ROG. And there was Brian O'Driscoll, who had not yet become a brand name with three letters just yet! The nickname BOD was a couple of years away still.

In Paris, where Peter had extreme physical and emotional experiences, March 19 was an afternoon on which he gave perhaps his greatest all round performance in an Irish jersey and he deserved to cap it with a try, but was cruelly denied one. .

'The pressure will be on France... nobody expects us to win,' Fester told the world before the game. Indeed he was not the first Irish captain to utter such a potentially self-damning statement. Except, this time, Fester was kidding.

Ireland believed, fully, that they would win.

It helped, of course, that the French were decimated by injuries to a total of nine first choice players, and that their half-back pairing of Fabien Galthie and Christophe Lamaison were amongst the pile of crocks. It was still France in those famous blue jerseys, and it *looked* like France from the very start.

They almost got a try from their winger, David Bory in the opening 60 seconds, but Cedric Desbrosse's final pass was judged to have gone forward. Emile N'Tamack chipped into the corner and our defence just held out. They scored a try on the 30 minute mark, and Gerald Merceron was kicking ably, putting over two early penalties. There was no question of the home team rolling over for anyone.

However... the French were in trouble. Big trouble every time 21 years-old Brian O'Driscoll got the ball. His pace and crazy change of direction was bamboozling, and he went over for his first try halfway through the half.

France led 25-17 when O'Driscoll went over for his third try, picking up the loose ball once Peter Stringer had been flattened by Abdelatif Benazzi and racing through a gap without one French player landing a hand on him. There was one point between the teams.

The game was just about up, with three minutes left on the clock, when the French went over the top at a ruck 41 metres from their own posts. David Humphreys, who had once again come in for ROG, hit the ball hard and true.

Ireland 27, France 25.

Sweet, sweet relief, and relief more than joy in finally proving that such a huge object as the French team was not *immovable*, swept over the Irish team.

By God, did they celebrate that night in Paris.

Eddie O'Sullivan had joined the management team, and Peter would say that himself and Gatty complemented each other perfectly – Gatty quietly spoken, and Eddie more aggressive and intense at team meetings.

Eddie was also a great fan of the white board. He would spend so much time detailing moves on the board, and plotting the downfall of the opposition. Not that Peter cared too much about that.

'That information is for the backs,' Peter always insisted. 'If we don't get the ball to them... it makes no f****** difference what's written on any board!'

He tended to tune out during these sessions.

Peter and Eddie did have a good relationship throughout his time with Ireland, however, and when Gatty was shoved to one side and Eddie took over the reins, he had individual meetings with all of the players.

Peter had already decided that his time was almost up, before Eddie asked him at their "one on one" what he was thinking?

'What are your plans, Claw?' Eddie asked.

'I'll play until the end of this season... then I'll retire.' Peter told him.

Eddie nodded.

'The jersey's yours for the season!'

It was incredibly fair of Eddie, as another coach may have wanted to start giving new players some experience up front as quickly as possible once he had it confirmed that his loose head was counting down the days!

Mostly it was because Peter always delivered the goods on the pitch, that he had earned this respect. Though new members of the management team sometimes found "Claw is the Law" a bit of an adjustment for them.

Mike McGurn had to come to understand the Claw's ways. And when Dr Liam Hennessy was brought in to advise on fitness regimes, he too had to go on a learning curve regarding Peter's unique status in the camp. Liam, for instance, had introduced cryotherapy – basically ice therapy – that speeds up recovery time from muscle strain and injuries, to the Irish squad.

It meant going to Spala, in Poland, and spending time in a chamber that was essentially a deep freezer. Athletes from all over the world were benefiting from this new science. Dr Hennessy wanted the Irish rugby players to fast track their way back to full health as well.

The team was fingered for a week of cold therapy.

But Peter wanted the sun on his back instead.

At this stage in Peter's career he knew that what he needed was a family holiday and a break from training – so he discussed this with Gatty and Brian O'Brien, who both agreed that Peter could take holidays at this time instead of going to Spala. But Liam, who was earnest and extremely thorough in his job, and was respected by sportsmen of all shapes and sizes and disciplines, had difficulty with this. He expressed as much in a letter to Philip Browne in the IRFU. He also sent a copy to Peter.

Peter felt it was wrong that Liam found it necessary to go over the heads of the national coaches, particularly as Liam was a new addition to the Irish management set up.

So Peter wrote back to Philip Browne, clearly outlining that all employees were entitled to a day and half of holidays for each month worked – therefore, he had a minimum of 18 days holidays due to him. He also pointed out that he had not taken any holidays that year – had trained every day, had matches at the weekend, and that the *rest* day after the match was a day spent travelling and this did *not* constitute a day off.

'I have not had a day off all year,' Peter stated.

He also pointed out that after discussions with his coach and team manager, a holiday was indeed something that all parties had agreed to at this stage of the season. Peter sent a copy to Liam, and the Clohessy family duly set off on holidays.

'It's too late to give ice treatment... to a dinosaur,' said Gaillimh, summing up the whole brouhaha perfectly.

While Peter earned this respect, he did not readily grant it to others.

It had to be earned.

That was his firm belief right through his rugby career.

Opponents were not granted his respect unless they doubly earned it. This meant that he had no fear of *bigger* opponents – in fact, the greater their reputation, the greater was the motivation for him to bring them back down to earth.

That was not just the case with individuals. It included his view of whole rugby teams as well. Even a team as big and brash, and brilliant, as the South Africans! And he introduced himself to them the following November.

The entire South African squad was in the middle of some drills at Lansdowne Road. They were in over-time, and Ireland were waiting to take to the field. Everyone was waiting when Peter came out of the dressingroom.

The South Africans were showing no signs of moving on.

Finally, they stopped what they were doing. But they did not start walking off the field. They got into a team huddle. And they stayed in the huddle...

'F*** this,' Peter remarked to everybody and nobody in particular, and marched onto the field.

He did not stop until he reached the South Africans and broke into the middle of their huddle.

'Right lads... yer time is up!'

'Move on...!'

If they weren't going to respect their hosts, then Peter was prepared to teach them a basic set of manners all on his own!

The first Six Nations Championship definitely brought Ireland out from beneath the bottom of the pile, though it ended with a million pound defeat!

In a move from the top of the PR drawer, it was announced by one business that one million pounds would be handed to the first Irish player to score four tries against Wales in Lansdowne Road. It wasn't likely to happen. Rob Henderson did not get his first pass until the second half, and Brian O'Driscoll had an equally quiet afternoon having to live mostly off scraps. Missed tackles were the story of the game. And there was a curious lack of aggression, and this was not unveiled until the game was long on and the Welsh held an 11-point lead.

It was amazing in itself that Ireland grabbed a 19-17 advantage. However, two penalties from Neil Jenkins in the last 10 minutes left the craziest and most fulfilling Championship that Irish supporters had experienced in a decade, engulfed by a sense of anti-climax.

One newspaper claimed Ireland were now top of Europe's "Second Division". Better than anyone else, but not really in the same league as the English and the French! Even after we'd beaten them!

Unfortunately, it was true.

Peter, disappointed or not, always had immense patience after games, and he was swamped by a crowd of autograph hunters after the defeat by Wales.

They were mostly kids.

It turned out one of the kids was Peter's own!

Luke became very upset after the game as Peter signed autographs for other children. He hadn't seen his Dad for two weeks, and when he joined Peter on the pitch after the game he expected his Dad's full attention.

Luke came with me to that game, and I was really glad to be able to send him onto the pitch to Peter, as I knew Luke would distract him from the pain of the loss.

He wasn't at all happy to have to share him with others. And it was hard for Peter to explain to a six year-old why that was necessary in public.

Munster, like Ireland, were also thinking so very differently at the turn of the Millennium. Everything that had come before, in the previous century, was old hat. And in the final months of that century – in the opening rounds of the Heineken Cup – Munster had demonstrated how serious their intentions were about taking charge of Europe in 2000.

We had Saracens, Colomiers and Pontypridd in our group pool, and we were making short enough work of the lot of them. When the group games were finished we had won five out of six games, we had scored 19 tries, and we had a points difference of 56. We also had real mettle, as shown in coming home from Vicarage Road with a 35-34 win over Saracens.

The single defeat had come in the final game, when Munster were already safely booked into the quarter-finals, at Sardis Road. We'd beaten Pontypridd 32-10 in Musgrave Park, but in their place, we got a reception we knew only too well ourselves.

'It was like playing Munster, in Munster,' stated Declan Kidney afterwards, '... and Munster came out on top.'

We had gone down 38-36.

We had led 36-31 with four minutes left on the clock. They threw everything they had at us for those four minutes, and then in the first minute of injury-time they stretched the Munster defence and stretched it further, until their centre John Colderley got over the line. Peter Stringer was clearly between the ball and the ground but the Italian referee felt that justice of some type should be delivered to the home team for their guts and glory performance.

We'd still earned home ground advantage in the last eight against Stade Francais. Tickets were at a premium. The Branch had only 2,200 tickets for sale to the public after clubs had received the lion's share.

Some of those tickets were on sale in Gleeson's Sports Scene 10 days before the game. On the Monday night, at 20 minutes to midnight, the first man turned up with his sleeping bag and a thermos full of coffee. By 7.30 a.m. there were over 1,000 people outside the shop door.

The owner's ticket allocation was slightly over 500.

Steve Gleeson handed out cloakroom tickets with the exact numbers – and told everyone else that there were no more. But very few people budged.

Most supporters felt they should hang around.

In case of some miracle?

After the game, Stade's Richard Pool-Jones spoke aloud of his team's cosmopolitan mix of eight different nationalities.

Gaillimh was unimpressed.

'We've got a lot of lads from all sorts of different places ourselves,' he stated with a straight face to his opponent.

'Australia... Limerick, Cork, Tipperary, Clare, Kerry...

'All sorts of strange places!' confirmed Gaillimh.

The winning plan was enacted with perfection.

Eddie Halvey was picked to target Stade's nervy throws to the front and the middle of the lineout, and John Langford was there to do the rest. Kidney wanted Stade's running game stopped... stone dead!

Done!

And it was decided that we should ruck the French pack off the field.

Also done!

Gaillimh won the toss and we played into the strong breeze.

Before Stade knew it, they were 12-0 down and victory looked a million miles away. Anthony Horgan got the opening try after a chase and catch by Dominic Crotty. Axel was carrying the ball forward and losing none of it. He and Peter also had a role in the second try. Peter made some hard yards for a fourth recycle, ROG dummied to Fester but fed Crotty, and he stepped between Fabrice Landreau and Diego Dominguez before skillfully handing off Conrad Stoltz.

With The Bull having to retire after 23 minutes with a cut, Peter had to move back to tight head, with Marcus Horan coming onto the loose side.

The second half commenced with Halvey hitting Pool-Jones right from the kick-off with a shuddering tackle that sent the Stade No.8 high into the air, and into reverse. The tone for the next 40 minutes was set. The game ended 27-10.

Munster got the worst semi-final draw imaginable.

Toulouse, in Bordeaux!

The last time Munster had met the French giants, three years before, in Toulouse, they had been taught a lesson in... everything about the game of rugby.

Toulouse 60, Munster 19.

In the season about to end, Toulouse had already won 17 of their 21 competitive matches. Bath had beaten them in their group when Toulouse were already through to the quarters. In France, they had won five of the last six Championships, and in the previous six months, only Brive had beaten them.

Toulouse looked *unbeatable*.

And they had one of the finest coaches in the world. Guy Noves was Declan Kidney's ultimate opponent, but the Frenchman let his mask slip a little bit when he told the media that Munster were a little bit of a mystery to him.

'I don't know this team very well,' he commented the week before, and then making a foolish miscalculation, 'I'm very happy to be playing Munster who are, in a way... the Irish team.'

Sure, there were players wearing both red and green that season, but Munster were a vastly different proposition to Ireland in April of 2000. Munster were not prepared to sit at the top of any "Second Division" in Europe.

The game was three-quarters way through when Mike Mullins returned from the sin bin after a deliberate knock-on. Toulouse were winning 18-17 in the tightest of contests, but, vitally, we had held them scoreless for 10 minutes with only 14 men on the field.

That was a declaration of intent that even mighty Toulouse could not ignore. They had tried to pulverize us for that 10 minutes, but in crash ball after crash ball, Munster had no shortage of volunteers to throw themselves in the wall of the defence. It was Munster who then moved up a gear. In a breathtaking end-to-end move with the ball passed from eight different pairs of hands, ROG took the final pass from Dominic Crotty and went over. Minutes later Jason Holland intercepted and went in for the decider.

'It's unbelievable,' Peter told the media after the game, deliriously happy and trying to make perfect sense of what had just happened, '... but we always believed in ourselves.'

Even more incredible considering Fester had to retire injured at half-time. We'd taken the lead in the first-half, letting Toulouse know that we were targeting a surprise victory, when John Hayes had rumbled over for a try. However, five penalties from Michel Marfaing allowed them to go in at half-time with a 15-11 lead. They had not broken our try line, and that would remain the case until the very end of the afternoon – their try was a consolation in injury-time from Jerome Cazalbou.

Declan Kidney was back to his teaching days after the game, working out some maths. He reckoned there were 2,500 Munster supporters at the game. He guessed it had cost them at least £400 each to get to Bordeaux and get home again. 'That's between £1million and £1.5million spent... to come down here and get behind this team.'

Peter and the lads were told about the likes of one supporter who had hopped onto a motorbike with a friend outside The Hurler's Bar in Limerick on the Thursday afternoon. The bike was outside the Stade Lescure on Saturday evening as the team started their slightly more comfortable journey home.

The team shared a jumbo jet with their own supporters.

They were also sharing a few well deserved drinks, as their coach was still doing his sums. Kidney had counted 28 and a half cases of 1.5 litres bottles of water... all gone over the three days the team spent in Bordeaux.

He said he did not know the weight loss of the entire group, but he imagined most of the lads had lost half a stone.

Peter was also £15 lighter when he arrived at Shannon Airport on the Saturday night. There were 1,000 men, women and children there to welcome the team home. This was another first. Peter and the lads were shocked by this display of support but it heralded the start of many occasions when Munster's followers showed their magnificent loyalty.

But when the people scattered, there were two clamped cars, one Peter's, and one belonging to the team doc, Mickey Griffin.

Northampton, on the Sunday, had needed to work right into injury time to finish off Llanelli in the other semi-final. They were 19-9 down at half-time. They also survived a late siege, and had somehow managed to set up a winning penalty kick. They just got through, 31-28 to the final in Twickenham.

They had "home" advantage, but Munster were bringing, pretty much, everyone from home with them to the game to even things out a little. The Branch sold 18,700 tickets for the game, 13,000 of them in Limerick. More Munster fans were mustering all over Ireland and Britain. More than 70 flights from Dublin, Cork and Limerick were scheduled to arrive at London's four airports in the 48 hours leading into the game.

Officials at Twickers were expecting 64,000 people at the final – they also anticipated that Munster fans would out-number their rivals by three-to-one.

Northampton were a different proposition to Toulouse.

Unlike the French team who had a trophy-room filled to the rafters, the Saints had never won a trophy in their 120 years of existence. Another difference was their size. Their entire pack was weighing in 16 stones heavier than the Toulouse eight – between 10 and 11 pounds heavier per man than Munster.

They also had Paul Grayson, who equalled Ronan O'Gara when it came to controlling a game with his boot!

In the "Hunger Game", therefore, the English team were also our equal – and destiny was something which both teams felt was on their side!

It was a blustery morning in London.

By the mid-afternoon the wind had died a little bit, but the surface of the field was greasy, and ideal conditions for a big juggernaut pack.

Peter Stringer and Axel were having to make the most of hurried possession, and their leader on the field, Pat Lam was orchestrating the whole game, it seemed, with complete authority.

It was obvious that Munster needed a bit of luck.

But the referee, Joel Dume of France was obliterating hope of that coming our way anytime soon – and his harshest decision of all was to sin bin Gaillimh in the final quarter of the game. It was clear to see that it should have been our scrum under the posts when Dom Malone fumbled his quick tap. Gaillimh pulled at him, and was out of the game until the 76th minute.

Worryingly, from early on, it had the feel of a game that might be the "one that got away". Peter sensed that Declan Kidney needed to make one or two bold decisions to turn things back in our direction. He also felt that Kidney had lost the game in the team meeting room at the hotel before the game, as he got the players too emotional – and Munster were halfway through the match before they were *themselves*.

More than that, Peter was adamant that Kidney should have brought on Killian Keane for ROG.

The opening 13 minutes were torrid. Nothing had prepared the lads for Northampton owning the ball for that long, but they did – having a 70:30 ratio of possession and spending 98% of that time in our half of the field. Somehow, we gathered our senses, and by half-time we led 8-6. But we would not get another score in the second-half. Jason Holland had struck a perfect dropped goal from nothing really, and Fester had been sent up the wing by ROG's skip pass. Fester got past his opposite number, Federico Mendez and support came to secure ruck ball. ROG played quick ball and David Wallace had a 20 metres run to the line. He took Alan Bateman's tackle and got over.

A kick to touch by ROG was blocked down eight minutes into the second-half by Don Mackinnon. We were penalized for being offside. Grayson put them back into the lead.

We had our chances. A sweet transfer from Fester put ROG through a gap and he was hauled down. We turned down the chance of a possible three points and went for a lineout maul against their pack. We came away with nothing, and ROG was wide with a penalty three minutes from the end, from close to the touchline, when the ball was blown fractionally off course.

After the final whistle, Declan took the team into a huddle. *The Fields of Athenry* was echoing around the stadium. Kidney told the lads they should feel proud of who they were and what they had done.

If you give something your best shot... then you have to accept the ending, he told them.

Hold yourselves up, he said.

The same way we accept victory, we will accept defeat, he ordered.

The huddle broke and the team stood in a circle in the middle of the pitch, feeling disorientated, and trying to make sense of what had just happened.

We had lost.

But the whole of Twickenham was flooded with chants of 'Munster... Munster' as though we had finally landed the greatest prize of them all. Peter's strongest feeling was that the team had let their supporters down.

Luke went onto the pitch, and climbed the steps with his Dad as he collected his runners-up medal.

It was the 60th anniversary of Dunkirk.

The retreat from London, on this occasion, was vast as well. The team was tired and bruised from the agonizing defeat when they made their way onto the balcony at Shannon Airport at 11.0 p.m.

Gaillimh held the microphone and he apologized.

'NO... NO...NO,' the huge crowd shouted back at him.

Gaillimh understood that the team's magnificent supporters did not see a shattering defeat, but, instead, thought of the 9-8 result as nothing more than a delay.

Right, said Gaillimh in response.

He told Tom Tierney, our reserve scrum-half to get up to the front and deliver a message to the supporters below.

Stand Up and Fight never sounded more reassuring than it did in the pitch darkness that Saturday night.

Frankie.
'You were damned unlucky to be around the same time as Fester.
'You were a workhorse... and a leader.'

– Peter

CHAPTER 20

Some of the team had to get back on their feet double quick

Ireland had a summer tour of Argentina, the USA and Canada, and Peter had agreed with Gatty that he would go to Argentina and the States, but he would not go on to Canada – a rest was what he needed after the season just ending.

On that tour he was called to task by the kangaroo court, a rare enough happening, since Peter was normally the one hauling others up to be quickly condemned. He was ordered to name the members of the touring party that he had just spent the previous two weeks with?

It was an impossibility!

In two weeks Peter could not have filed away that many names, even if he was living with them 24 hours a day, but he didn't do too badly. He was making a decent fist of it, until he came to "T-Bone".

The court would not accept that "T-Bone" was a man's name.

Full name... please, the court ordered.

Peter hadn't a clue.

He passed on that one... and named his next team-mate... "Topper".

This too was refused by the court.

How the f*** would I know the name of a new full-back... and he from Leinster? Peter thought to himself.

Peter also fell a third time.

For not knowing the names of his three teammates – Tyrone Howe, James Topping and Peter McKenna – Peter had to strip off…

Then he was told to sit in a bucket of ice.

In the Argentina game, Fester took a knock on the head. It was coming up to half-time when Peter heard Fester shouting something at him.

'WHO ARE WE… PLAYING?'

'Argentina!' Peter responded.

'You stupid f*****,' he added affectionately.

Fester was not finished with the conversation.

'Who is winning?' Fester asked.

'Not us,' was Peter's reply.

There had been a kick ahead by Ireland, and the ball was just touched by an Argentinian player, who played Peter onside.

The South African referee, Andrew Watson penalized Peter for being offside. At the post-match function the referee made his way over and apologized to Peter.

'A lot of f****** good that is to us,' Peter told him.

Argentina won the opening game of our tour of The Americas, 34-23. But we bounced back to win 83-3 against the US when Mike Mullins scored three tries in a 10-try haul in Manchester, New Hampshire – but, one week later, in Fletchers Fields in Ontario, we struggled to a 27-27 draw with Canada.

It was not, all told, one of Ireland's more successful tours.

For the US game Eimear Danaher and myself flew to Boston, and Gallimh and Peter hired a car and came to collect us. It was holiday mode for the lads really as Gatty was using the tour to give the newer guys a run.

The morning of the match Eimear and myself were heading to a nearby shopping paradise in Kittery. Peter was not happy about me driving over there, even though I argued that I had driven in America before, many times when he wasn't with me.

He wasn't playing that day against the States, he was on water boy duty and so he insisted on driving us – we timed the journey on the way down, and left in plenty of time to get back for the match. What we didn't factor in was that we had left in the early morning when there was no traffic, and on our return we hit peak time and traffic was totally jammed!

We were getting closer and closer to kick off time, and there was no sign of the stadium. We finally ran into the ground five minutes after the game had started.

The team had decided, when there was no sign of their "water boy", that they would meet him with complete silence. Nobody would talk to him.

He felt badly enough turning up late, but felt a right b******* altogether when they all ignored him.

And he was up in front of the kangaroo court again.

The charge?

Going off on his own little holiday!

Back home, the November Internationals had Japan and South Africa back-to-back. We totted up another 10 tries against the Japanese, when Peter also got in on the act in a game which marked his 40th cap for Ireland – though the back's coach, Eddie O'Sullivan said they only *allowed* him that because it was his big day, otherwise they wouldn't have given him the ball.

Martin Murphy of the IRFU, who was always very kind to us, invited Luke to be the team mascot that day against Japan. He walked out onto the pitch with Peter ahead of the team.

Briano's wife, Olive was beside me in the stand.

She turned to me with tears in her eyes. 'Isn't that a fantastic picture... you must be so proud?'

'I suppose so,' I replied, but I wondered why Olive found it so emotional and I didn't?

Time must have made me sentimental though, because now that Luke has just turned 21 years old, when I look at that famous photo on my office wall, I smile and feel an immense sense of pride at the expression on Luke's face as he looks up into his Dad's eyes as *Amhran na BhFiann* was played.

A week later we lost 28-18 to the South Africans.

***

For the last two years of his playing career, Peter valued every single day he had with Munster. The atmosphere within the camp was truly remarkable. To a man, they were bonded. No man complained about another man, ever!

The strength of their commitment to each other was so perfectly measured that it didn't matter that the coach wasn't one of the boys. The only person I heard Peter complain about was Declan Kidney.

Peter continued to struggle with Declan's half-coach, half-teacher presence – and, in my opinion, Declan also struggled to figure Peter out. It did appear that Declan admired Peter, but he seemed equally frustrated at not being able to control him like a teacher would one of his pupils.

Peter had left school at 15, while Declan was a schoolteacher first and last, and an exceptional coach in between. He had even started coaching colleges rugby at 19 years of age and when he graduated he returned to Presentation Brothers in Cork where he won four successive Munster Junior Cups and then four Munster Senior Cups in five years. He had coached Ireland Schools to a Triple Crown, and Ireland Under-19s to a World Cup win.

Sometimes, he struggled to differentiate between boys and men!

The Munster team was staying in The Burlington Hotel one weekend and, as usual, they had a designated team room in which they had their meetings, watched movies, and generally hung out in privacy. The evening before check out they had ordered pizzas to the room in which there happened to be no bins, even though someone had pointed this out already to the hotel staff.

At check out time one of the managers of the hotel complained to Kidney about the state that the lads had left the team room in. And Kidney's instinctive schoolteacher response was to tell the lads in no uncertain manner that the state of the room was unacceptable.

Peter, however, was having none of this nonsense.

He was outraged on two counts!

One – how dare the hotel treat a valuable customer in such a manner, especially when it was their own fault for not providing bins when requested!

Two – how dare Declan treat him and his teammates like a crowd of children who misbehaved!

Peter stormed up to hotel reception and asked for the Duty Manager. He proceeded to tell him that it was their job to provide bins, and it was their job to clean the room. And in light of the poor service he informed the manager that he was 'f****** lucky to be getting paid by Munster at all'.

Declan and Peter were simply not always on the same page.

Though, even Declan was brought into the "family' at times, especially when his boys would surprise him.

As Gaillimh and Peter did during a game against Connacht, in Galway, when the two old men of the team did indeed act like schoolchildren. Peter explained afterwards that he just felt a bit 'giddy' during the game. And he couldn't help himself.

Gaillimh was running back to join play and, as he passed by, Peter heel-flicked him and sent him flying for about 15 yards.

The two of them cracked up.

And when they got into a lineout a couple of minutes later and took one look at one another, they cracked up again. Declan was definitely not impressed – two of his senior players with tears of laughter running down their faces in a lineout?

He stood in the middle of the dressingroom floor once everyone trooped back in, and had his hands on his hips.

'If I ever see one of my players heel flick another player again,' he began, '… especially one of his own players…

In fairness, Declan could not finish his own sentence.

Instead of promising what he would do, he left the room laughing

Spring of 2001 was a lost opportunity for Ireland.

The outbreak of Foot and Mouth possibly cost us a Grand Slam. The Six Nations started bang on track with an anticipated win over Italy in Rome, 41-22. And since this was the Irish team's first time to play Italy in the Eternal City in the Championship, they were invited to go and see Pope John Paul II at The Vatican. Brian O'Brien had the team up at the crack of dawn.

The management was all ready and very excited to be having a private audience with the Pope – Peter, as I could have guessed, wasn't too pushed one way or the other, but he was soon weak with laughter when the team discovered the *private audience* turned out to be 'us… and 5,000 others'.

They had also arrived much too early, so Peter was in and out regularly with Hendo, who would score a hat-trick of tries against the Italians, for a smoke.

Each time they left "Briano" was having palpitations in case they were late back. For one who wasn't bothered whether he was there or not, it was typical for Peter to land right behind the left shoulder of Pope John Paul in the group photo. In one of the shots the doc, Mickey Griffin is looking taller than usual and a little uncomfortable, due to Peter giving him a massive wedgie as the photo was being taken!

They weren't all irreverent though, and Rala had spent many days practicing a Polish saying that he had picked up from some Polish guys who were painting his house at the time. He had it off to a tee.

And he had rehearsed it to Peter many times. When he finally met the Pope he was star struck and couldn't manage to open his mouth. As Plan B, Rala decided that he would kiss the Pope's ring, and Fester reckoned he knocked a couple of Cardinals out of the way before the security guards intercepted him.

I would end up with fond memories of that trip to Rome. It was my first time, and as well as having fun sight-seeing with Francine Mullins and Nicola Wood I got to have dinner the evening of the game, all alone with my husband.

Meeting the Holy Father had not changed Peter. He was sin-binned late in the game, but he also picked up an injury and decided not to go to the team dinner – we enjoyed room service instead.

Two wins on the trot were recorded against France a fortnight later, and the manner in which we handled them in front of our own crowd showed that Gatty had built a team which was good enough to fight it out with the French and the English for the Championship and, who knew, perhaps even win a Grand Slam.

Three of the best penalties from ROG settled everyone in the first-half. We led 9-3. But instead of waiting for the French to throw something special at us, it was Ireland who went for the kill once the teams were back on the field. ROG kicked another penalty after four minutes, and then in a sparkling 10-minute spell Brian O'Driscoll bolted down the left flank for a try, ROG converted, and ROG kicked another penalty.

There was a confidence, and a solid composure, about the performance – even though the French got in for two late tries from Fabien Pelous and Philippe Bernat-Salles. We were never in fear of losing.

And 22-15, and two wins out of two, had Gatty aiming higher.

But, suddenly, we were sitting out the Championship when Foot and Mouth closed down all sporting events in the country for several months, and put a stop to large groups travelling in and out of the country also.

Our visits to Murrayfield and the Millenniun Stadium, and the chance to really have a crack at England at Lansdowne Road, were postponed until the autumn.

Luckily, Munster already had plenty of good work done and dusted by the time of the "close down". We had been grouped with Bath, Newport and Castres in the Heineken Cup – and had won five out of the six, losing to Bath away. But a double victory over another proud French team had the team's confidence bubbling.

We beat them 32-29 in their home ground, even though they flew out of the box and were winning 20-6 early on. Nobody panicked or fussed on the field, and ROG masterminded two beauties of tries for Anthony Horgan and David Wallace.

We landed in Castres on a charter flight, and as we disembarked we came across French officials with a table filled with sandwiches. As I walked down the steps of the plane, an official asked… 'sandwiches?'

'No thanks… we brought our own,' one of the lads in front of me replied. We soon understood that they were confiscating the packed lunches from Ireland because of Foot and Mouth.

We needed to beat Castres again, in Thomond Park, to make certain of a home quarter-final and were perfectly business-like, without being flash or particularly brilliant, in winning 21-11.

We were almost on first name terms with the French club, as we would meet them again three times the following season – and finish up winning two games to one!

We rolled through our group, in truth, and Munster were the team to beat in everyone's eyes.

Even the supporters were getting a little carried away.

In Newport on a cold January evening a chant started in the crowd and grew and grew, until even Peter looked up at the stand.

'Who let the Claw out... who... who, who?'

A portion of our supporters were mimicking the hit song of that year... *Who Let The Dogs Out?* Peter, I noticed, gave a wry smile.

But I could tell he wanted it to stop!

Biarritz brought a big pack with them to Limerick for the quarter-final at the end of January. They were Northampton's size, and spelled trouble.

The game turned into a try fest, a good old fashioned slugging contest until one team was left standing. They scored the first try on seven minutes, attacking the short side on a ruck outside our 22, when Christophe Milheres touched down. Four minutes later, ROG threw out a long skip pass, Alan Quinlan caught the ball spectacularly off his toes and Axel was left one-on-one with their winger, Bernat-Salles. It was Axel's first of three tries in the next hour.

But Biarritz' second try came on 15 minutes when Stuart Legg went over in the corner, and it was 2-1 in tries to them at half-time.

Seven minutes after the restart Mike Mullins took a short ball from ROG, straightened perfectly and crashed between two defenders. The ball was recycled twice. Quinny saw a number advantage to us and threw a long pass out to Gaillimh. He set up Axel for the corner. Two tries each.

Fifteen minutes later John Kelly made a mini-break, and collected his own chip. The ball was recycled. ROG dummied and raced through a gap. The pack drove on and the ball was worked back five metres from their line. Axel squeezed over in the corner to make it 3-2.

ROG was kicking spectacularly and even though Biarritz stormed through our lines for two more tries in the last 10 minutes, and won the try fest 4-3, we had already carved out a winning lead. We were four points up with minutes remaining. ROG brought daylight between the teams. It was 38-29, and Gaillimh summed it up by saying it takes a great team to come to Thomond Park and score four tries, and it takes an even greater team to concede those four tries and still win!

'I'm good friends with Peter,' John Connolly informed the media. 'He's going to send me over some Munster tapes, and that's good… that'll help…

'And I'm going to send him a law book in return!'

The draw for the semi-finals had been made in The Sugar Club, in Dublin – Leicester, Gloucester, Stade Francais and Munster, and we were ball number three. And we came out last. The ball before us was Stade.

We had another trip to France to prepare for in April, but the French had three months to smell revenge for their defeat in the quarter-finals the season before. And John Connolly, our old friend, and Peter's old coach from Queensland, had a big smile on his face – and all the time in the world to start plotting!

Eimear and myself decided to make a trip of it for the semi and John kindly offered us his apartment in Paris. We flew to Lille, met John and collected the key, and headed to Paris for two days of shopping.

We returned the morning of the game.

Times had changed. Peter may now have been respected by the game's authorities, but his wife was also being treated royally – Pat Geraghty was with the team as Munster Press Officer and he couldn't have been nicer, insisting on organising a lift to the match for us.

John Connolly was a happy man all week. He made light of the fact that he spoke no French, but insisted that if he spoke very slowly there was a chance that half of his team might understand what he was saying. He joked that Stade had not been able to even win the toss in Limerick the year before.

Only a man so extremely confident could have been that happy.

On our side, Declan Kidney was admitting that the team had unfinished business in Europe after losing the 2000 final by the slenderest of margins, but Munster had some problems. Quinny was injured and Donnacha O'Callaghan was coming in for his European debut, David Wallace hadn't played in nine weeks since Ireland had played France, Axel had played only one and a half games in that same period of time, Peter Stringer two and a half games, ROG three times.

It was not ideal.

Also, the pitch in the Stade Lille Metropole had been described in one newspaper as a "sodden pudding'. The good news was that there were 8,000 Munster fans in the place! One of the charter flights even took in Farranfore Airport to pick up 100 Kerry supporters!

Mudbaths were not to the team's liking.

In the previous 12 months we had gone down twice in similar slippery circumstances, to Northampton and Bath, and from the start we struggled to control our ball in Lille. We handed possession to Stade a dozen times exactly from our own lineouts and scrums – but we still had the winning of the game.

ROG was left to rue three penalty misses, though nobody could blame him. One was into a strong wind, one was from almost the halfway line, and another did seem to curl inside the far upright before gingerly been declared wide by the touch judges. ROG, nevertheless, still had the courage to step up and nail his last two penalties.

We also were denied a perfectly legitimate and brilliantly executed try from John O'Neill, which inexplicably the touch judge, Steve Lander ruled against. Those points, with 30 minutes remaining, would have been like extra fuel to our pack. It would have brought us to within two points, 16-14, and if ROG had kicked the conversion we would have been level. We had the wind at our backs in that second-half – and we stopped them from getting a single score in that 40 minutes.

Lander did put his hand on his heart in the 24 hours following – but as Peter always liked to say, 'f*** all good that is to us now!'

'I felt that the ball had gone into touch in goal,' Lander explained, '... and that it was not a try. If I got it wrong, as it appears I did… I am sorry!'

There was no official in the sky with a monitor for the Heineken Cup in 2001. With no TMO, Munster had to live with Lander's decision, and get on with winning the game the hard way.

We were 16-6 down at half-time after Cliff Mytton crossed for a try in the 35th minute, and we needed every little thing to go our way in the second-half, instead of meeting such cruel luck over and over again.

A one point defeat was excruciating. Anything but a one point defeat – and 16-15 was just too close to the bone as a reminder of the Heineken Cup that had fallen through our hands the previous season.

It was the end of the road for John Langford. He confessed that nothing in his long career in two hemispheres had prepared him for such intense disappointment. Peter said he would do one more year. But there was a fear that lads on the fringes of the team, Jeremy Staunton and Donncha O'Callaghan, might look for opportunities elsewhere.

Once again, the lap of the pitch after it was all over was something that every last man felt in his heart could not be avoided.

All Peter wanted to do was to retreat to the dressingroom and bury his head with everyone else, but they owed it to their supporters to thank them.

Everyone was in a state of complete shock.

I hung around to meet Peter, instead of getting on the supporters' bus and making my way to the airport. This proved to be a big mistake. When Eimear and I left a deserted stadium we quickly realized that we were in the middle of no man's land.

We wandered the streets, hoping to find a taxi – and we bumped into Donal Lenihan doing the same. We were all rushing for the same flight, so when we found a taxi first, we pleaded with the driver to let the lads jump in with us.

It was a strange coincidence.

This was the year of another Lions Tour and everybody understood that Peter was strongly in the running. Donal was manager of the Lions, with Graham Henry as coach. Peter was playing some of his best rugby ever, even though he didn't play particularly well against Stade earlier that same day.

The Lions squad was due to be announced after the semi-final.

'I'll get you to the airport, Donal... seeing as how you'll be getting Peter into the Lions!' I joked.

The procedure at the time was that the Lions' management would, by midnight on the Sunday before the squad was announced, ring those who were in contention for a place but had not made it!

It was 11.55 p.m. and Peter still hadn't got a call.

He thought that Donal and Henry may have overlooked his bad display in Lille, but then, on the stroke of midnight, the phone rang.

It was "Mannix"... Donal Lenihan.

He explained that because of his bad day out in the semi-final Peter wouldn't be going on the tour to Australia. This was Peter's third time missing out on the biggest honour in the game but, in truth, Peter never massively desired to go on a Lions tour.

'Of all the guys,' Donal said in an interview a couple of weeks later, 'I probably feel more sorry for him. There's no question he should have been selected in '93, and in '97 he was selected and couldn't make it.

'Now he was as close... as close can be.'

Again, as Peter would say... 'F*** all good...!'

The selection had 18 English men, which was fair enough, but it was inexplicable that 10 Welsh also made it through compared to just six Irish Lions! Ireland had won five out of their last six Championship games, and even though the Foot and Mouth debacle had stopped the team in its tracks – and also hurt Munster's preparation for Stade Francais – it was a questionable party that was finally assembled.

Luckily, for the Lions' management, they had the sense not to overlook Brian O'Driscoll who duly lit up a losing tour.

'The Bull.
'So many great memories, thank you!
'When you begged me to go loose head in South
Africa was one... and then there was the more
worrying time when you nearly got Gaillimh
and myself shot outside a diner in America...
because you called an African American Macy
Hayes because she was as big as you!
'She was going to stick a cap in you're a**
boy!'

— Peter

CHAPTER 21

In August 2001, Peter and his new business partners opened Peter Clohessy's Bar at Howley's Quay, and a few months later the Sin Bin Night club was unveiled. So for the last year of his rugby career, Peter went back to double-jobbing.

The bar opened at just the right time – Limerick was booming, and Munster were the uncrowned kings of Europe.

There was no problem filling the three sections of the big premises, and his mainly silent business partners were thrilled with the instant success. Like everything Peter does, he gave it his all, learning the tricks of the trade in record time, and he managed the 60-plus staff without any great fuss. At one point he reckoned there must have been someone standing in the main street of Bangladesh with a sign that said, "Hiring at Peter Clohessy's" because only people from there were applying for work! Despite cultural and language problems Peter was still able to train his new staff, perhaps a testimony to his time with the Turks in Russia!

Shortly after the opening in September, it was time to complete the Six Nations matches that had been postponed in the spring.

The opening game to Scotland cost Ireland a Grand Slam as we lost 32-10 – no doubt about it, the summer break had a lot to answer for. But Murrayfield was also, without question, not our cup of tea. We'd now lost there 38-10, 30-13 and 32-10 on our last three visits.

Next up was Wales in Cardiff. We hammered them 36-6. Trevor Brennan was back, which always made Peter happy. He liked Trevor's passion.

When Trevor ran onto the field to replace Mick Galwey, Peter made it his business to have a quick word with him.

'Now Trevor... no penalties!'

Ten yards later, as he was walking by Fester, he received more advice.

'Cool and calm Trevor... no penalties!'

If Ireland weren't going to win the Grand Slam, then we were certainly going to do our best to make sure the English didn't win it instead. Going into their second International in eight days, the huge question was would the team believe in itself right to the very last minute?

We did, emphatically. This was a very good English team that had Jonny Wilkinson, Jason Leonard, Simon Shaw, Mike Catt, and Will Greenwood in their number, but they were missing Lawrence Dallaglio and Martin Johnson.

Ireland won 20-14, and the fans loved it.

That year I had decided to train as a Reiki master teacher with Francine, Mike Mullins' wife. I had completed the earlier levels and was taking to my new vocation like the proverbial duck to water.

I loved doing something for myself.

In a hectic life that revolved around everyone else, my time at class in Francine's was precious, and Peter knew never to phone me while I was there. I do believe that there is no such thing as coincidence, and that synchronicity is at play at crucial times in our lives. Life is a classroom, where our biggest challenges are our greatest opportunities for growth. But we don't notice that growth has occurred until a situation presents itself and you notice yourself reacting in a way that you knew you wouldn't have before.

However, it was still a surprise when just after my important Master teacher class, we were putting the kettle on in Francince's kitchen when she played her voice messages – and I heard Peter looking for me. This was very unusual as he was in Irish camp in Northern Ireland at the time and he would never call me at Francine's.

I rang back immediately.

'The guy who killed Aileen... he just escaped,' Peter told me.

My immediate thoughts were... *Oh, no...they didn't rehabilitate him, the prison service had him for seven years... and did nothing to change him.*

'How do you know he escaped?' I asked.

'Scotland Yard rang the IRFU,' Peter replied.

'They are releasing it to the press tomorrow,' he continued.

'You'd better warn Helena (my Mam) and Nana. "Briano" wants you and the kids to come up here to us.'

'What?

'Why on earth would we go up to your camp?' I asked.

'Just to be safe,' replied Peter.

'That's ridiculous... I'll chat to you later!'

I hung up.

I turned to explain to Francine what I had just heard.

'The guy who killed Aileen was in an open prison,' I told her, '... and he only had three months to go to probation. They clearly didn't do any psychological work with him over the seven years... otherwise he wouldn't have bothered escaping.

'Isn't that very sad? Imagine if prisoners were taught Reiki while they were inside... they would have all the time in the world to practice it...

'... and they would have the opportunity to change their future lives in the process...'

Francine smiled back at me.

Then I had an 'A-ha' moment!

'Wow!

'I never would have guessed that would have been my reaction... how cool was that?'

I then told Francine that "Briano" wanted me and the kids to go to the camp. This led to another moment – was I mad and were they right?

Or were they being over dramatic?

I decided that we were in no danger whatsoever, and the only thing I had to consider immediately was how to tell Mam, Nana, Howard, and our uncles – and how best to minimize the upset that this press release was going to cause them?

A few hours later I rang Peter.

'Well love… what are you at?'

I knew by his reply that he was a bit off.

'Nothing much,' he said, '… finished training a while ago… where are you?'

'I've just been in with Mam... and told the lads,' I replied. 'Mam is upset but the lads and Nana didn't say much. I hope the papers don't go to town on it again, for their sakes.'

'Ok then love… I'll call you later!

And he hung up.

A little while later I realized why he had been a bit *off* – he was on the way home and didn't want to tell me. They had sent him home from camp to be with us in case anything would happen.

It was nice to see him, but I still didn't get what all the drama was about. The guy who killed Aileen had no reason whatsoever to come near us. What did fascinate me though was the timing of the news, and my reaction to it. I guess my own journey into personal development had a good deal to do with that, but also I realized that Peter's natural refusal to mull over stuff and be dramatic had rubbed off on me over the years.

Some years later, Peter got a call from a tabloid newspaper asking him what he thought of the sentencing of Laurence Hughes?

'Who?' asked Peter.

'Laurence Hughes… the guy who murdered your sister-in-law?'

'I've no idea what you are talking about,' said Peter.

Apparently after he escaped, Hughes fled to Germany where he murdered a man, and he had only just been extradited back to Britain and sentenced to life. At that stage my Mam, Nana, Gena, Lar and John had all passed away, and a quick call to Howard was all I had to make.

Someone sent us a clipping of the newspaper a few days later.

Neither of us gave it any more attention that it deserved.

Two seconds.

That autumn saw the start of the Celtic League.

This meant that the number of matches doubled for Munster players, and it also meant that the same players would have to start saying their "good-byes" to their clubs! There was also a new boy in the Munster ranks before the team started into the unfinished business of becoming champions of Europe.

His name was Jim Williams. John Langford had gone back to Australia and Jim, a former Australian International and ACT Brumbies star, had joined in his place.

The lads decided to call him "Seamus".

From day one Seamus played like a Munsterman. 'We taught him so much at Munster,' Peter announced when Seamus went back home, '… that he became forwards coach for Australia!' Before that, of course, Seamus would play over 30 times for Munster in the Heineken Cup over five years, and take up a place on the coaching team.

Seamus' first Heineken cup game was in his new home, Thomond Park – and against our old friends, Castres.

Munster won 28-23 and played as nervously as a team coming into the Heineken Cup for the very first time. The lead changed hands seven times – but crucially we took it for the fourth time after Dominic Crotty returned a poor chip by Gregor Townsend with an immaculate 70-metres touch. ROG tidied up a tight game with two penalties. Castres would finally get their revenge in the return game when we thought we had landed into the quarter-finals, losing 16-13 with seconds left. We turned the ball over and they got the winning try – and a home *quarter* – with the last play of the game. Our visit to Castres would also have Peter back in the middle of further controversy! That was down the road.

After our victory over Castres we had Harlequins away, led by Fester. We won even though we still didn't play very well, but the team was now streetwise, and winning was becoming a habit. We still didn't deserve to win as clearly as 24-8 suggested. Marcus Horan started against Bridgend, and Peter came off the bench late on to replace John Hayes. Munster won 16-12 and the following week had the return game at Musgrave Park where we really showed the gulf in quality between the teams. We were worthy of every point in the 40-6 victory.

By the start of December the knockout stages of the Celtic League were underway. We beat Llanelli, and then Ulster in the semi-final, but in the final at Lansdowne Road Leinster were the first team to lift the trophy, winning 24-20.

It was always hard to lose to Leinster, and them more than anybody, but the defeat straightened the team's head out and doubled the resolve for the Heineken Cup. That was the Cup that mattered.

We had Harlequins coming to Thomond Park for their return game.

That day Peter led out the Munster team as he earned his 100th cap, and as he ran onto the pitch the Thomond Park faithful gave him a standing ovation.

Was he emotional?

'I felt like a spare p****... the lads deliberately delayed coming out for the laugh, so I was left on the pitch alone for about 20 seconds.

'And Gaillimh breaking his h*** laughing in the tunnel.'

The historic nature of that win was quickly passed over, however.

Instead, Peter found himself centre-stage with Castres No.8, Ismael Lassissi, at the end of the final group game.

Lassissi was cited for biting Peter's arm. Peter was in the dock for allegedly abusing the Ivory Coast International and using racist remarks.

The two of them had become entangled during a scrum.

Peter caught Lassissi's jersey to stop him breaking away. He hit out at Peter's hand, but Peter would not let go. Lassissi then bit into Peter's arm.

When the scrum broke up Peter shouted to the referee.

'That dirty black b****** is after biting me!'

'I didn't see anything,' Tony Spreadbury replied, '... so I can't do anything about it!'

But then Gregor Townsend butted in.

'He's being racist... !' said Townsend.

Peter was having none of that.

'I was just describing who it was...

'... he's the only black man on the pitch!'

Peter needed some medical attention. The teeth marks were clearly visible through the blood on his arm, but Spreadbury was adamant that as he had not witnessed the incident he could not take any action.

Just before the 48-hour deadline passed after the game, Munster cited Lassissi. And Castres lodged a counter citing, and their president Pierre-Yves Revol jumped into the middle of the row making all sorts of mad allegations about Peter's conduct on the field.

'He is provocative and a cheat,' declared Revol. 'It is clear where responsibility lies in this affair… that is with Clohessy.'

Revol said that nobody could prove that there had been a bite. But he did say that Castres had a witness to the abusive remarks, presenting Townsend as someone who had been told by Lassissi what was being said to him.

Munster brought their solicitor Olan Kelleher, Mick Galwey, Jerry Holland and Pat Geraghty to the subsequent hearing in Dublin – Castres just had Revol with their player. But Lassissi apologised to Peter. He also broke down in tears – and Castres withdrew their racial abuse claims before the hearing began.

After two and a half hours, the ERC declared that 'the case brought against Ismael Lassissi of Castres Olympique for biting was found proved'. They suspended Lassissi for twelve months. Castres and their player, under ERC rules, had 72 hours to consider lodging an appeal.

It seemed that was the matter done and dusted.

Lassissi had apologised to Peter, the allegations against Peter were dropped, and even though Peter had the right to take legal action he had no interest in going down that path.

The controversy then rolled on and became extraordinary, however.

The ERC notified Munster late on a Tuesday evening that they would be holding an appeal hearing the following Thursday. Munster requested a postponement as they were travelling to France that same day – and naturally Peter needed to be present at any appeal.

The ERC denied the request.

The only new evidence was the testimony of the Castres doctor, a pathologist, who claimed that the injury to Peter 'was not consistent with a human bite'. In the initial hearing there was evidence from the Munster team doc, Mick Shinkwin, and there was supporting photographs – however, the three man panel of Robert Horner and Bob Taylor from England, and John Owens from

Wales decided the argument of the Castres doctor was convincing.

Lassissi's ban was lifted entirely and he played for his club that weekend in the Heineken Cup quarter-final against Montferrand.

Once more in his career, Peter had broken new ground for the game and exposed more flaws in rugby's system of justice. But he didn't whinge. Like always, he threw the controversy over his shoulder and headed into the next game.

A week after coming home from Castres, on February 21, 2002, Peter ran out at Lansdowne Road for the Six Nations opener against Wales, and to earn his 50th cap for Ireland. Luke was the team's mascot and accompanied his Dad onto the pitch.

As is customary Peter led out the team that day – a day that happened to see a first cap in the superb career that Paul O'Connell is still enjoying.

Luke was also interviewed by the media.

He was asked who was his favourite player?

'Fester... Dad... and ROG,' replied Luke, but his Dad was only number two! Guinness, as match sponsors, had printed life sized paper masks of Peter, with "Believe" written across the forehead.

It was so very strange to look across at the East Stand, and see thousands of Peters! Reaching 50 caps for Ireland was a huge milestone then with games in shorter supply. Only Mike Gibson (69), Willie John McBride (63), Fergus Slattery (61), Paddy Johns (59), Phil Orr (58), Brendan Mullin (55), Tom Kiernan (54), Donal Lenihan (52) and Moss Keane (51) had done it before.

Nowadays 100 is the new 50!

That evening before the official dinner, his Irish teammates made a special presentation to Peter. They insisted that he sing a song, and he obliged giving them his personal rendition of Sinatra's *My Way*.

He did feel privileged that he had made it to 50, considering the long and winding road he had taken to get there. And how times had changed – in the week running up to his 50th cap every paper in the country had articles celebrating his rugby career. One even had a complete supplement dedicated to "The Claw".

It was fitting, I suppose, because it was the media who had christened him "The Claw" in the first place. His nickname had simply been "Claw", because in Limerick Clohessy is pronounced Clausey, so it was naturally shortened to Claw. We could only smile years later when it was inferred that he was called "The Claw" because of how he played!

The tributes from his teammates were an appropriate recognition of an incredible character. And that, for me, was the important distinction, because there have been many talented and great players over the years, but not so many with such an amazing strength of character as Peter.

The true measure of a person is the impact they make at a personal level, in their connection with others, and not necessarily the success they have enjoyed or a long string of worthy achievements. Peter has always made an impact no matter what task he has attended to! He rarely says no to any request for charity work, and he then follows through in a completely understated way, with no pomp or ceremony.

Usually, of course, after showing up at the last minute, often making an off the cuff speech, and leaving quietly.

That day against Wales was also Eddie O'Sullivan's first as Irish coach.

He had taken over from Warren Gatland at the end of 2001, and included in his coaching team were Niall O'Donovan and Declan Kidney.

Gatty's departure showed how ruthless the old game had become. Peter had always felt that the IRFU were not happy that Gatty was a players' man, and that he was not someone who was easily controlled by the higher powers in the Union.

Peter also knew that Warren Gatland had something special, and he was not surprised that Gatty went on to prove himself a world class coach.

Eamonn Coghlan, Ireland's great miler, had invited Peter to a fundraiser for Crumlin Children's Hospital. There was an auction that evening, and the main item for sale was a VIP trip for two to Silverstone for the British Grand Prix.

Peter has always been a softie for kids, particularly the poor children who battle illness. So he began bidding on the Grand Prix weekend. When it got to €7,000, I intervened.

'Really Pete, you don't even like Grand Prix racing!'

'Doesn't matter,' he replied, 'it's for a good cause.

'I'll use it as a promotion in the bar!'

He duly paid €10,000 for the weekend, and then forgot all about it. A couple of weeks before the Grand Prix the Eddie Jordan promotional company – Eddie had donated it, as Eamon Coghlan is his first cousin – called Peter to ask for the names of the two people that would be attending.

'By the way, we're going to Silverstone,' he told me when he came home.

'That's sacrilege Pete... neither of us give a toss about Grand Prix,' I told him, 'and there are tonnes of people who would give their eye teeth to be there... would you not offer it to someone else?'

'Ah, f*** it, I haven't time to think... sure we could do with a weekend away,' he suggested.

With that, we arrived at Stansted Airport, and a chauffeur picked us up and took us to our hotel. Our itinerary for the weekend had also been cc'd to another couple, John and Isobel Stronach from Scotland, who were being looked after by the same promotional company.

The next day we were tagged on our wrists and had ID around our necks, and chauffeured to the trial runs, sharing the journey with John and Isobel who were avid Grand Prix fans – they were excitedly talking about various drivers, and the Belgium Grand Prix in particular where they had to walk miles to get to the track.

They were puzzled as we just listened and didn't offer any opinions. When we got to the corporate section, which is in the centre of the track, the roar of the engines was unbelievable. We followed John and Isobel who were running to the stand to have a look.

Peter sat there for approximately thirty seconds, then decided he had seen enough and announced he was going to find the bar. We left an even more puzzled looking John and Isobel in the stand. They relished the atmosphere.

The corporate arena was incredibly impressive, with champagne in abundance. In our Team Jordan section there were rucksacks packed with goodies for each of us. We were enjoying the atmosphere in the sunshine watching the world go by, when the other pair came down to join us when the trials were over. We were chit chatting together, and Isobel excitedly was pointing out lots of TV personalities.

I was never really one for TV and I am astonishingly poor at recognizing people, so Isobel would say, 'There's so-and-so from Eastenders', and I would reply, 'Really?' I did recognize Sarah Ferguson, but that was about it.

At this point we could clearly see the Stronachs were really confused and trying to figure out what on earth we were doing there. At one point Isobel asked, 'Do you mind me asking... do you have TV where you live in Ireland?'

'Yes, but I don't watch it very often,' I replied with a smile.

Myself and Peter had a giggle about all this as we got ready for the La Dolce Vita Ball that evening. To my last day, I'm sure we will never witness an event like it again. We were chauffeured with the other couple to Stowe School. We drove up the two-mile driveway. Perched on pillars were models draped in white robes, dancing in a way to make them appear like they were floating in the wind.

'Look at those girls!' I said to Peter.

'They are not girls,' he told me, 'They are Goddesses!'

There was more champagne on the lawn outside the biggest marquee I have ever seen, as the Royal Philharmonic Orchestra serenaded us. Being chauffeured made us feel important, until we noticed that the "car park" for the helicopters was much bigger than the one for cars! Guests in tuxedos were landing in their own helicopters. Peter was more interested in the canapés the waitresses were serving. He was scoffing them, and he particularly liked one type so he asked the next waitress, 'What's this one, love?'

'Caviar, Sir,' was the reply.

We could tell that the Stronachs were gathering the momentum to ask us why we were there, when a guest approached Peter for an autograph.

'Ok, lads... who the hell are ye?' they asked.

We burst out laughing, and explained how we had come to be at the event. Isobel then admitted that when she had received the itinerary and saw the names Peter Clohessy and Anna Gibson-Steel had also been cc'd, she was panicking about what to wear – she reckoned with a name like that I must've been very posh!

A little later that same evening they told us that John had brain cancer, and that his friends had arranged this special Grand Prix weekend for him. They had one boy Jack, who was three years old, and they were both in their 30s.

The entertainment was Craig David, followed by Puff Daddy, then Atomic Kitten. There was no bar, just Dom Perignon, and I learned that evening why wealthy people drink good champagne, because Peter drank seven bottles, never got stupid drunk, and had zero hangover the next day. Just as well all drink was included in the event. There was an auction that evening, and in light of how we had ended up there I had Peter under strict orders not to even touch his nose! The main item at the auction was a replica of the event itself donated by the event organizers – it sold for £750,000 sterling!

On the way to our table, Eddie Jordan spotted Peter. They had met each other many times through Fester, and Eddie had invited Peter to many Grand Prix races over the years, but Peter had never accepted.

'What the f*** are you doing here, Claw?' said Eddie.

'How come I didn't know you were coming?'

Peter explained himself. Eddie then invited Peter to go to the pits for the start of the Grand Prix the following day.

'You don't give a toss about being in the pits,' I said to Peter over dinner, 'would you ever ask Eddie if John could go… it would mean the world to him!'

Eddie didn't hesitate when he heard about John's illness and I can honestly say that made the whole trip for us.

John cried in the pits, and Isobel said it was the most perfect weekend ever. In fairness to the Jordan management they arranged for John and Isobel to go to Monza later that summer as well. The Monday after that weekend, however, when they got back to Scotland, John went into hospital and never came out again.

I got a call from Isobel in September to say that John had passed on, but that he had got so much mileage telling all his visitors about the special weekend he had spent with a really gentle giant called "The Claw".

'Paul O'Connell.
'Australia have John Eales as their Nobody...
but Paul... you are our Nobody... you are
perfect too.
'An out-and-out professional, you have been
more intensely dedicated to rugby than any
man I have known. Good job you have Emily
and Paddy, otherwise you would eat, sleep and
drink the bloody game.
'You have been some ambassador for Limerick
and Ireland.'

                                    — Peter

CHAPTER 22

After seeing off one of the greatest English teams of all time, there was more than the normal thimbleful of confidence that we could finally record an historic victory over the All Blacks. Beat them for the first time ever?

Why not?

The greatest team in the world of rugby were in Lansdowne Road at the tail end of 2001. And Gatty was a proud man sending an Irish team that he had built into a serious and respected International force out against his own country.

He had every right to be!

But little was he to know – nor did the team that was willing to face into stone walls on his behalf have an inkling – that his last game as Irish coach was upon him.

Gatty was about to be axed.

It did not make any sense. To Peter and the players there was no explanation which could be given for such a decision, not that the IRFU were extremely bothered about explaining their actions to the team!

Nobody could have done more than Warren Gatland in his time as national coach. It showed in the week ahead of the All Blacks game. "We have a chance,' stated Fester. It was a very different comment to the one he had made four years earlier when he said our chance of winning was 25-1.

Then we'd been beaten 63-15, not that Fester had thrown in the towel – he bagged a couple of tries before leaving the field injured at half-time.

This time was so different.

As usual, Peter was mostly unfazed by the ceremonial Haka. In fact, he believed that the All Blacks should not be allowed to do the Haka outside of their own country. If opposing teams do not have the right of reply, the All Blacks are given an unfair advantage before the ball is even kicked off.

The old ground was buzzing early on that Saturday evening as both teams left the field. We'd seen an epic contest. We lost 40-29, but we'd scored more points than ever before against the All Blacks. What's more, we had managed something both South Africa and Australia had failed to do in the Tri-Nations – we crossed the New Zealand line three times.

Two of those tries, by Kevin Maggs and Denis Hickie were mouth-watering. The first came after a big Shane Horgan tackle on Jonah Lomu. It also came from a strong scrum. David Humphreys took Peter Stringer's pass at speed. Brian O'Driscoll made a break. Eric Miller and Mal O'Kelly supported brilliantly. Humphreys worked some magic, and Maggs held his line and snatched the try.

The game was on.

Horgan had his greatest game in an Ireland jersey. Girvan Dempsey was brave and smart. Axel was immense. Eric Miller was immense. Fester was immense. And Humphreys was making Andrew Mehrtens look like a new boy out of his depth in the famous black jersey.

It was that good.

For 40 minutes the scrum was in total control, and Ireland were playing the biggest name in the game off the park. Hickie's try just after the break put us 21-7 in front – then two minutes later the monster in those same jerseys was awake and kicking. Reuben Thorne went over for them, and six minutes later Doug Howlett also touched down.

A dropped goal from Humphreys made it 24-19, but the whole balance on the pitch has changed by that point. It showed when we lost three successive line-outs on our own throw. They also outscored us three tries to one in the final run-in. But it had been inspiring, and more than intoxicating.

Irish supporters were walking on air leaving the ground.

It had been some 12 months.

We had started the year ranked eighth in the world and finished it sixth. We might have won a Grand Slam only for the arrival of Foot and Mouth. We had a record win in Rome, and first back-to-back wins over the French since 1973. Brian O'Driscoll was on fire for the Lions down under, and when the Six Nations recommenced in the autumn we were the first team to beat England in 16 matches. After that we went toe-to-toe with the All Blacks.

As a year goes, it was close to spectacular by Irish standards. And then six wise men – Eddie Coleman, Syd Millar, Noisy, John Lyons, Eddie Wigglesworth and Philip Browne – decided to dispense with the services of Gatty.

After the opening game of the 2002 Six Nations, Eddie O'Sullivan surely was the most relieved man in Lansdowne Road. He had beaten Gatty's 36-6 record win over the Welsh from 12 months earlier. In fact, we'd streaked by it and landed 54 points on the chin of the Welsh team.

'I'd have taken 1-0 at ten to two this afternoon,' stated Eddie, '... the way that wind was blowing out there!' There were six tries to decorate the day of Peter's 50th cap. Tails were up heading to Twickenham a fortnight later.

Twenty minutes into the second half in Twickers Peter was standing in a line-out across from his pal, Jason Leonard.

'Claw,' shouted Leonard, 'I hear you won't be around after the game for a few pints? You're going back for a wedding... or something?'

'I'd leave f****** now if I could!' Peter replied.

Fester had organised a taxi to leave straight after the game to get Peter to Heathrow for the last flight home to his business partner, Brian Smith's wedding in Cork. I was picking him up at Shannon and driving down.

I never met a man more delighted to be home on the night of an Irish game. The whole afternoon had been one of the old horror shows that Peter and Fester and everyone else thought were things of the distant past.

England could have scored in the opening minute but, that apart, the first quarter of the game was smooth enough from Ireland's point of view, but then, all hell broke loose. Jonny Wilkinson, Ben Cohen and Will Greenwood scored three tries in a 10 minute spell. Austin Healy should have made it four, but lost control of the ball after crossing the line, but Joe Worsley made sure of No.4 just before the break. It was 31-6. It ended 45-11.

In his last season as an Irish rugby player even Peter would have found it hard to dull the pain through the rest of the evening and early morning in London.

There were three games left in the green jersey.

The first two passed by in a flash at Lansdowne Road, Ireland beating Scotland 43-22 and then having it a little tighter against the Italians, but still romping home 32-17. Brian O'Driscoll grabbed his second hat-trick of his Irish career in the first game, running 80 metres for his second try after a typically brash interception.

The team had gone go-kart racing a few days after the defeat in Twickenham, and the therapy had worked, even though Brian and Shane Horgan joined Peter on the sidelines after been banned for dangerous driving.

Peter, funny enough for a man about to put his feet up, was in the form of his life. He'd never played better for Ireland than he did in the two games. He never enjoyed himself more either.

As he left the pitch at Lansdowne Road for the last time, with 10 minutes remaining in the game against Italy, the supporters gave him a standing ovation.

'Go on Claw,' shouted ROG, '... you have to give them a wave goodbye!'

ROG then cracked up laughing.

He knew that Peter never wanted to be the centre of attention.

Peter hesitated.

ROG refused to let up.

So, Peter turned to the crowd in the Lower West Stand, and gave his first and last wave in the old ground.

On his last day, he was not going to put in a performance which might have anyone saying that his time was up!

Also, French coach, Bernard Laporte had one change in his line-up – and he was putting his greatest prop, Peter de Villiers in at tight head. Peter knew his last game for Ireland would be as ferocious as his first day out in Paris those few short years before.

It had also all begun with the French in Dublin nine years previously, the men he had always found the toughest opponents of all. To be fair the French had voiced a tremendous respect for Peter over the years – strange, since Peter was notoriously outspoken in his dislike of anything French, though that would change and come full circle very quickly in his retirement years when he happily found France to be his favourite country of all!

Our traditional travel party of Meg, Noel, Geraldine and Austin, travelled with Luke and myself to Paris for the match. In an effort to entertain our eight year old, I had booked dinner and a magic show on a boat for the Friday evening. And, at the last minute, Nicola Wood who was now pregnant with Alexander, and Brian and Kitty Smith, decided to join us.

It was another of those memorable evenings, and it was Nicola's first introduction to Geraldine, and she never forgot it! Nor did the magician who was there to entertain us after our dinner, as he was heckled and abused by most of us, and snored at by Daddy Noel.

The following day, Nicola and myself and Luke took the official bus to the match. The traffic was chaotic, and we were still a good distance from the ground with 10 minutes left to kick off.

I really wanted Luke to be there for the start of the game, and I thought I remembered a short cut, so the three of us jumped off the bus and started running. Luke took great pleasure telling his Dad all about this afterwards.

'Mam made the bus stop...' he began.

'We got off... and ran and...

'... every time I stopped she gave out and made me run again...

'She said we were going to be late... and we got to the turnstile...

'... and... the bus was there before us!'

Gasping for breath we got to our seats for the French national anthem. At 36 years of age Peter was about to say his goodbyes to International rugby. All week his French opponents were glowing in their words.

Louis Armary, whom Peter counted as the toughest opponent he had ever faced, was especially flattering.

'We wondered if he was human,' said Armary, '... he went off the rails so much that it made us think he was mad!

'But... in the world of the prop there is always huge respect for a warrior like Clohessy!'

Franck Tournaire also said he would never forget Peter Clohessy.

'He would pull your jersey, he would stamp on your toes,' recounted Tournaire. 'But as a fellow prop I know that the game is, above all, a personal duel with your opposite number... and you do anything you can to win it.

'Clohessy was a great prop... a tough character.'

Even Olivier Roumat, the man whom Peter would always be most closely associated with from 1996, had a word.

'He was a persistent pain in the neck over the years!' Roumat declared.

'He was fiercely determined... a handful, and had such a big heart that he could take an awful lot of punishment. Never mind the stamping incident... what remains is the memory of a fine player whom we all respected.'

Though, the French knew that Peter had earned their kind words for other reasons as well. Neil Francis remembered the close-up view he had of Peter's first game against the French in 1994, and wondered how Peter had survived.

'It was really two against one,' stated Franno. 'And they – Armary and their hooker Gonzalez – really worked him hard. Their weight was bearing down on him the whole match and, at the break-up of a lot of scrums, Armary's head would come up and belt Claw right in the face.

'Everyone picked on him.

'If he was on the ground... he got stood on. He was seeing stars by the time he came off.'

Whatever else, Peter had indeed done it *His Way*.

Ireland's coaches knew that most of all.

'I think they broke the mould with Peter,' said Eddie O'Sullivan. 'He's an amazing character. He will leave a big, big, hole in the team when he goes... and it's a big pair of shoes to fill, not just from a rugby point of view, but for personality... leadership.'

Gerry Murphy owned up to being the man who *inflicted* Claw on the world. 'I'm afraid I'm the man, yes,' said Murphy. 'When he came in to win his first cap against France in Dublin, Mick Galwey and a few others got onto him about the French scrummaging... and how it was, eh... slightly different.

'That he had to be prepared for anything.

'He went into the first scrum and was thrown back two steps... you could say those were the only backward steps I ever saw him take.'

Murray Kidd had first come across Claw at club games in the early nineties. His club, Garryowen used to scrummage against Young Munster in training. 'He must have been pretty young in those days, but he always looked pretty old to me,' stated Kidd, recalling one session in Tom Clifford Park especially.

'We were there about two hours... on New Year's Day... p****** wet, and we had Barney O'Kane, a huge man at loose head.

'Every time Barney got the hit Claw just turned his shoulder and dropped everything into the mud. Every time Barney got a poor hit Munsters stayed up and pushed. It was a long day.'

Peter was in Queensland when Brian Ashton first came across him. 'The logical place to send Irish convicts!' stated Ashton.

'But I suspect the experience did him the world of good... it opened his eyes to a different sort of rugby. When I first met him he wasn't the sort of player I expected at all in that he could play football as well as do all the essential bits of a tight five forward.'

Warren Gatland took a year and a half to be able to understand one word from Claw's mouth. 'Paul Wallace and Nick Popplewell were the first choices when I took over, but we brought Claw to South Africa in '98. He was a tight head but what impressed me was when we needed cover for the bench in one game he pops up with, "Oh, I'll have a go at that!"

'He had no problems switching over.

'I've a huge amount of time for him and I'll always remember him coming up to me in the changing room after a game against Wales and saying, "I took a punch for you… and it hurt!" With an old head on his shoulders now there are probably a few games he would like to have again.

'I'd like to have had him in those early days!'

We were hammered that afternoon by the French.

44-5!

The giant scoreboard never looked so mean.

The French wanted their Grand Slam more than they wanted to wish Peter Clohessy a bon voyage. The day was one of glorious sunshine and with the warmth on their backs the home team took off!

The last words from de Villiers before the game were for Peter. 'I have a lot of respect for him,' he insisted. 'It is an honour for me to play against him in his last game!'

And with that de Villiers and Peter, whatever about the rest of the game, and the numbers going up fast on the scoreboard, went to work on one another.

They were never going to let us get close to a hat-trick of victories over them. Two minutes and 15 seconds after the opening whistle the French moved the ball left, right, and then left again. They sucked in our defence, before Serge Betsen romped over the try line, with a two-man overlap sending a message to their opponents that they were in one of those French moods.

Fester got a try after 12 minutes, but they had four more up their blue sleeve. Even the Irish in the Stade de France decided to sit back and enjoy it, long before the match referee, Paddy O'Brien from Australia sounded the final whistle.

The mood in the Lutetia Hotel on Boulevard Raspail was subdued, to say the least. The next morning the team was heading back home, but Luke and myself spent the day exploring Notre Dame, and the Arc de Triomphe, before we got our evening flight home. It was a strange, lonely feeling as we walked the streets of Paris. It was similar to the feeling I had had that day in the bank before the Australian trip in 1994, and I hoped I was just experiencing a bout of melancholy because Peter had finally retired.

The next day, however, made sense of that feeling when Peter came very close to retiring from life.

The petrol explosion in the back field which burned so much of his face and arm rocketed Peter back into the headlines.

'Everyone who has ever supported me.
'My coaches, trainers, bagmen, physios
and doctors... from Community Games right
through to the end of my career... thanks
for putting up with me and my bad habits,
and for showing me the way and allowing me
to become a professional.
'Munster supporters... you are the best in
the world. It is because of each and every
one of you that Munster rugby is the success
that it is today. It was your hard earned
cash that brought ye overseas... to follow
what was an average team to begin with!
'And because of your loyal support, ye
created a world-class team.'

                                        – Peter

CHAPTER 23

We had made it back to the semi-finals of Heineken Cup by *kicking out* the team that had broken our hearts 12 months earlier.

It was the third time we had met Stade Francais in as many years and, in many ways, the meeting in 2002 was the *deciding* game! We'd the added incentive of undoing the wrong that had been visited upon us in the semi-final the previous spring when John O'Neill's perfect try was ruled out.

At the end of the season, Peter was going, as were Declan Kidney and Niall O'Donovan, and John Connolly had also let it be known that he was also calling it a day with Stade. Knuckles was heading for Swansea. So, the quarter-final in Stade Jean Bouin at the end of January was extra significant all round.

We probably did not realize just how vital the game was until it was all over. There was hardly a dry eye in the house jammed with 12,000 fans after a pulsating 85 minutes, and with Gaillimh being passed from shoulder to shoulder by our supporters, as he clutched the Munster flag, we all finally released our breath. We had done it, 16-14.

It had been a tense few days, not helped by the fact that Stade had got up to different bits of mischief. They had someone try to record some of our lineouts, and they hung around when they were due to leave the stadium and give us some privacy. Luckily, this only angered our lads.

All of that emotion came out in the first-half when we had a big wind at our backs, but a 16-3 lead was dicey in the circumstances, especially considering Diego Dominguez, their out-half, was able to launch any ball from within 60 metres of the goalposts.

We needed every one of those points, and special praise was due to ROG and Anthony Horgan for their brilliance in manufacturing our try. ROG dazzled with the ball, and Horgan came blazing from the blindside wing to take his pass. He straightened and accelerated through Nathan Williams' tackle and brushed aside their full-back, Sylvain Jonnet and got the ball down between the posts.

At half-time, Declan asked the lads what they wanted to do?

Do you want to try and defend this lead, he asked?

Or, do you want to attack?

The right answer, and the one Declan wished for, saw to it that we came out on top – and we controlled possession for so many long periods in the second 40 minutes that stretched out to 45 minutes thanks to referee, Nigel Whitehouse. But it was a long half of rugby after Christophe Juillet scored from a ruck close to our line seven minutes into that half.

We let them know, immediately, that we were not going to lie down. Peter charged 40 metres from a clever lineout variation. Two rucks later John Kelly seemed certain to score after Dominic Crotty cleverly chipped forward, but Stade got back and blotted out the chance.

It was all hands on deck.

Midway through the second-half, Axel heard someone shout, 'Oh… s***!' He quickly grabbed a hold of Dominguez' jersey as the Munster defence was opened for once. It was a close thing. Minute by minute, we fought to make it to the finishing line. Dominguez kicked a penalty on 74 minutes to leave just two points between the teams.

On 80 minutes, Peter was called ashore by Declan.

The French crowd booed their faces off.

Peter waved.

Others were watching the game in the little stadium. In Leicester, Martin Johnson was impressed.

'That performance in Stade was one of the best, and maybe even the very best in the history of this competition,' stated the Tigers' and England captain.

Beziers airport was a small, regional place for Munster's giant support to make its way through. Three months had passed since the quarter-final victory over Stade. We were back in the company of Castres. There were 9,000 Munster supporters on their way. The team was in situ – but nobody longer than the team's kit manager, Noel "Buddha" Healy who had set off the previous Tuesday in his red van with "Munster Rugby" emblazoned on the sides.

In that three months, Munster had only been able to come together five times as a squad, though the previous weekend Declan Kidney finally enjoyed some quality time with his players by taking them off to The Inchydoney Hotel in Clonakilty for the weekend.

A brass band and a TV crew filmed our arrival in Beziers, but at the airport the tour operator that I had flown with was taking the rest of the passengers north of Beziers. I was going to my hotel at Cap d'Agde which was south. At this stage, the Heineken Cup had instilled a love of France in me, and although I didn't have a word of French I knew I would find a way to my hotel.

There were no taxis at the tiny airport, and the only person left was one of the camera crew.

'Where could I get a taxi?', I asked the man.

'There are none here… but, where are you going?' he asked in broken English. I told him.

'That's on my way… I will give you a lift!' he volunteered.

People in France liked Munster supporters.

Peter called while I was in the car.

'Where are you, love?' he asked.

'I'm just on my way to the hotel,' I told him.

'A lovely man offered me a lift… there were no taxis.' I replied.

'What the f***…

'F*** sake, Anna… he could be a mass murderer!' shouted Peter.

'Well, even if he is… I've caught him off guard. I'm safe… stop worrying!'

'Stay on the phone until you get there!' he ordered.

I told him not to be daft and said goodbye.

When I got to the hotel, I found the tour operator hadn't booked a room for me, but again the angels were on my side, and Kathy O'Donovan, Fiona Steed and a few more of the girls were sharing a big room. They invited me to stay with them.

The weather was super, and that meant beach time. I was studying at the time, so I was happy to leave the rest of the girls and head to the beach with my books. There I met with the dedicated Fiona, John Hayes' wife as she did her training for the Irish womens team on the beach.

Everyone was excited, and giddy.

The fact that Peter had burnt his arm and that he would now be playing against Ismael Lassissi again led to all sorts of wise cracks.

'Nice of you to barbecue the arm for him this time, Claw!'

There was also a t-shirt that someone handed me at the game.

"Bitten, Burnt, but not Beaten."

After his final match for Ireland, and before *potentially* his final match for Munster, Peter had gone up in flames while trying to set a blaze in a field down from our house. He was a lucky man to escape with his life.

And the last thing he should have been thinking about for many weeks, if not months, was a game of rugby.

But, Peter's recovery had been incredible. He went from being written off completely for the semi-final, to having an outside chance. The days passed and he was good to go, but even though the coaching staff had built a protective covering for his arm Declan Kidney was still working on "Plan B".

Peter, meanwhile, was housed in the team's chateau on the outskirts of Montpellier. As the clock counted down to the Heineken Cup semi-final he was less worried about his own fate, and more concerned with his wife hitching a lift with a serial killer!

The day of the match was baking hot, but the Beziers City Council had been warned of the size of the "Red Army" and had erected tents all around the town. The place was a sea of red that totally swamped the Castres support. It was due to hit the high 20s by 3.0 p.m. kick-off time.

On the field, the sight of Ismael Lassissi raised temperatures even higher, and when he got the ball in his hand in the opening minutes there were red jerseys queuing up in his direction.

The opening 40 minutes was about containing Castres, and shaking off the cobwebs of only one game in the preceding three months! We trailed 9-0 after three penalties from Romain Teulet. But Quinny kept calling everyone into the huddle, and Gaillimh kept talking to everyone. Gaillimh reminded everyone it was all about mauling, and mauling, and running the clock down.

We also worked our way upfield.

An intercept and run by Quinny led to a chance for three points. ROG kicked the penalty on 39 minutes, and he kicked another one on the stroke of half-time. A 9-6 scoreline was more than ideal, and Castres knew as they trooped into their dressingroom that they had fluffed the chance of putting any daylight between the teams.

They were not happy.

Mauricio Reggiardo, their prop, bumped into The Bull from behind in the tunnel. He escaped with his life, but his team would pay a bigger price in the second-half – a half that began only after the referee, Chris White ordered the teams to come back out of their dressingrooms separately – when Castres found Munster even further pumped up for action.

'You see Gaillimh crying at half-time, as he was speaking to us,' Donncha O'Callaghan, who had come in as a blood substitute in the first-half for Axel, remarked afterwards, '... that would shake you to your bones!'

In that second-half, Gregor Townsend was the first to crack – after having David Wallace in his face for far too long! Three penalties from ROG had us 15-9 in front with the game entering the final quarter. It was 18-12 after 80 minutes. Then John Kelly nailed Castres' coffin tightly with a try that ROG converted. Their final effort and one last consolation try hardly mattered apart from making the home scoreboard, showing 25-17, a little more respectable.

After the game Peter did something he had never done before. He went into the opposition changing room. His purpose was to shake hands with Lassissi, and he duly handed his match jersey to him.

In return Lassissi gave Peter his jersey which now hangs in Small Claw's Bar with the caption, 'Don't bite the hand that beats you.'

When Brent Moyle and Peter were sin-binned by referee Chris White, they were put sitting beside each other on a bench at the side of the pitch – another little thing that would be changed due to Peter!

Peter, as usual, wanted to have the last word.

As they sat there holding their drink bottles Peter turned to Moyle.

'If you were any f****** good,' Peter commented, 'you'd be playing in your own country (South Africa)!'

'And if ye were any good… ye might have beaten us,' replied Moyle.

Peter had no retort.

He did the only thing he could do, and squirted his water at him!

The joy after that game was very special. I felt it was extra personal because Peter had yet again overcome all the odds in recovering from the burning accident – plus victory meant that his final game would be an opportunity to finish in style with a Heineken Cup medal.

I did what I had never done before. I climbed the fence around the pitch with Fiona, and ran onto the pitch to congratulate him.

We were travelling back on the team flight that evening, so Peter and I were heading through security together. When we came to the scanners, the security guards called Peter aside to go behind the screens.

'F*** it,' he muttered to me, 'the dirty b******* are going to get their own back... and strip search me!'

Thirty seconds later, he came back looking relieved.

'They just wanted an autograph!'

The following week, journalists from all over Ireland and Britain were in search of Peter again, one last time.

Another Heineken Cup final.

His last game of rugby... ever.

He told them he had not thought at all about the final being his last game. He said he might stay involved in the game, or he might not. Maybe work as a scrum coach, maybe not. He said he'd no regrets about anything in his career, apart from Munster being a little naïve when losing two years earlier to Northampton.

'We thought we had won it in 2000, before we left the dressing-room,' he admitted. 'In the back of our heads, we thought we had done it already.

'This time, we know that we have a game to play!'

Luke and Jane came with me for their Dad's last game.

Jane had a red t-shirt with "My Dad's No 1" proudly printed on the back. We travelled over on the team flight on the Thursday before the game, and I hired a car to take the kids to the coast until Saturday as I knew they would be bored in Cardiff for the few days.

The morning of the game we stopped to say 'Hi' to Peter at the team hotel on the way to the ground. As usual he was nice and relaxed, strolling around with his coffee and fag.

We were itching to get to the stadium.

Peter, on the other hand, was like a man who had all the time in the world.

Our seats in the stadium were perfect and Jane was enthralled with the carnival atmosphere, and was mesmerized by the acrobats who were performing from the closed roof of the stadium.

Munster supporters were ready to celebrate. Over 15,000 people had looked to make their way to Cardiff by ferry. A total of 31 chartered planes flew out on the Friday and Saturday from Farranfore, Cork, Limerick and Dublin. Others were taking scheduled flights to London and Birmingham.

It had taken 16 matches and two years to get back to a Heineken Cup final. It was Gaillimh's last time to lead the team out the dressing-room door. He knew it was going to be an emotional occasion.

And Gaillimh knew he needed, to the best of his ability, to keep a lid on it. 'It's going to be emotional stuff,' he admitted, 'and I'm emotional at the best of times... so I don't want to think about that.'

Peter, Frankie Sheahan and The Bull were facing Graham Rowntree, Dorian West and Darren Garforth. On Peter's side of the scrum it was a battle of the OAPs, as Garforth was also 36 years of age. Both teams had packs brimful of passion, so there was no advantage for Munster in that department this time. Equally, both were unflashy and sprinkled with some Aussie influence. And both teams saw themselves as unpolished and grizzly at the best of times – no doubt about it, it was a contest in which our lads did not have an upper hand in any corner. They also had a sprinkling of Irish genius in the presence of Geordan Murphy.

It was going to take one, deep, heartfelt, completely error-free performance to make sure of winning the big one, finally.

The lineout was always going to be a worry.

It had not been our strongest link in the chain all through the season, and Leicester had serious ability in Ben Kay and Martin Johnson. We probably complicated our throws too much, trying to out-manoeuvre the pair of them. We did manage to rob three of their throws, but we also coughed up eight of our own, a huge cost in terms of quality possession. It left us with few attacking options in the first-half. That cost us, and more heavily than the two late penalties which ROG was unable to nail. He had been so good all through the game, until his first misses. His kicking and reading of the game was excellent, and included three successful kicks which left us 9-5 in front.

There were crucial turning points in the game, however.

The first was a helpful penalty Joel Jutge of France gave them and against Frankie for not releasing the ball, when we were on top and pressing home our advantage. The referee gave them lots of room at the breakdown, especially in tacklers not rolling away, and a series of penalties helped them to gain control at a crucial stage in the contest.

With 20 minutes to go, Austin Healy slipped through ROG's tackle and scored their second try – Murphy had scored their first. We were left fighting an uphill battle after that.

It was 15-9 and we needed a converted try to win the game.

In injury-time we finally had an attacking scrum in front of their posts. It was last chance saloon. And what happened next left us outraged and indignant in the stands, and in homes all over Ireland, but on the field there was a wearying acceptance that the team had not done enough to land the biggest prize.

Neil Back flicked his hand at Stringer and diverted the ball into the Leicester side of the scrum. It was cynical and illegal, but Leicester had no intention of apologising – and Munster's coaches and players were not asking!

Back should have been penalized and sin-binned, and if he had and Munster faced a seven-man scrum, perhaps the dream would have lived on for a few seconds more. However, the referee had decided for some reason to position himself on the blind side of the scrum. He saw nothing.

Stringer was left surprised and dazed as the final seconds played out. He did not know what to do, or think. The whole team shared his disbelief. Nobody was irate, or angry, or cared to point an accusing finger at Back.

Back, meanwhile, was doing all the talking. He denied he had cheated. He said his action was not the turning point in the game. He stressed that Leicester had scored two good tries, and that the better team had been crowned champions of Europe. He said too much, in truth, but not a soul in the Munster camp had the stomach or the desire to disagree with him.

Peter would also say that Leicester were the better team on the day. He felt they matched our passion on the pitch, and around the stadium he also felt their fans equalled the noise of the "Red Army".

Our lineout was poor. Ben Kay and Martin Johnson cleaned up, but our scrum was solid. Peter was playing well, and I couldn't understand why

Declan Kidney called him ashore so early.

'I thought I had more left in the tank,' Peter insisted afterwards, and felt that Declan was wrong. 'I think that was Declan's way of finally having the last say over me!'

He was not angry.

Neither was he devastated by the action of Neil Back.

'At the end of the day,' he accepted, 'you do what you have to do to win.' Peter believed that if a Munster player had done the same thing he would have been hailed as the hero of the hour.

We both knew in our hearts that Leicester were the better team on the day.

Peter had left the pitch with his head hung low, and in the dressing-room he sat there alone for sometime.

Someone looked in at him.

He couldn't remember who?

'Claw, come on out... get your medal,'

'What for?' he replied quietly.

'I already have one of those f****** things at home!'

With that, the coaching staff decided to leave him alone.

He never did collect that medal.

Cardiff Airport was a disaster that evening.

Only 12 desks were open.

And the place only had one small café!

There were plenty of disgruntled supporters sitting on the floor, hanging around and longing to be home in Limerick and Cork, and so many other parts of Ireland. The team flight was three hours late departing, but there was still a crowd at Shannon Airport at 1.0 a.m. to welcome the lads.

I went home with an exhausted Luke and Jane, and Peter didn't show up on the radar until 11.0 a.m. the following morning. They had drowned their sorrows all night long at The Sin Bin.

This last time, after his last game, I wasn't going to complain?

‘To Luke, Jane and Harry.
'Luke and Jane... I'm sorry that I missed a lot of your earlier years because of rugby, but on the other hand ye got to see the world, and ye have grown into two fabulous young adults.
'As for the other little tyrant, Harry... because you were a late arrival, Anna said, "he's all yours!" My magnet and I have great fun together, and as I have the time now you are my farming apprentice and a great help for doing the handy jobs.
'This book is for ye, and ye'r children.'

— Dad

CHAPTER 24

We headed to Majorca the following Tuesday for a week with the kids. It was a welcome break.

Our new-found freedom, for both of us, was very exciting. Being able to decide where and when we would go somewhere was a novelty that we totally embraced. The world was ours all of a sudden.

We could do anything.

And we could reunite with our friends.

One of those reconnections was with Ray, Trish and their four kids.

Ray had bought a massive RV from America – just like the one in *Meet*

The Fockers actually. They were excited to have their first holiday in it, so we decided to rent a regular size motorhome and do a tour of Kerry and Cork with them.

We drove in convoy. I followed our motorhome in the jeep so we would have transport when we were camped at the various sites. Peter and Ray took off on that holiday where their friendship had left off years earlier. We arrived at the camp site in Skibbereen first, and the owner looked at our motorhome and said, 'That's a big one... I hope it will fit!'

'You think this is big... wait 'til you see the one that's coming behind us!' replied Peter.

Within ten minutes of parking up the boys had created mayhem when Ray attempted to plug in his RV but it kept tripping out the fuse board at this particular site.

Genius Peter had an idea.

'Ok Ray, I'll hold up the trip... and now try it?'

With that, the entire campsite was plunged into darkness. They had managed to blow the main fuse board for the entire park. That was the start of a very adventurous week. Of course what else were they to do now? Sitting outside between the two motorhomes they proceeded to tuck into the wine. By morning it was clear we had outstayed our welcome, and we decided to find a more suitable location!

The Kingstons had introduced us to a fantastic campsite near Caherdaniel a few years previously, so we decided to head up there. Trish, Dawn and Harry came with me in the jeep, and the boys and Jane divided themselves between the two camper vans. Upon arriving at Caherdaniel we pulled into the wrong site!

There was no way to turn the RV around, so Ray had no other option but to reverse it back up the hill, at which point an oil seal went in the gearbox and oil flooded all over the place. When we finally got out of the campsite, we headed for the one that we should've been in – down a very narrow road, so we sent Darren and Luke ahead to stop the oncoming traffic. When Ray got to the bottom of the hill, he shouted to the boys to jump in as he knew he couldn't stop with the gearbox.

Luke didn't make it, and ended up walking the couple of miles to the next campsite, and was not impressed. Neither were the Ryan triplets, who were 15 at the time, and had just been to busy Salou on their summer holiday.

Now they had been catapulted back in time to a crossroads, with one shop and one pub.

'You've got to be joking us,' they asked.

'… how long are we staying here?

'What are we supposed to do here?'

Peter broke the tension first.

'Don't do it all on the first night now, lads,' he advised them, '… ye'll spoil it for yourselves!'

Here we were with a broken RV, and five bored teenagers, in a remote part of Ireland and it started to p*** rain!

Out came the cider. We had a great night and the Kingstons joined us. The teenagers didn't torment us either, so we suspected they had nicked some of the cider. That night we didn't care!

The following day it had dried up. We were sitting out between the two campers, and Ray took out his guitar and started playing.

Ah… now, this is holidays! I thought.

'What is it that you do anyway, Anna?' Ray asked me.

Like many of my friends the Ryans had only a vague idea that I did *something alternative*, but not many of them asked me.

'Actually, I've just learned this cool new system that allows us to check with your subconscious mind what might need to be balanced in your system,' I replied.

That stopped the singing!

'Go on… that sounds interesting… will you do it now with me?' asked a curious Ray.

'Sure, why not,' I agreed, 'I could do with the practice.'

I was undaunted by the audience of teenagers and Trish, who gathered around to watch. In this system we use bio-muscular feedback, by pressing on the arm to determine where there is *imbalance* in the body, and then by using specific techniques we can instruct the body to rebalance itself. So, off I started, and Ray asked me to tell everyone what I found. There were a couple of things.

But then I told him, 'Your left ankle needs a balance.'

He replied, 'No... you're wrong... it's my right ankle, remember I snapped my right Achilles' tendon last year?'

'Ah well, not to worry anyway,' I continued. 'It makes no difference, this isn't about diagnosing... it's about using energy to rebalance your system so that you don't develop an illness,' I informed him.

As soon as I had finished the sun came out for the first time that week. Everyone made a mad dash for the beach.

Peter ran into the water at one stage, and Ray took off after him with the intention of acting the maggot. But, before we knew it, Ray was being assisted out of the water by Peter.

Ray had snapped his left Achilles' tendon!

He looked at me.

'You are only a witch... after that!'

I immediately put my hands on his leg.

'What are you doing?' he said, panicked, '... my leg is on fire!'

'Don't worry, it should help with the pain,' I replied.

Ray rang Mickey Griffin, our doc, who knew Ray well enough to know that if Ray said his Achilles' was gone, it was gone. An hour later, Mickey rang back.

'Ray... you are booked in for surgery at Limerick Regional tomorrow, and do me a favour and don't show up with a high alcohol blood count!'

Ray and Trish headed back to Limerick, and the next day Ray was fasting all day waiting for surgery. Meanwhile, Peter had picked up a gastric bug and spent the day running to the toilet on the campsite. Again it was pouring rain, so I took the kids into Kenmare for the day to entertain them, and leave Peter in peace. When we got back to the campsite that evening Peter was still ill.

'F*** it... let's go home love,' he advised. 'I'm like a dirty old man going up and down to the toilets!'

The toilets were beside the kids play area. The funny part was, there had been much banter over the few days about using the toilets in the campers – Ray had issued a directive to his lads that they were not to use the camper's toilet, and there had been all sorts of threats from Peter about surprise attacks being made on Ray's toilet.

I let Harry run around for a while at the campsite as he had been in the jeep all day, and Peter headed off with Luke in the camper back home. We left the lonely sight of Ray's abandoned broken-down RV in the middle of the campsite behind us.

The rain on the way back home was unbelievable, and as the kids were asleep in the back I passed the long dark journey on the phone between Ray, who was still waiting for surgery, and Peter who was on the road about an hour ahead of me. We were all in good spirits laughing about what else could possibly have gone wrong on the trip.

'You know what Anna,' said Ray, 'I think my leg is improving.

'Something is going on…

'In the scan it is snapped… but it feels like it is healing?'

'Make sure they do another scan before you have surgery then!' I told him. As I described how sick Peter was, we were weak laughing at how totally disastrous the week had been.

I had just hung up when, suddenly, I was surrounded by water.

I was at Newcastle West driving behind a big articulated truck – I looked to my right and a Micra was floating past! I didn't realize that the river had just burst it banks, and I was in it! Again, I was blessed, as my angels took care of us because the *artic* truck ahead of me was making a path in the water. And just as I got out of the flood, the *artic* took the right hand turn for Dromcollogher!

'You won't believe what just happened…?' I informed the boys.

The next day they scanned Ray's leg and noticed that there was a thread visible that they hadn't seen the day before. They decided to put a cast on his leg and wait two weeks.

Ray called me.

'Anna, I don't know what you were doing to my leg, but I think it's working… and can you do more when the cast is on?'

'Yeah sure, Ray. I'll see you tomorrow,' I promised him.

We did a couple of sessions, and when Ray went back two weeks later to get the cast off his Achilles' tendon was completely healed. At the request of a research programme that I knew about in the States, Ray got the scans for me and I sent them off.

The experience with Ray taught me a lot about the power of energy healing.

***

Peter had almost always refused to *do* corporate speeches. However, when the call came for him to talk at the Bermuda Rugby Association's annual dinner dance, that was a different story. An all-expences paid trip to Bermuda?

Not to be sniffed at. We were very well looked after by Shane Coman and Daniel Greenslade, whose grandfather had been held in some standing there, and Daniel took us to his beautiful home, where he still had all the original horse and carriages that were used in Bermuda. He brought us on a tour of the island in a Clydesdale-driven carriage which was exquisite. Being at the Greenslade's beautiful home, with the stables and sand arena, gave Peter the inspiration to want to ride again. We had needed to move house for the previous couple of years, but because Peter was away so much we simply didn't have time. Now we were actively looking for a site that was near water – we were working on getting one at O'Brien's Bridge. After retirement Peter had bought a new boat and was clearly searching to fill the gap that rugby had left.

His adventurous spirit still needed nourishing. He was after all an adrenalin junkie for the previous 15 years, and a sudden withdrawal from that can cause physiological issues. Not that Peter noticed or spoke about it in such terms.

'What is it you really want to do now, Pete?' I had asked him in Bermuda. He did not reply for a few minutes.

'Farming... I wouldn't mind doing some farming.'

As a teenager, he had worked on his Dad's small farm in Kilkee, and he had very fond memories of that time. The day after we arrived back from Bermuda, Peter saw an advert for a farm in Murroe that was up for auction three days later.

'Where's Murroe?' I asked.

'You know where Glenstal Abbey is... near the Clare Glens?' he replied. I had a vague recollection of being there once as a teenager but that was it.

'Will you come out and have a look?' he asked.

I told him to go on his own, but also asked if there was not a farm any closer to where we had been living? We had lived in Annacotty since we had got married in 1988, and we were happy there. It was a good location, the kids were happy in school, their cousins all lived nearby, so I was in no rush to move *out to the country*, disrupting that status quo. So, I began driving around the back roads near us in Annacotty hoping to find some farmland around there.

'Will you come out and have a look at this place,' Peter said to me the next day. 'I think you'll like it?'

We went out and I reluctantly looked around the old farmhouse, where the bachelor who had recently passed away had been born and raised. It had potential for sure, but still it was miles away! I did, however, love that there was a river on the farm, and a beautiful glen beside it.

Still, this was the country.

I was a *city* girl.

Two days later Peter went to the auction on his own.

'Well,' he informed me, 'we bought it!'

'Ok,' I replied, '… and how do you feel about it?'

'Not sure!' was his reply.

'Jesus… if you're not sure we are in trouble… because I'm certainly not sure!' I told him.

'What happened at the auction anyway?'

'There were lots of people there but only two of us were bidding,' he explained. 'And afterwards everyone clapped!'

This clapping worried me.

'Oh, God, why did they clap?

'Do they always clap at auctions?

'Or did they clap because it was you… or worse… did they clap because you paid too much for it?

I was a headful of questions.

'Don't know… but it's done now!' he replied.

My life experience has taught me that sometimes things are just meant to be, and that decision was one of the best Peter was ever *guided* to make. Shortly after he bought the farm we began in earnest planning the house, and we started spending plenty of time out there, as Peter immediately bought horses and started plotting the farm.

He was in his element saving the hay, just like he had remembered as a child. We were blown away by the welcome that we received from our new neighbours, it was not something we had ever experienced before. One day, a couple of weeks after he had bought the farm, he was bringing bales of hay out on a trailer for the horses. A bale had fallen off unknown to him – the next day the neighbours presented it to him in black bags. They had gone onto the road and gathered up the fallen hay for him.

At the same time a local man, Tony McGuire called over to ask Peter to sign a jersey that he wanted to raffle at a fundraiser for Milford Hospice. His wife, Anna had just passed away from breast cancer and he wanted to thank Milford for the care they had shown to them.

Tony and Peter struck up an immediate friendship that was to lead to many life-changing experiences, and not just for us. Tony and Anna had three boys, Kevin, Seamus and Dermot, and the latter two boys worked with him in the agri-machinery business. He also had one daughter, Geraldine, who was just 15 at the time.

The McGuire lads were always on hand to help Peter getting to know the locals, and help with farming matters. Meanwhile, Geraldine would call over to our place regularly with Tony. Herself and Jane became incredibly close, despite the age difference, and they filled the gap of not having sisters by becoming *sisters* to each other. Geraldine became a part of our family. She came on trips abroad with us, and worked part-time in the bar in town while she finished school.

She has become an incredible addition to our family.

We had never felt as *at home* anywhere else as we did when we moved to Murroe, and my only complaint was that there was no restaurant in the village, as we had to travel for dinner if I didn't feel like cooking. I mentioned this to Peter a few times. The village is missing a bar and restaurant, I told him. Think of the parents visiting the boarders at Glenstal, they have to go to Castletroy to eat? Would we not consider opening a business out here?

Geraldine's grandfather was the blacksmith in the village, and their family home was on the main street – they owned a large plot beside the house. Tony mentioned that he was going to sell some of the land. From that, Crokers

Bar and Restaurant was born. It is more than just a business, it has given a heartbeat to the village. For starters, it has been a meeting place in which three of the McGuire children have met their partners.

Peter asked Angie and Eimear if they would like to take a partnership in the business, as a way of thanking them for the loyalty over the years. Eimear then met her fiancé, Tom Sparling at Crokers, and Peter was honoured with the task of *giving* Eimear away at her wedding to Tom. It is a hub of activity and the new energy coupled with the fantastic contribution of Fr. Simon Sleeman from Glenstal Abbey has transformed the community.

Peter restarted the "Mary from Murroe" festival and through my involvement in that I got to know my community for the first time in my life. This was joined hand-in-hand with my opening the only Holistic Centre of Excellence for training therapists, with the blessing of being situated on the magnificent grounds of Glenstal Abbey. Geraldine went on to train on the full-time programme and is now a fully qualified Holistic Therapist. The connections that have clicked together since we moved to Murroe are amazing, and we couldn't be happier anywhere else in the world.

Geraldine met her partner, Paul Coffey at Crokers, although she had met him with her brothers before, but never socially. Crokers crystallised their relationship, and Peter found his new partner in crime! Paul has always adored farming, although he worked as a sales representative. He was always coming over to give Peter a hand around the farm, and they get on like Mutt and Jeff despite the age gap between them. It was a natural transition when Geraldine and Paul moved into the farmhouse, on the basis that Paul would help with the farming. Peter adores coming home from work and pottering around the farm with Paul, and they have a great laugh together. Again, I believe these *coincidences* are, in fact, life's miracles.

That August, a few short months after Peter had retired, we were in Kilkee quite a lot, as the children loved it there and we now had time to enjoy it. One beautiful day we were messing about on the boat, when Peter got a call.

It was Toulouse.

They wanted to know if Peter would join them for the start of the new season?

'What do you think love?' he asked.

'Well, why did you retire this year?' I asked him back, 'you could have played longer here if you wanted.'

'True... yeah.

'No... I've had enough!'

He called them back to say no thanks.

A week later we were back in Limerick, it was pouring rain and, suddenly, a few months in Toulouse was looking a whole lot different. There was the added attraction that Trevor and Paula Brennan were living there.

'Gosh Pete,' I told him. 'I bet if you go to Toulouse... you'll win a Heineken Cup medal with them.

'Wouldn't that be hilarious?'

He called Trevor, who confirmed that it was a fantastic club, and he assured Peter that he would love it there. Peter called Toulouse back but they had just signed a prop earlier that same day!

Some things, after all, are just meant to be, but it would have been a curious extension to Peter's saga.

As I've explained earlier, I had only seen Peter *do fear* less than a handful of times, though he did it twice in the same week in 2006, when my waters broke two months early and there was a rush to get me to Cork.

That morning Jane who was seven at the time had surgery in Limerick on her teeth – the two of us were in bed for the afternoon as she slept off her anaesthetic. I had been feeling a little strange. I woke when my waters broke, and rang my doc, Miriam O'Callanan to ask her what I should do?

'Grab your bag... and head to the hospital straight away!' she ordered.

'Really, Miriam,' I replied, 'can I not go until later... I'm very tired.'

'Absolutely not... you need to go now!'

I looked out the window to see where Peter was?

He had been cutting the grass, but there was no sign of him now. But Luke was out there, so I asked Luke to find Dad for me.

Peter sauntered in.

'We need to go to Cork love, my waters are breaking,' I told him.

'Well have to take Jane with us,' I continued, 'we can't have her waking up from the anaesthetic with someone else... oh, and will you pack a bag for me?'

Miriam had said I shouldn't move about too much.

'F***... what will I pack?' was his reply.

I listed out some things and, meanwhile, I rang Eimear and told her to follow us in her car, so she could take Jane when we got to Cork. We dropped Luke into Mags on the way. As we came out of Charleville, I felt something *come away*.

It felt like a balloon in my pants. Peter became very anxious and wanted to pull over at the side of the road.

'Keep going... and pull in at the garage.' I told him. He pulled in and ran to find where the bathrooms were. Unfortunately, it was too late, and as I stood out of the jeep my waters fully broke. This hadn't happened to me before so I wasn't sure what had *come away*.

Peter came back to the jeep to find me standing there.

'Quick... quick... let me see?' he asked.

'See what... you eejit... get in and drive!'

I was laughing. And I will never forget the sight of a young lad, who had stopped washing his white Honda Civic – and was watching this whole scene with his mouth wide open as we drove off.

Peter was very anxious, but I found the situation hilarious as I had never seen Peter like this before. The more anxious he got, the more I laughed.

'F*** sake... stop laughing... you'll lose more!'

Suddenly my husband was an obstetrician!

I rang Eimear. She asked me was I laughing or crying? I told her what had just happened at the garage.

'Please tell me you've got spare trousers with you?' asked Eimear.

'I don't know... Peter packed the bag!'

This sent me into more laughter.

Peter was getting crosser, and crosser.

We got to the hospital and the lovely Mr Corr, who had looked after my pregnancy with Jane came to explain. He told me it was a serious situation and that I was in the hospital to stay.

'The longer you can hang on to the baby the better,' he continued. 'If you go into labour before 32 weeks we will have to move you to another hospital – our neo-natal unit isn't equipped to deal with younger *premmies*.'

This was a little inconvenient for me, as I had 30 students registered for training in Limerick the following weekend, and I didn't have anyone working for me at the time. So, much to the disgruntlement of the nursing staff, I had to do some work to get things sorted. With me in the right place, Peter began to relax.

I suggested that he go home with Jane and that he could come back in a couple of days. Funnily enough, as Eimear drove Jane to visit me in the "Bons" Jane pointed to a building on Western Road.

'What's in there?' she asked Eimear.

Eimear read the sign and answered, 'That's the Erinville… it's a maternity hospital.' At the time most of the windows were boarded up as it had been due to close the previous year, but this was delayed 'til 2007.

'Wow… state of it,' replied Jane. 'Imagine if Mom ended up there!'

Out of the mouth of babes.

Two days later I was getting ready to go to sleep for the night, and I went to the bathroom and I haemorrhaged. I rang the bell and the next thing I knew I was in an ambulance on the way to the Erinville! I was accompanied by Nurse Fiona, who I had gotten to know since my admission. At the Erinville, I was prepped for an emergency section.

'Peter is here,' Fiona told me.

'Will you bring him in for a moment?' I asked.

'But… where was he?' she asked.

'At home, in Murroe.' I replied, 'why?'

'Because I only rang him 40 minutes ago!' said Fiona.

'That'd be right!' I said, 'now, can he come in for a second? He won't relax until he sees that I'm ok!'

I had never seen Peter so fearful, but funnily enough I was totally calm. Though I did say a little prayer.

'Ok, angels, I would love for my baby and I to be ok… but if that's not meant to be, I accept it.'

With that I, for once, was the one who felt no fear. Good job I suppose, because Peter had enough for all three of us! Thankfully we were blessed when a tiny Harry arrived at 2.40 a.m. – he was not much bigger than Peter's hand at 2 kilograms.

They took Harry off to the neo-natal unit, and as the surgeon was stitching me my body started to go into shock. I started shaking, but yet I felt totally calm. I wanted to move my arms to get rid of the "DTs", so I asked the surgeon how long more he would be, as I wanted to move.

'Thirty minutes,' he replied.

I need to get rid of this shaking, I told myself.

I turned to Peter.

'Don't talk to me for a minute… I'm just going to do something.'

And, with that, I started focusing on my breathing. After taking three deep conscious breaths the shaking stopped. I was amazed, and turned to Peter in my surprise and happiness.

'Can you believe how fantastic this energy work is?'

He murmured something vague in reply.

The following day, Eimear brought Luke and Jane down to see me. She hadn't told them that Harry had arrived. There was great excitement but, unfortunately, the closest they could get to him was watching through the window of the neo-natal unit. I settled into the Erinville, and despite the fact that the building was literally falling apart, the staff were superb, and I felt very blessed that Harry was getting the best care. Two days later I was very aware that Peter was still very stressed, so I suggested that he go for a night out in Limerick. I told him to leave the kids at our house, and stay at our good friend, Angie's place instead. That way he could have a good *blow out* and lie in the next day.

I got the drunken, 'I love you' phone call at about 5.0 a.m. Peter was on his way back to Angie's. He was in the mood for chatting, but I had to go because the nurses in neo had called down to tell me that Harry needed a feed. When I got to the ward Harry was fast asleep, so I sat on the chair beside his incubator, with him cradled in my arms.

The sun was just rising and streaming in the window onto my face.

Will I close my eyes, I thought, *and have a little snooze?*

But, then I replied to myself, *No… stay awake!*

Wherever that 'no' came from, it was an absolute blessing, because I suddenly noticed that Harry was turning blue in my arms!

I called the nurse.

'Is he gone a funny colour?' I asked.

Immediately they whipped Harry over to the oxygen. He had stopped breathing. With the oxygen he started breathing again, and the neo nurses reassured me that this often happened with "premmie" babies, as their brains would simply *forget* to breathe.

I was unsure what to do about Peter.

I certainly didn't want him driving to Cork with all of that drink on him, nor did I want him panicking for the third time that week.

So I hatched a plan and rang Angie.

'Let him sleep 'til midday,' I told her. 'Don't tell him what has happened, but tell him I need clean pyjamas as soon as possible.' This way he would get to Cork quickly, but safely. Then I rang Clodagh Kingston, and burst out crying as the reality of what had just happened hit home. To be fair to her, she downed tools and came to the Erinville to sit with me.

Peter arrived at 2.0 p.m., and I had decided that I wouldn't tell him until we were in the neo with Harry.

'What's up love?" he asked.

'Nothing, just a bit tired,' I replied.

When he had Harry in his arms, I told him what had happened. Tears welled up in his eyes and we both grew to a new level of realization that day, about how blessed our lives had been. Those three times are still the only occasion that I have ever seen Peter fearful. Even a couple of years later, when the thatched roof of Crokers went on fire, he reacted better than the trained firemen, as himself, chef Tom Sparling and Willie Ryan, climbed onto the burning roof and managed to extinguish the flames with the help of Paul Coffey, and some other locals on the ground.

When the fire brigade arrived they couldn't believe that they had saved it – in their experience once a thatch takes fire the whole building usually goes with it. But as everyone was re-living the drama of the fire, Peter shrugged his shoulders, and bought everyone a few pints and dinner.

He had already moved on with his life.

***

Four years after Peter had retired he turned forty.

I decided that I would surprise him on two counts. One with a big surprise party, but also I set about making a surprise documentary around his rugby career as his 40th birthday present.

Peter hadn't had a testimonial to conclude his career, that wasn't his thing, so I thought it was a good opportunity to double up his 40th as a "retirement party" as well. And Ray Ryan, tipping his cap to the great Christy Moore (who also appeared in Peter's documentary saying a few kind words, and singing *Nancy Spain*) sang the following:

He's no ordinary man,
He'd skin you if he can,
Pound for pound he's every woman's dream,
Married to Anne, he looks like Desperate Dan,
It's a buck ape wouldn't have him on his team.

Now, Peter is his name,
The man they couldn't tame,
The wild one that loose heads feared the most.
And in 1993, twas plain for all to see,
The Claw would soon be Ireland's toast.

In Parc De France one day,
Our Pierre was to play,
With Meg and Daddy Noel up in the stand.
As he mimed Amhran na BhFiann,
He was proud to wear the green,
And we all thought the Pierre would be grand.

Then Roumat hit the deck,
And The Claw said what the feck,
As he launched his silver kings into his pole.
A steady flow of rouge,
Came out of Roumat's bruise,

But the sad thing was our Pierre had to go.
Au revoir,
Au revoir Pierre,
Au revoir Pierre, Au revoir Pierre

Now his career was put on hold,
Because Pierre was so bold,
Half a year for a thing so near, is not that bad,

Down under he would go,
With the silver kings on tow,
To Queensland, we all thought that he was mad.
And Sunday's poisonous pen, had struck him down again,
With reporters twisted words a waste of time
How that journalist could write,
All that septic shite,
The holder of the pen commits the crime.

G'day Pierre, G'day Pierre, G'day Pierre,

Then back to Erin's Isle,
Came the bold Claw with a smile,
To serve his club and country best he could,
With the passion and the pride,
This man you couldn't hide,
One had to say that Peter Claw was good.

With the blink in his eyes, he gave us four great tries,
And caps to cover heads of fifty-four,
Happy Birthday to you,
I'll finally say adieu,
To the famous one we wish a hundred more

Bonjour Pierre, Bonjour Pierre, Bonjour Pierre.

So many great friends and teammates contributed to the documentary over many months. I was thankful to them all. Of primary importance was that it was all done in secret. This is not as easy as you'd think, as it involved filming in six different locations in order to catch up with the various guys whom Peter had been involved with over the years. We started in October and the final editing began in February, in time for his party in March.

There was a Heineken Cup game at Thomond Park, so I used this opportunity to book a room at The Castletroy Park Hotel, where we would film Ned Van Esbeck, Mannix and Killian Keane, as they would all be in town for the game. At the same session we were going to film Ray playing the song.

Howard, Ray and the film crew arrived at the hotel before me, and were in the room by the time I got there. When I asked at reception which room I was in, I did notice that the receptionist looked oddly at me.

When I got to the room, the lads were weak.

'Did the receptionist say anything to you?' Ray asked.

'No… but she did look a little odd… why?' I asked.

'What have you done now?'

Ray was more than happy to explain what he had told the same receptionist upon arrival with the film crew.

'There's a room booked in the name of Anna Gibson-Steel…

'We are here to film a porn movie!' Ray had told her.

And Peter kept ringing me for stupid stuff that morning.

'Where's Jane's shoes?'

'Where's Luke's jacket…

'… and where are you anyway?'

I had to keep ducking out of the room to take his calls. I found that the hardest bit, the constant covering up. I nearly got caught in December. We had a room in the Clarion Hotel in Limerick, and Mickey Griffin, Paul O'Connell and I can't remember who else were doing their bit that day. Later that evening the Kingstons were coming up to town to join us, and we were going with them to see Christy Moore in concert - we had arranged to film Terry and Christy at Dolans before the show.

Peter's sister Mags called him to ask if he could get tickets for her for the show that evening? But when Peter called Mick Dolan he was informed that we were on the guest list already.

Peter rang me.

'How are we on the guest list for Christy Moore?'

I was afraid he smelled a rat, particularly as I had been *missing* all that day.

When he arrived into Dolans he anxiously looked around, certain that I was going to surprise him by having a party in December when he wouldn't have been expecting one. After a while he relaxed, safe in the knowledge that his instincts were wrong. 'Who's that!' he urgently enquired, when my phone beeped during the show.

I knew he could see, so I replied, 'Mickey Griffin.'

'Why is he texting you?'

'Never mind,' I said, as his suspicions rose again. That was the closest I came to getting caught, and of course he had forgotten all about it by the time March came around. As I was pregnant with Harry at this stage, I said, 'Let's double up your 40th with the christening later in the year!'

He seemed happy at that.

I had purposely booked a holiday for us in Tenerife the week leading up to Peter's birthday, and Eimear and Angie were prepped to post the invitations as soon as we left the country. The Friday was St Patrick's Day, and Ireland were going for a Triple Crown victory against England on Saturday – the party was planned for the Sunday. Unfortunately, my plans went a little haywire while we were away because An Post changed their system, and on the Monday all Limerick post was now re-directed to Cork for sorting. This caused a huge backlog, and with Friday being a Bank Holiday it meant that many invitations were never delivered, and others got theirs the week after the party.

I was back ducking and diving during the holiday to be on the phone with Angie and Eimear, to explain who was who on the guest list, so they could try to phone everyone.

We arrived home on the Saturday, the day of the match, and I had arranged with Angie that she was cooking dinner at our house as a welcome home – her husband, Pa was coming over and we would try to keep the lads in the house, otherwise I knew someone was going to let the cat out of the bag.

258 CLAW // CHAPTER 24

By Sunday I was getting confident that we were going to pull off the surprise. I snuck out to get my hair done and, on the way, I phoned ROG.

'Well done yesterday, ROG... will ye make it to the party tonight?'

'Of course we're coming,' ROG replied, 'but Claw knows... right?' he asked.

'No ROG... I swear he hasn't a clue!'

'Have to go Anna... see you later!'

Again the angels were looking down on me. At that moment ROG had hung up because he was just coming off the flight home, and the RTE news cameras were in front of him.

'Will you be celebrating tonight ROG?' he was asked immediately.

He smiled.

'We'll be celebrating alright... but I can't say where!'

I had told Peter that my cousins were visiting and Mam wanted us to go to dinner with them. While we were away a new carpet had been put down in The Sin Bin, so on the way to the *dinner*, I asked could we stop, so I could see how the carpet looked. 'Ah no... if we go in there, I'll end up doing work,' said Peter.

'Come on...' I pleaded, '... we'll go down the back stairs... so we won't meet anyone.'

It was an absolute joy to catch him.

He was completely shell-shocked, and overwhelmed. It took him about an hour to get back to himself, and then I told him we had another surprise. The video was fantastic, thanks to the lads. He was dumbfounded for the second time in quick succession.

The night was fantastic fun. The Ireland boys were safe in the knowledge that they could celebrate out of the focus of the public eye. Though poor Rala and Dixie had some trouble. That week was the first time that the Ireland gear van went by ferry for an International. Rala, however, refused to miss the party and travelled through the night.

He arrived at The Sin Bin at 3.0 a.m.

Rugby also helped to confirm what I now know to be true about the power of energy, as an Energy Medicine Teacher. In fact, in my teaching, I often use the perfect example of the 2006 Heineken Cup final.

We brought Luke and Jane to that final in the Millennium Stadium in Cardiff, flying to Heathrow, and stopping at LegoLand to break the journey for the kids. Being heavily pregnant with Harry at the time, I was happy to babysit while Peter went out in Cardiff the night before the game. The atmosphere on the streets of Cardiff was special, as the growing red army of supporters descended.

In O'Connell Street in Limerick they had erected a massive screen and closed off the main street, and had a party there for all those who couldn't make the trip.

When the game began the atmosphere was electric, but we were under pressure from Biarritz from the start as they scored a try two minutes in. ROG narrowed the gap with a penalty, then Halstead scored and the "Red Army" raised the roof of the Millennium Stadium. We were level midway through the half. Then Stringer left Serge Betsen for dead and touched down. ROG's conversion gave us a half-time lead, 17-10.

When the second half began, the supporters were exhausted.

Oh no... wake up everyone, I thought to myself alarmingly, *or this final is going to slip away from us as well.*

The energy in the stadium was gone – and the Munster players seemed to be exhausted also. The flair wasn't there. The single defining moment that won them their first title then came, not on the pitch, but through a moment of inspiration on behalf of the Sky TV producer.

It perfectly demonstrated the power of positive energy – an energy that is not bound by time and space. On the big screen in the stadium we saw the cameras pan the crowd in O'Connell St in Limerick, and the Munster supporters there were *dead* as well.

However, once they saw that they were on TV they went bananas and started jumping up and down, and cheering – and in that instant that positive energy transferred not only to us in the stands, who could feel it, but more importantly to the players on the pitch.

That energy lifted the spirits of Munster at that instant, and beyond doubt that's what won us the game. Paul O'Connell spoke of it afterwards. Indeed Biarritz must have noticed it also because Sky since then have a directive that if they are showing one home town, they must show equal footage of the other team's home town also!

On the final whistle, that day, it was one of the rare times that I have seen Peter actually cry.

Munster 23, Biarritz 19.

He was overwhelmed that we had finally won it.

He wanted to join the lads on the pitch, so he made his way down from his seat. But the stewards were having none of it. They refused to let him on to join the lads as he had no official tag.

In that moment there was nobody going to stop him but, thankfully, he didn't have to resort to brute force. Stuart Barnes, who was working for Sky and was standing there, gave Peter his press pass. It was fitting that he got to join the lads on the pitch that day, as the journey to success had been conceived so many years earlier.

After Peter had finished with rugby we occasionally went to matches, but that was about it. But in 2013 Trevor invited Peter to go on the Lions Tour as part of "Trevor Brennan Tours".

'Well love, what do you think?

'Would you come with me? asked Peter.

I was not sure. Winter time was the wrong time to get the best of Australia, I thought. But I also started thinking about bringing the children with us?

'Then I wouldn't mind, at least they'd get a chance to see the country!' I said. Peter renegotiated his first class ticket for four standard seats, and off we went.

It was like stepping back in time for me, to a time that I had long ago forgotten. Peter's job on the tour was to entertain the supporters, so that meant it was his job to go drinking every night!

But I knew before I agreed to go that this may be challenging for me.

I also asked my good friend, Michelle Murphy if she would like to *pop* down to join us for some of it – as an air hostess she can literally pop around the world whenever she feels like it. Michelle was now a part of our family, and often joined us on trips.

As we queued at the Emirates desk for check-in at Dublin Airport, Harry pointed to the huge poster overhead.

'I want to fly bed class,' he said.

The poster was an advert for Emirates Business Class seats that open into beds. I truly hope that Harry retains the ability to manifest his wishes, because amazingly Mark Pinsent – Trevor's business partner – had organised an up-grade for us. The four of us lived it up, with Harry adapting like he was born to fly this way. He was outstretched, with his eye mask on, as the cabin crew asked, 'Mr Harry… can we get you anything?'

The flight to Dubai was a dream. Then we had a few hours to rest at the airport hotel, before flying onto Brisbane.

There were many 360 moments on that trip for me. I had first arrived in Brisbane 19 years previously for Peter's first rugby tour, with Daddy Noel. As then, our first resort stop was Surfers Paradise – beside the beach on the *specific ocean*.

Many memories came flooding back, as we had also gone there again in 1997 with Mam, Daddy Noel, Meg and Luke, and it was surreal as Mam and Daddy Noel were now at their resting place. Looking at Harry there was also strange, as Luke had also been a young boy at that time in '97.

Later that day Michelle arrived, and Peter went straight to work.

I had absolutely zero interest in being at the pub, and getting over the jet lag asap was my priority.

It was amazing how Peter so easily slipped back into his "rugby role", though, of course, he was in good company with Trevor, Quinny and Brent Pope.

Harry's seventh birthday was that weekend so we took him to DreamWorld as his birthday present. The next day the tour party sang *Happy Birthday* to him, and he and Jane took to touring like his Dad. They had a blast. Harry would get on the bus and sit beside whomever he chose, and would entertain them with all the news of his day. A socialite, just like Peter. Michelle and Jane were the same, and each day they made new friends, while I was happy to take a back seat.

Knowing how tours work and the slagging that goes on, I had said to Michelle to just say she was my sister if anyone asked?

'But Trevor knows you don't have a sister!' she replied.

'Just do us all a favour and introduce yourself as my sister!' I told her.

I should have known not to waste my breath.

At the first opportunity some of the curious tour members asked Trevor who was who? 'Oh, Anna is his wife... but Michelle is his mistress,' Trev informed them with a straight face, '... and they're all ok with it... for years!'

The tour was heading to Melbourne for a week and I knew I had no business in a city with the kids for a week. Also I knew I'd need a welcome break from *Party Peter*, so I had booked the kids, Michelle and myself a break in my favourite place.

Noosa.

We took the bus to Surfers Airport, where the tour was catching its flight *down*, and we jumped into our hire car for our own peaceful mini holiday. Quinny was standing with Peter as we drove off.

'Best of luck looking after Peter for the next few days,' I shouted at Quinny, '... he's all yours!'

After the game in Melbourne it was all to play for in the last Test at Sydney. We were heading to Cairns for some welcome sunshine first for a few days. It was there that Jane and Harry became good friends with Mary Kate and her two boys – Harry had found partners-in-crime and followed them everywhere.

Down in Sydney the match atmosphere was amazing. Our niece, Jessie Clohessy and her boyfriend, Shane (who happens to be Billy Meehan, the Honda 50 fame's nephew) showed us around Bondi. And Jessie drove us out to John Langford's house where we had a superb barbecue. If we hadn't the kids to remind us, there is no way we would have believed that it was 12 years since we had been together. Rugby is like that, and the friendships forged between players are akin to soldiers who have battled together. It is an everlasting bond.

Then, into the middle of the barbecue, walks Gaillimh. The General who had planned so many rugby battles for the troops!

Peter wanted me to go to the final Test match. But at €400 per ticket, I was much happier to send Jane with him for the experience that I knew would last a lifetime for her. To me it was just another game.

But it was another full circle moment for me as I stood at Darling Harbour waving our tour and thousands of others off on their fantastic *booze cruise* transfer to the stadium – and I didn't feel even the tiniest regret that I wasn't with them. Harry, Jessie and myself had our dinner, and from our hotel room we watched the fireworks display over the harbour, before settling down to scream our heads off at the TV as we cheered the Lions to victory.

This time we left Australia with no regrets.

A few weeks after the Lions tour we headed to France for Paul and Emily O'Connell's wedding. We flew to Toulouse and had two good nights out with Trevor and Paula.

Instead of hiring a car, Trevor offered us his Mustang.

I thought a Mustang was a precious vintage car.

'God no... we're not taking that,' I replied.

At the same moment, Peter said, 'Thanks Trev... that'd be great!'

We went to collect *Sally* from the street across from Trev's – and then I realized what it was, apparently every man's dream car! It had to be true because, at every traffic light, drivers of cars beside us would signal for Peter to rev the engine so they could hear it!

Now that's all fine and well when Peter was driving, but of course as soon as we got to the town where the wedding was it was party central time again, which meant I had to do the driving.

It was a fantastic venue, and the square in the town was a re-union of a group that had been living in each others ears for over a decade. The craic was fantastic, but the heat was searing – even at 1.0 a.m. when we were leaving for our hotel.

Of course Peter insisted I drive around the square and give some of the lads a spin in *his new toy*, though I was not in the least bit comfortable as I had to repeatedly respond to cries of... 'Rev it Anna... rev it again!'

We were seated at a pub in the square before heading to the chateau for the reception. ROG pulled up with a few of the lads in a Renault Clio.

'Spot the difference,' announced Donncha, '... between a racing car and a Toulouse car!'

Then up showed Gaillimh in a UK registered soft-top Mercedes.

The two old men were having the last laugh one more time. Only Claw and Gaillimh could manage to acquire two *high-end* cars for free… in France!

EPILOGUE

How appropriate that this final chapter is being penned in the South of France, another 360 as we holiday in our favourite place!

I feel very grateful that these writings have already exceeded my expectations, before even going to print. As I read the unedited version to Peter, Luke, Jane and Harry on this holiday – which was a blessing in itself, as we are rarely together without distractions these days in our busy lives – it validated my reason for writing it in the first place.

Both Peter and myself were very surprised to discover that all three of our children didn't know most of what was in this book. Not just that, but we were laughing out loud together, which has created new special memories for us.

This is an added bonus that I hadn't expected.

Which brings me to thanking those who inspired these musings in the first place. Luke, Jane, Harry and, of course, Peter. In writing a story like this, it allowed us to do a review of the last 30 years or so, and the greatest achievement of all in that time has been the blessing of our children and the family that we have created.

Luke is now 21, and has excelled since finishing school – like Peter, life experience has allowed him to grow more than formal education. Luke has always been a natural leader and decided to work in the bar with Peter after school, and he has taken many initiatives since.

He has learned how to manage a bar, has created his own events management company – using the skills he displayed as a 10 year old, when he regularly organised rugby tournaments, complete with trophies, team kits... the works! – is a self-taught DJ, qualified as a security guard, and manages the social media for the bar.

Like Peter also, Luke is a good people person, has a great sense of humour (when he's in the mood), and has a very soft centre. During Peter's playing years as a small child he was an absolute pleasure, and never once complained despite all the travel he used to do.

Jane has the ability to light up a room with her smile and can make fun in a bucket. Like Luke, she inherited the people person trait from her Dad, and is also a natural leader. She does enjoy school and learns easily – by 14 she was qualified to teach piano. She also is a good basketball player and footballer, when she makes the time from all of her activities to train!

She is great company and a joy in our lives.

With Harry – yet another leader, as long as we all follow – everything is cosha! He is Peter's shadow and best friend, and if Peter was a sucker for Luke and Jane he is a complete sucker for Harry's requests. Like the other two he is also very sociable and has made Murroe his own.

So far he is enjoying rugby, GAA and horse-riding. He has a messers sense of humour, and melts hearts. We are incredibly blessed that all three are growing up to be children that we can be proud of – as Fester said, 'Your kids are fantastic... despite their parenting!'

Peter and I were chatting over dinner one evening, and I said, 'Life is like a play... and we are now at the intermission having completed the first act...

'Being 47 and 48...' I continued, 'the best we can hope for is a second half that lasts another 40 plus years!'

He looked at me.

'Maybe by then,' he replied, '... they'll have figured out how to keep us alive for 200 or 300 years.'

'Perhaps, but at any rate, our spirit lives forever.'

He looked at me again.

'Well, if I'm coming back again,' he said, 'I want to be me again... I wouldn't change a thing!'

So the mission is accomplished, and I have recorded the history of this first act. The final words should, of course, go to Peter, Luke, Jane and Harry...

Luke wrote this about Peter...

'My first memory is of being on Dad's shoulders as he went up the steps in the stand at Twickenham to collect his medal in the final against Northampton. In the changing room he started crying, and because he was crying... I cried. I remember him throwing his medal into his gear-bag.

As a kid I could never understand why people always came up to Dad with a pen and paper for him to sign it, it would annoy me because it would take time away from him and me. I guess I was jealous.

Anytime I have ever wanted anything he always said, "yes".

The triplets (Ray Ryan's boys) always remind me of one time when we were all in Arthur's Quay having breakfast. They saw a scooter in the shop, and Ray told the lads they weren't getting it – in fairness, Ray would have had to buy three of them! But I was told that if I ate one sausage, I could have the scooter. I didn't even really want it – I only asked 'cos the lads did!

Everyone used to ask me what it was like to have a famous Dad? Or they would say, "You think you are great because your father plays for Ireland".

I never understood that either, as my father to me was the same as their father was to them. He's more than just a Dad to me, as he is now my boss at work as well. He's also my best friend, and he's good to talk to because he always listens to new ideas, and thinks about it for 30 seconds and then gives me his decision – which is usually the answer I wanted anyway.

Thanks for everything so far, you really have looked after me more than enough.

Love, Luke.'

This is what Jane has to say about Peter…

'My only memory of Dad playing was the day I wore the red t-shirt with "My Dad's No. 1" printed on the back.

In 2006 I knew he was a real softie when I saw him cry for the first time, when Munster won the Heineken Cup final at the Millennium Stadium.

I remember people saying to me that Dad stepped on a French man's head, but I had never seen it. It was only recently that I saw it, on video and I thought it was hilarious that he was out of rugby so long for doing it. When people ask me what it is like to have Peter as my Dad, I always say, "He's just Dad… its normal to me".

As a Dad he is fun and very funny, a sucker, and very generous. Sometimes he is funny for the wrong reasons, like when he loses it with someone in traffic. I feel very lucky because everything I've ever asked for I got – and I know who to ask if I'm looking for something too. He always gives in… eventually.

He is very handy for DIY jobs or teaching me normal things, like swimming, riding a bike, horseriding – and some extras, like how to drive when I was nine!

On holidays as Mom read this book to us, we had a great laugh as I found out loads of things I never knew. Which seems weird because a lot of people already know this stuff about Dad, and I didn't.

Already Dad has given me lots of special memories and I know he'll give me many more.

Love always, Jane.'

Harry was to the point, like Peter…

'I love my Daddy and I always will.

My Daddy was a great rugby player.

I love you.'

And Peter...

'When I read this book, it brought back many memories that I had forgotten. Some made me laugh and some made me emotional.

If I had the chance to do it all again, would I change anything?

No... though perhaps one thing... I wish I hadn't started smoking!

As good as it was to get paid to play rugby, I didn't do it for the money. I did it because I loved the game. But the best part was all the friendships I made along the way, many of whom Anna mentioned in the book, but there are many more important friends that I made during those years that I should mention.

And I did so by putting a few words together for each of them at the beginning of each chapter in this book.

To those I have not mentioned, I'll get you in Anna's next book...

To my darling wife, who has stood by me through thick and thin, and all the ups and downs of my career, what can I really say?

She is always there for me, especially in the hard times. I have no doubt whatsoever that if we hadn't met, things would have been very different. She has been my rock always – even though she may have hopped that rock off me many times, when I thoroughly deserved it!

Only for her this book would never have happened and I really enjoyed it as it brought back many great memories. She has always been right in the career making decisions hence the title of the book should be "She Was Right".

Love forever, Peter.'